EVIDENCE BASED INCLUSION

IT'S TIME TO FOCUS ON THE RIGHT NEEDLE

DR. LAURAN STAR

Copyright
LS Publishing
Copyright © 2022 Dr. Lauran Star

No part of this book may be reproduced or transmitted in any form by any means: graphic, electronic, or mechanical, including photocopying, recording, taping or by any information storage or retrieval system without permission, in writing, from the authors, except for the inclusion of brief quotations in a review, article, book, or academic paper. The authors and publisher of this book and the associated materials have used their best efforts in preparing this material. The authors and publisher make no representations or warranties with respect to accuracy, applicability, fitness or completeness of the contents of this material. They disclaim any warranties expressed or implied, merchantability, or fitness for any particular purpose. The authors and publisher shall in no event be held liable for any loss or other damages, including but not limited to special, incidental, consequential, or other damages. If you have any questions or concerns, the advice of a competent professional should be sought.

All rights reserved.

Hardcover ISBN: 979-8-88831-435-7
Paperback ISBN 979-8-88831-144-8
Ebook ISBN 979-8-88831-145-5

Why Now

Organizational thought leaders have gone out of their way to utilize the terms workplace diversity, inclusion, and equity to mean whatever their business outcome measures. I have had many arguments with thought leaders in this space on how we define workplace diversity, and for me it is always going back to the basic written definition, as it is important to understand what we are measuring and looking for. Throughout this book, I aim to level set definitions as they are written.

So, what does workplace diversity mean today? Workforce diversity refers to an employee's affinities that make them unique to the organization. The characteristics of these affinities can include gender, race, ethnicity, religion, age, sexual orientation, sexual identification, veteran status, disabilities, physical abilities, socioeconomic status, education level and ideologies. It may help to think of what I call the Affinity Iceberg, where certain affinities (or as SHRM calls them, "diversity traits") are visible above the waterline of an imaginary iceberg and others are invisible (below the waterline). What's visible? Things like age, physical traits, and behaviors—but there are plenty that aren't immediately visible, such as marital status, military experience, values, beliefs, culture, religious affiliation, and more.

Table of Contents

Foreword 1
Introduction: Why This Book 5

Section 1—Clearing Up the Confusion of Diversity: A History of Striving and Failing 13

Chapter 1: The Broken Platform of Diversity 14
What Does Workplace Diversity Even Mean Anymore?
Quick History of Diversity
Workplace Diversity Is Broken
The Risks of Focusing on Diversity Initiatives
Focused on the Wrong Needle

Chapter 2: The Lenses of Diversity Are More Than Gender and Color 32
Typical Lenses of Diversity
Hiring Untapped Potential
Lenses of Workplace Affinities
Diversity Is More Than a Social Movement

Section 2—Evidence-Based Inclusion 57

Chapter 3: It All Starts with Culture 58
Organizational Culture
The Cultural Misalignment
Measuring Culture
The Inclusive Culture Value
Leadership Drives Inclusion, Not Human Resources

Chapter 4: Inclusion Is More than a Trend—It Is a Must............... 74
What Has Happened to Our Workplace?
The Role of ESG in Inclusion and Diversity
Transactional vs. Transformational Diversity
The Damage of Quota Attainment
Intersectionality: A Critical Lens in the Workplace
Getting Your Supports Ready

Chapter 5: Pivoting to an Inclusive Organizational Culture 86
Is Your Organizational Ready to Pivot?
Inclusion: More Than a Trend, It's the Foundation
The Business Case for Inclusion
The Pivot
Organizational ID&E Maturity Model
Measuring Inclusion
Barriers to Inclusion

Section 3—The Inclusion Paradigm® 107

Chapter 6: Driving Awareness: The Foundation.............................. 108
The Inclusion Paradigm®
The Foundation
Moving Forward with Inclusion

Chapter 7: The Business Imperative: The Framework.................... 126
Shore Model of Inclusion
The Framework
Moving Forward

Chapter 8: Inclusion as the Intersection of Employee Engagement and Culture: The 4 Pillars........................ 146
Pillar #1: Leaders
Pillar #2: Human Resources
Pillar #3: Organizational Development and Learning
Pillar #4: Managers

**Chapter 9: Inclusion Immersion—
Resulting in Performance Outcome**.. 163
   Intent Leading to Immersion
   Human Resources Dashboard—Measuring Diversity
   Measuring Inclusion
   Wrapping the Inclusion Paradigm with the Return on Investment

Section 4—Equity and Trends 179

**Chapter 10: To Be or Not to Be:
Equality vs Equity Is the Question** 180
   The Difference Between Equity and Equality
   Equity in the Workplace
   Risks of Workplace Equity

Chapter 11: Future Trends in Inclusion, Diversity & Equity.......... 191
   Evidence-Based Initiatives
   Impact of Inclusion on the Community
   ID&E Trends
   Your ID&E Journey

Appendix A: Dissertation Abstract 204

Appendix B: Training Framework 205

Appendix C: Inclusion Paradigm Human Resources /
   Demographic Dashboard 206

Appendix D: Glossary 210

Appendix E: Intersectionality Exercise 212

Appendix F: Culture / Engagement Survey 216

Appendix G: Listing of Tools on Book Website 220

Endnotes 221

Acknowledgements

This book could not have been written if not for the support from some amazing people.

My amazing editor and book coach—Kate Hannisian—Blue Pencil Consulting, and graphic designer Lisa McKenna—Arrow North; your coaching, continued support, and amazing editing and ability to know the exact look and layout that speaks to my readers—Thank you!

To all the organizations that allowed me the honor of impacting your organizational culture, —Thank you!

To my readers, thank you for providing a platform for growth. Continue to have the courage to be curious about the beauty in the world.

My amazing family Rico, Raff, Lena and Bella and friends Kathleen Burns Kingsbury, Gina Abudi and Maria Lynch—who often were a sounding board for many chapters, providing insight and love, attempted to keep me sane and focused while I worked on yet another book. One more I promise—Thank you and I love you!

Foreword

*If you don't understand your culture,
you don't understand your business!*

Last May I gave a keynote address to the New England Human Resources Leadership Forum on why the HR community must **Step Up** and **Step In** to an expanded leadership role. Given the many challenges employees and employers are facing with the disruptions of the COVID-19 pandemic, rapid digital transformation, and changing work attitudes and working locations, the HR community must take the lead in navigating this shifting business landscape.

At the end of my talk a very articulate and passionate HR professional came up to me and said something like: *"OMG! You need to write the foreword for my new book on inclusion, diversity, and equity so people will finally understand that an **inclusive culture** is the foundation for achieving the benefits of diversity."*

Dr. Lauran Star needs little help in making a strong business case for an inclusive culture. This book uses clear thinking, case studies, and most importantly, an evidence-based approach to the fact that without a culture of inclusion, money spent on improving diversity metrics and ratios will be short lived. Just as fish can't survive in polluted waters, diversity of thought and ideas will die in a culture that doesn't accept and respect differences. If new employees don't feel included or valued, they won't stick around! And if they do, most will quietly become part of the old culture. In noninclusive organizations, it is better to blend in than stick out.

My big takeaway from this book is the fact that diversity and inclusion are not the same! Yet everywhere you turn today in business and the media, the terms diversity and inclusion are lumped together, or worse still, used interchangeably. Lauran makes a compelling case that diversity is a metric (actually several different metrics), while inclusion is the way peoples' differences and ideas are treated. Without an inclusive culture, studies show that increasing the mix of gender or race (or any other diversity metric) does little to improve business performance.

A bad culture will defeat a good person every time.

My culture journey began in early 1980 when I was asked by the new management team of the Three Mile Island Nuclear Plant (following a major nuclear accident in 1979) to help build a safety culture that would be world class and sustainable. While a technical issue led directly to the partial core meltdown in Unit 2, the genesis of the accident was a culture of exclusion! The Three Mile Island Nuclear Plant was literally an island of silos—departments that didn't respect or communicate openly with each other. Ultimately this culture led to poor operational communications and the accident that derailed nuclear energy in the US for decades. While employee engagement was high, and people were technically excellent, it was the silo culture that laid the groundwork for the accident. Over the next two years we built a culture of cross-functional teamwork, respect and open communication that helped the power plant restart and run safely for the next 29 years.

Over the past 40 years of working with leadership teams on culture improvement, business turnarounds and strategy execution, it is clear to me that the best culture is one that supports the strategy and employees. But what is culture? Culture is more than vision, values and beliefs. Culture is an ecosystem of causal factors (e.g., policies, work practices, leadership, training, compensation, and peer pressure, etc.) which interact to influence how people behave at work. People join a company with their own individual values, beliefs and work habits, but most are quickly acculturated by the system, peer pressures and management demands.

Yet an effective culture must adapt to new business conditions. As the business world changes and new competitive pressures emerge, leaders must actively reshape culture to align with new strategies and organizational structures. An easy-to-see example is during mergers and acquisitions (M&A): when an acquisition reshapes the organization, the culture must shift to align with the new organization and strategy. But how to change culture?

Change the system, change the culture.
Change the culture, change the outcomes.

Using the tools of ecosystem modelling and identifying those causal factors that influence employee behaviors and attitudes, it is now possible to build a visual model of how culture impacts employee behaviors and business performance. Visually mapping the causal factors of culture helps identify hidden business risks inside an organization, thus giving leadership clear insight into how to reshape and improve culture and business performance.

Here is an example of how a culture ecosystem map can provide executives with insight into potential culture-related business risks and where to focus culture change efforts.

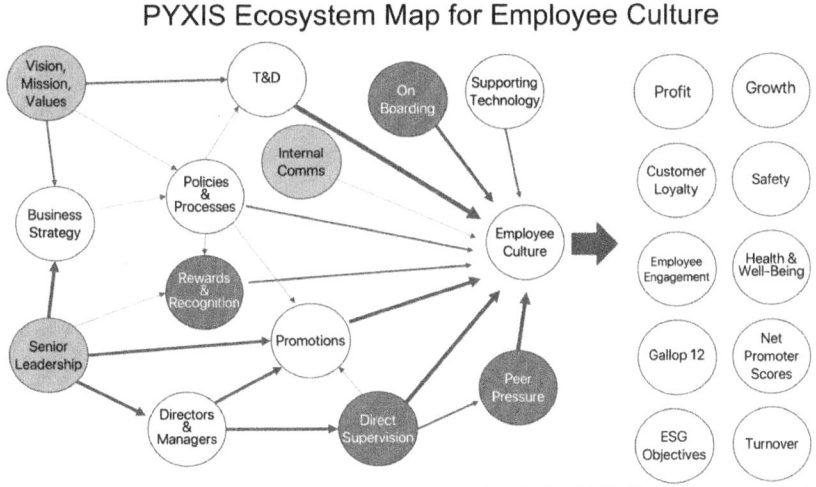

PYXIS Ecosystem Map for Employee Culture

Copyright 2022 © PYXIS Culture Technologies Ltd.

Currently, my team at PYXIS Culture Technologies are building visual culture ecosystem maps, using quantitative and qualitative company data, for such important business issues as safety culture, cybersecurity culture, risk culture, innovation culture, and customer culture. With the help of Dr. Lauran Star, we hope to develop in the near future an inclusion culture ecosystem map as well.

Besides exploding the myths of DE&I and bringing a common-sense approach to this important topic, Dr. Lauran Star provides another important takeaway in this book: the addition of an effective and evidence-based model for building an inclusive culture that supports and empowers the business benefits of diversity and equity.

What I most like about this book, however, is its straightforward, matter-of-fact, evidence-based, no-BS approach. Refreshing and insightful. I will leave you with a few of my favorite passages. I know you will find many more as you read through this great new book.

- *Companies often latch onto the newest ID&E buzzword in part because it is easier than admitting, "Hey, our diversity efforts have not worked."*
- *Perhaps the greatest risk of diversity initiatives that are done poorly is lost trust.*
- *Please let me reaffirm, diversity initiatives are not one-size-fits-all and may often alienate many of those in the room.*

Dr. Lauran Star has pulled back the curtain of misunderstanding and given us all the gift of her clear thinking on and expertise in inclusion, diversity and equity. I hope you find this book as useful as I did.

–John R Childress,
Chairman, PYXIS Culture Technologies Ltd.
Author: **Culture Rules!** and **The CEO's Guide to Corporate Culture**

Introduction: Why This Book

I have spent the last 15-plus years researching, applying, and building inclusive organizational cultures while shouting from the office space...

- Stop focusing on diversity—it's the wrong needle in advancing diversity, equity, and inclusion!
- Diversity is an affinity trait, a workplace metric of measurement within an organization!
- If you are looking to drive diversity and equity within your organization, you must start with inclusion!
- It is time to stop the craziness and focus on the organization's culture as the driver towards diversity!
- Intersectionality is a critical lens for thriving employees!
- Diversity training does not shift attitudes and behaviors—it is an increase-in-knowledge tool!
- If you are focused on just gender and people of color, you are missing the bigger picture!
- The business case for diversity is BUILT on inclusion!
- Stop throwing diversity initiatives at the wall to see what sticks—we need to focus on evidence-based inclusion, diversity, and equity solutions!
- Equality and equity are NOT the same thing—pick one!

And during these 15-plus years, I have helped organizations successfully navigate the diversity landscape and create a sustainable inclusion and diversity strategy and culture. This navigation is built on evidence and return on investment, resulting in saving precious time, energy and money. Where other companies are struggling, these organizations are thriving and enjoying the benefits of inclusion, diversity, and equity. Are you listening now?

Here's a little bit about my involvement in this work. I began my journey into the field of inclusion and diversity back in 2007, with my focus on inclusion first, followed by diversity. This was well before diversity and inclusion were considered the "it" factors, before buzzwords began to be profit areas for consultants, and before organizations truly recognized the value of inclusion in the workplace.

I dove into this field well before all the confusion around diversity and inclusion hit the marketspace. At every corner I asked why: why diversity first, why that program, what is the goal you wish to achieve? The answers to these questions pushed me forward academically as my master's degree focused on leadership and ethics and my doctorate is in industrial/organizational psychology with a specialization in inclusion and diversity. I am the first inclusion and diversity workplace psychologist in the United States—to date only four of us exist. I am a workplace inclusion and diversity practitioner, strategist, psychologist and researcher with over 15 years of success building sustainable organizational inclusion that leads to improved workplace diversity and maybe equity / equality. To clarify for a moment, evidence-based equity vs. equality is a whole other book—coming in 2023. To level set—from here on, ID&E refers to inclusion, diversity and equity (or equality). However we will not touch upon equity or equality until Chapter 10.

Again, I must emphasize that my focus has always been on inclusion first, then diversity, regardless of the attention certain buzzwords were getting.

Yet the confusion around ID&E continues to grow in the workplace and many of my counterparts are feeling diversity fatigue and frustrations. So, I decided to write this book in hopes of decreasing the confusion around inclusion, diversity, and equity or equality (what the industry calls DE&I but I'm calling ID&E because I believe we need to focus on the right needle), and to help give you—the human resource professional, leadership, management, and the inclusion and diversity practitioner—evidence-based tools for your organizational success. Please note, I have removed the "E" from the "inclusion and diversity practitioner" title, as we are focusing on inclusion to drive diversity. I am hopeful this book will help you by providing solid evidence of the need to **stop focusing on diversity** and get you to **pivot to inclusion**. It will help you level set your organization on what inclusion and diversity mean to the organization as well as how the business case fits in.

Why now? Like many of you, I am frustrated by seeing organizations spend time and money on programs, training, and initiatives that have not been proven effective. Frustrated seeing my fellow practitioners suffer from diversity burnout. As an evidence-based inclusion and diversity psychologist and strategist, I am knee-deep in the thick of ID&E. Like many of my peers, I have decided enough is enough!

Please stop throwing diversity and inclusion initiatives at the wall to see what sticks or moves the needle within your organization. Instead, let us focus on evidence-based initiatives that will drive your organization to thrive.

It is time to stop all the noise and begin to build sustainable solutions for creating an inclusive organizational culture that will drive more than diversity and equity, one that will also drive organizational growth, performance, job satisfaction, employee retention, and so much more.

Today's organizations must adapt to the rapidly changing economy and business workspace. Now more than ever, the need to attract, retain, manage, develop, and coach an inclusive workforce is critical to an organization's success. However, many businesses are unsure where to start and may not have the expertise to drive such a transition. According to the Massachusetts Institute of Technology, US organizations spend a combined average of well over $8 billion annually on diversity training, with a focus on improving diversity; however, there is no evidence this spending is working to achieve that goal.

Read that again: $8 BILLION dollars a year spent, focused on diversity, with no evidence that this is money well spent. We know the business case has been made for organizations to have a diverse talent pool AND an inclusive organizational culture. Yet, can we agree maybe, that diversity is not the needle we need to look at for a diverse organization? How do we get to a place where we have inclusion, a diverse talent pool AND an inclusive organizational culture? Here's how: **Evidence-based inclusion and diversity** must become a standard practice within the global business workplace, AND inclusion is your foundation for diversity and equity.

My Focus on Inclusion Is Based on Evidence

This book is focused on evidence-based practices and proven solutions that have defined returns on investment. We need to stop reacting in the workplace and become proactive. inclusion and diversity practitioners need to stop throwing DE&I at the wall hoping to see what sticks. The evidence presented throughout this book is both timely in thought leadership and supported by peer-reviewed studies that reinforce best practice behaviors. Research is critical and much more is still needed.

In my doctoral dissertation I examined the overall impact diversity training has on the workplace and employees, both from training structure and behavioral shifts through perceived organizational justice (see the abstract in Appendix A). In my research, what surprised me the most was the overall lack of evidence that diversity alone has a solid business case. *In four separate meta-analyses of over 200 diversity training studies, not one study could make a solid business case for diversity without inclusion being one of the criteria for being part of the study.* Essentially, I found that an inclusive organizational culture had to be present *before* diversity of affinity factors could be counted. Again, the business case was made; however, the business case is dependent upon there being an inclusive organization.

In studies where the inclusive culture was missing, no diversity benefit was noted, and in fact the research showed the exact opposite. Furthermore, every study I reviewed had a measurement of diversity, separating out the different affinities. That's the percentage of black people, percentage of white people, percentage of women, percentage of veterans, percentage of people with disabilities. However, you cannot really articulate an organization's success or increased profit margins based solely on affinities, as affinities are utilized as a metric. Yet, when a company has a strong, inclusive organizational culture and diversity among its employees, the company is thriving. We need both; keeping in mind that without the foundation of inclusion, the whole house falls and what organizations are really looking for in diversity (diversity of thought) is not present.

The purpose of my dissertation (a quasi-experimental quantitative study) was examining diversity training content and design to determine if there was a significant change in employees' perceptions of organizational justice. My dissertation is the largest diversity training study done to date outside the academic walls, meaning the study was done within a large STEM firm with over 600 employees.

There is more … In 2020, I complied a 10-year comparative review of over 150 organizations that actively hired consultants to create diversity solutions to address low workplace diversity numbers. The results showed that for 92% of those organizations that hired a consultant, the symptom was low diversity, but the actual problem was the lack of an inclusive organizational culture (based on the correlation of turnover, employee engagement and organizational culture survey). More to the point, these organizations, while focused on diversity solutions, demonstrated an increase of turnover, and a decrease of employee engagement results at year-end. What is more problematic, of the 92% that lacked an inclusive culture, only 22% wanted to work on inclusion (you'll find the full details in Chapter 4).

Again, I ask why are we focusing on the needle of diversity? Why is diversity and inclusion so confusing? Where does an organization focus? There is a lot of misleading information out in the world on inclusion, diversity, and equity. Back in 2010, I did my master's thesis on "The Business Case for Diversity," and in every peer-reviewed article on diversity and business, I found a common theme: an inclusive culture was present. Diversity is a measurement of different affinities; diversity is a measurement tool. It cannot measure impact because there is no way to remove the impact of organizational culture. That solidified my thoughts that yes, while diversity is important, without the inclusive foundation, you're just cycling employees in and out of a company. They simply won't stay if they don't feel included.

Book Overview

The first section of this book examines today's business practices that focus on diversity. This will help demonstrate first why diversity is broken and costing organizations money—in short, how the situation got to be the mess it is today. We'll look at how diversity is more than gender and color and we'll untangle the confused business case of diversity versus inclusion. We'll also look at where diversity initiatives have failed and why.

In the second section, we'll set a new stage and explain how to focus on diversity and inclusion based on what works with today's workforce. To help organizations pivot their focus to inclusion (rather than diversity), we'll define it and explore the barriers, and provide you with an evidence-based model with supporting data on inclusion, diversity, and equity. We'll show you what workplace inclusion looks like and examine intersectionality as well as other affinity groups organizations often miss. Topping off this section is a chapter on culture. I highly recommend you continue your reading on culture, as culture is dynamic and always changing.

The third section focuses on a proven path to build an inclusive culture that will increase diversity and equity: The Inclusion Paradigm.® This paradigm will help your organization create a framework of success. The Inclusion Paradigm has been researched and vetted within many successful organizations—building both inclusion and diversity that sticks. In spending the last 15-plus years focused on evidence-based inclusion, I've developed a research-based and application-proven workplace inclusion model that provides a clear pathway for creating an inclusive organizational culture. The model is an innovative scaffolding of steps that have been strategically layered, resulting in sustainable success. The model also recommends inclusion initiatives that have proven to have the desired impact of driving inclusion within the organization. This model is based on research into workplace culture, diversity, equity, and inclusion, followed by real-world application with proven, measured results. **Be sure to visit this book's website (https://www.drlauranstar.com/evidence-basedinclusion) to download complimentary PowerPoint slide decks, general policies, training tools, and more.**

Of course, we wrap up with a short section on equity and future trends in ID&E. Honestly, equity is a topic worthy of its own book (coming soon), but we need to begin addressing the "E" in ID&E.

My hope is that this book helps to decrease the confusion around inclusion, diversity, and equity, and that it gives you evidence-based tools for your organizational success. For the last 30 years or so, diversity and inclusion has been a best practice guessing game and it's costing the workplace billions. Imagine if you had that money as profits in your pocket instead! What's more, when the industry used up the weight of the word "diversity," the industry switched it to "inclusion," then "equity," and now "belonging." Nonetheless, the underlying problem remains this: how do we build an inclusive organizational culture that will attract and retain a diverse workforce, leading to equity? It is time to stop the craziness and focus on the organization's culture as the driver towards diversity.

Building an inclusive organization takes work, so if you're ready to roll up your sleeves, then I hope you will enjoy and be inspired by this book. It's filled with funny and sometimes shocking stories, as well as evidence-based solutions you can put to work as you pivot to build your inclusive organization.

Please feel free to email me with any questions. I understand all too well that there is confusion and at times you may feel strongly about many of the points I raise. So please email me and I can help you understand what the actual evidence tells us. Lauran@DrLauranStar.com

Inclusion is not something that can be the responsibility of just one person within the organization; it takes the whole organization. And it's not a one-and-done, check-the-box initiative; it is an ongoing journey. Let's get started!

Book Key:

Level set Icon: Level setting terminology, definitions, and goals

Website Icon: The goal of this book's website is to continue to reinforce, define and provide tools and evidence on ID&E. Think of it as a place to ask questions and share ideas without being sold to. It is all about evidence-based inclusion, diversity and equity, and filled with articles, PowerPoints, strategies, tools, training materials, and more. **https://www.drlauranstar.com/evidencebasedinclusion**

SECTION 1

Clearing Up the Confusion of Diversity: A History of Striving and Failing

We have been focused on workplace diversity for over 60 years—and to date we have little to show for it.

1

The Broken Platform of Diversity

We are so focused on diversity we are missing the bigger and impactful picture of organizational culture, and this does a disservice to the end goal of diversity—diversity of thought.

What Does Workplace Diversity Even Mean Anymore?

If you were to do a web search on the term "workplace diversity," you would find several very different results. Some definitions combine diversity with inclusion, others with equity, and then again, some define diversity with no business sense whatsoever. Some sites list the affinities (i.e., diversity is the number of people of color working for an organization), while others argue the business case of diversity is tied with inclusion (one of the main points of this book is that it should be the other way around). There are thousands of articles that mention diversity first and follow with whatever point they are trying to make; but as I read these articles, I constantly ask, where is the evidence? With all the different definitions, interpretations, and comments, it's no wonder the platform of diversity is broken, as we are continually re-defining it—it's a moving target.

To make matters more challenging, often organizational thought leaders have gone out of their way to utilize the terms "workplace diversity," "inclusion," and "equity" to mean whatever their business outcome measures. I have had many arguments with thought leaders in this space on how we define workplace diversity. For me, it always goes back to the basic written definition, as it is important to understand what we are measuring and looking for.

Throughout this book, I aim to level set definitions as they are written. **Diversity, inclusion, and equity do not mean the same thing.** That's why we need to approach each with their own focus and goals. As you read, you'll see the 🅒 **Level set Icon** = Level setting terminology, definitions, and goals.

So, what does workplace diversity mean today?

🅒 **Workforce diversity** refers to an employee's affinities that make them unique to the organization. The characteristics of these affinities can include gender, race, ethnicity, religion, age, sexual orientation, sexual identification, veteran status, disabilities, physical abilities, socioeconomic status, education level and ideologies.

It may help to think of what I call the Affinity Iceberg (see Figure 1-1), where certain affinities (or as the Society for Human Resource Management calls them, "diversity traits") are visible above the waterline of an imaginary iceberg and others are invisible (below the waterline). What's visible? Things like age, physical traits, and behaviors. But there are plenty that aren't immediately visible, such as marital status, military experience, values, beliefs, culture, religious affiliation, and more.

🅒 *Workforce diversity is also a means to measure affinity groups in the workplace;* it's a *metric*. However, can you set workplace outcomes based on that affinity metric? No, because it is a measurement metric. There is no correlation between affinity groupings and business outcomes. Let me restate this by asking some questions:

How is having an organization with a staff that's 38% women "better" than an organization with only 10% women? How can you prove it? How do you remove the variable of organizational culture? What if I were to add that the company staffed 38% by women had an attrition rate of 60%, while the company staffed just 10% by women had an attrition rate of just 11 percent? The bigger question is this: how do we measure the overall impact of diverse thought, as that is what these women bring to the workforce, because that's what matters? In a nutshell, you really can't do that, and you cannot place affinity groups in a vacuum and expect measurable results. As a researcher myself, I tend to stay away from making "claims" that one affinity group can do more or better than another.

Figure 1-1 The Affinity Iceberg

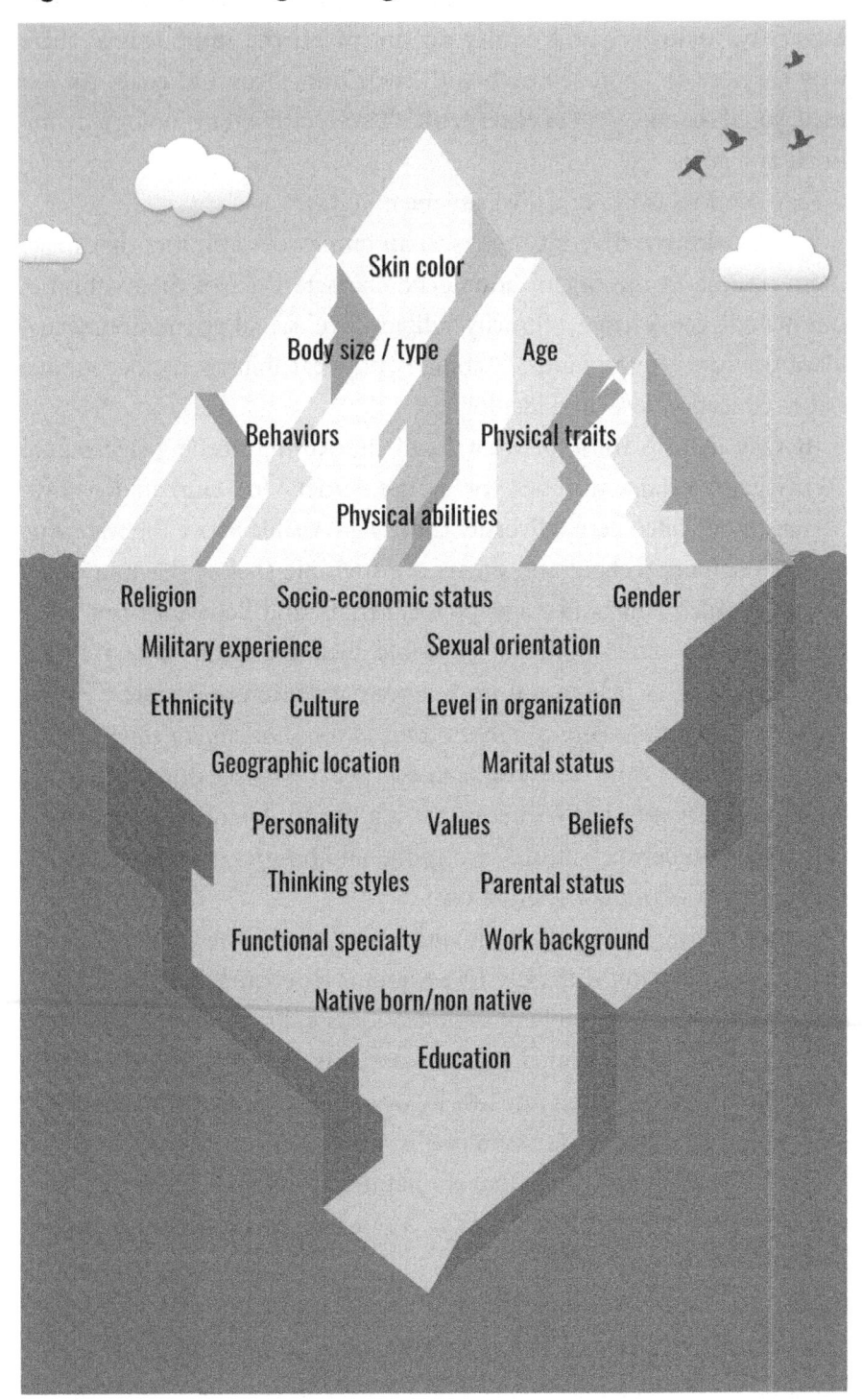

Skin color
Body size / type   Age
Behaviors   Physical traits
Physical abilities

Religion   Socio-economic status   Gender
Military experience   Sexual orientation
Ethnicity   Culture   Level in organization
Geographic location   Marital status
Personality   Values   Beliefs
Thinking styles   Parental status
Functional specialty   Work background
Native born/non native
Education

The reason organizations want diversity in their ranks is for diversity of perspective and thought. Let's look at the United States Armed Forces as an example. Why? It's an organization where the diversity of thought is important. It is not that one skin color will fight harder than another or solve problems better. The Armed Forces have a structured inclusion model—once you sign the contract, it is more than a challenge to get out. I am not saying it's a perfect model, but having served in the military for 10 years, I will share that I never struggled with a glass ceiling, knowing my value, problem-solving, or getting paid my worth. Why? I learned from those around me—we were all in similar boats with different perspectives and were encouraged (okay, the Army *demanded* it) to learn from each other and embrace the difference.

The goal of workplace diversity is to have a diversity of perspective and thought and that, combined with an inclusive organizational culture, leads to innovation, problem-solving, job satisfaction and so much more.

Yet, "diversity in the workplace" is a bit of a moving target and has been for the past fifty years. Part of the reason for the moving target, as I found in researching my doctoral dissertation, is that the history of diversity in the workplace shifts every 10 years with each new generation, plus the laws around diversity are constantly changing. Add globalization as a partial driver for the diversity message within organizations, and you can start to see the confusion.[3]

From 1960 to 1979, the goal of workplace diversity was diversity compliance, due in large part to the Civil Rights Act of 1964.[4] Affirmative action was the cornerstone of diversity hiring and organizations were focused on conformity with that. Increased workplace diversity during the 1980s led to the birth of diversity training in 1987. While compliance was still a goal, it was from training rather than affirmative action.[5] The focus of diversity and diversity training from 1980 to 1999 was to foster sensitivity and understanding. From 2000 and beyond, the focus of diversity shifted to specific affinities rather than the individual employee. The diversity focus has shifted slightly from ethnicity to gender inclusion in the global workplace.[6]

Today, workplace diversity leans more toward inclusion, as the definition of diversity has become more encompassing and confusing. Workplace diversity blends its definition to include inclusion—yet they are different. Workplace diversity is defined as acknowledging, understanding, accepting, valuing, and celebrating the vast differences within the workplace regardless of age, class, ethnicity, gender, physical and mental ability, race, sexual orientation, and spiritual practice.[7] It is no wonder we are confused. As you read, please keep in mind that diversity and inclusion are NOT the same thing.

A Quick History of Diversity

For some perspective on this, let's take a quick look at the recent history of diversity in terms of efforts to improve it—in our workplaces and our communities.[8] In the 1960s and 1970s, we saw civil rights protests and the introduction of affirmative action programs and the establishment of the US Equal Employment Opportunity Commission (EEOC). In the early 1980s, the focus switched to diversity, and was a compliance-focused activity targeted at bringing women and minorities into the workplace in a greater variety of roles. Diversity was seen as a business initiative rather than an imperative. Then in the 1990s we started to do "sensitivity training" with a focus on gender and minorities. This decade also saw the introduction of the Family Leave Act and the Americans with Disabilities Act. In the 2000s, businesses began to appoint "chief diversity officers" and we saw the start of Employee Resource Groups (ERGs).

From 2010 on, the focus began to include protections for LGBTQ+ individuals, response to the Black Lives Matter and MeToo movements, and the introduction of the somewhat inappropriate notion of "belonging." As a new buzzword when consultants tired of "diversity," "belonging" is part of the inclusion definition—more on that as we go. Throughout these decades, the focus of diversity efforts has also been influenced by which generational cohort has been advocating for new ways of thinking (see Figure 1-2).

Figure 1-2
History of Diversity

1960's-1970's — Diversity
- Anti-discrimination
- Civil Rights
- Affirmative Action
- Regulations
- EEOC

Early 1980's — Diversity
- Compliance focused
- Bringing women & minorities into the workplace
- Glass Ceiling
- Fitting-in
- Diversity seen as business imperative

1990's — Diversity & Sensitivity
- Sensitivity training
- Gender & Minorities
- Family Leave Act
- Americans with Disabilities Act Signed into law
- Generation X

2000's — Diversity - Focus on Gender - 60% of women in the workplace
- Chief Diversity Office
- Diverse Workforce - increase in ethnicity in workforce
- ERGs

2010-2020 — Diversity & Inclusion
- Black Lives Matter/Me too Movements
- LGBTQ+ Protection
- Millennials
- Belonging

2021-2030 — Inclusion & Equity
- Generation Z
- Millennials are turning 40

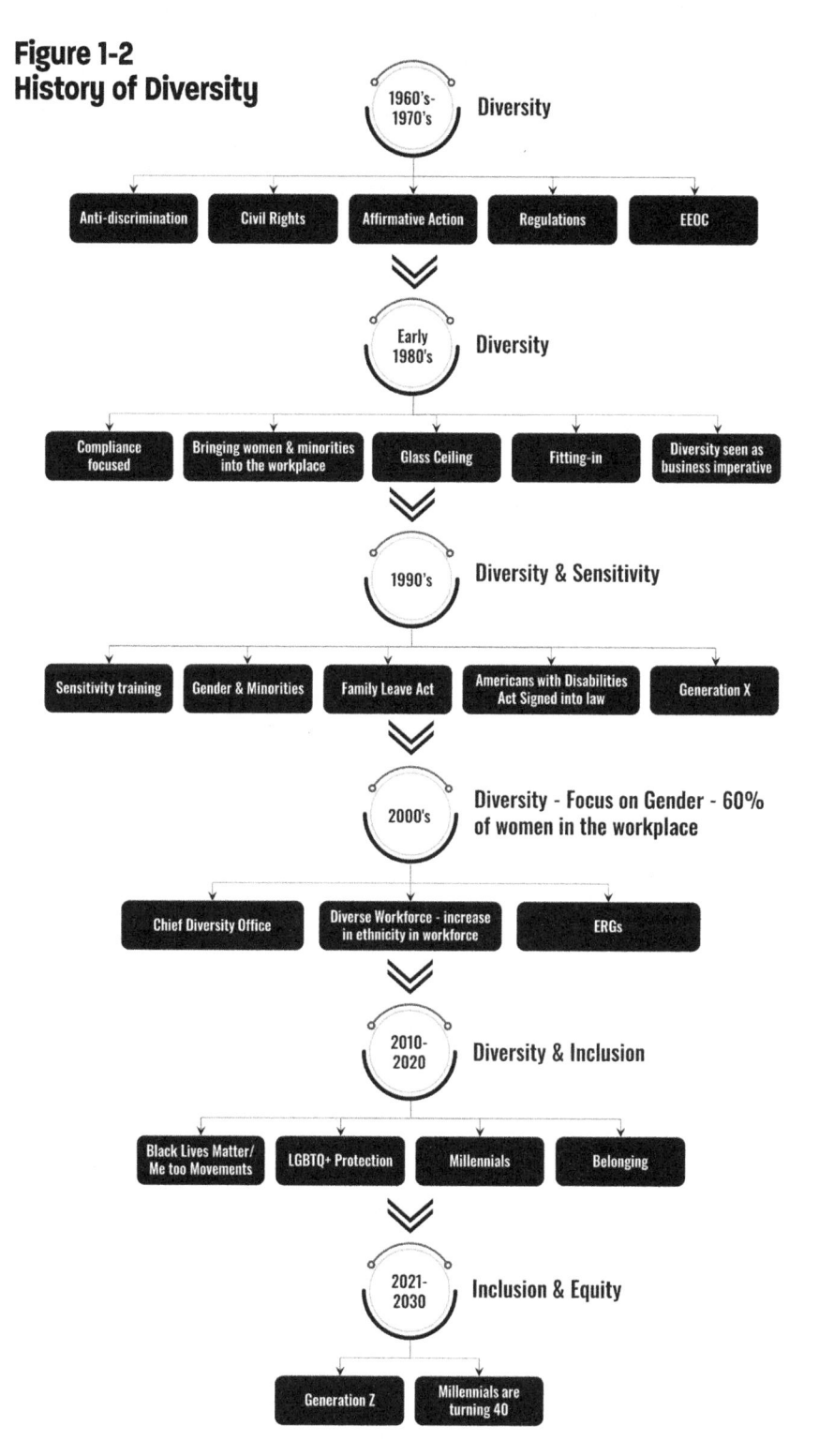

DR. LAURAN STAR

Even in reviewing the history of DE&I, the focus has been on laws and affinities rather than the "how." It is no great wonder why many in the field advocate that diversity comes first, and then you build an inclusive, effective organization. *I strongly disagree.* If your workplace culture is not inclusive, you will not keep the diversity you currently have. Here is one reason why inclusion is the foundation of ID&E. The inclusive workplace truly is an example of "if you build it, they will come." Through my work with companies, I have seen that if you build an organization that is inclusive and values its people, they will come—and stay. If you have inclusion, that means you are interacting with and utilizing the affinities people bring to the table in terms of diversity of thought and perspective, and *that's* what we are utilizing in business. I'm not talking about skills, because those are learned. I'm talking about perceptions and experiences. For example, people may be able to share barriers they've experienced, and that can illuminate something for the company.

No matter what industry you're in, diversity in the workplace is critical to organizational success, as the desire to understand the customer's perspective is an imperative (no matter who your customer is). For example, in the healthcare space, it is imperative the workforce shares the same diversity as the people it treats. I was fortunate enough to work with a large healthcare partnership organization where they were committed to inclusion first. They built it and yes, the employees came. They are one of the largest healthcare providers in the Northeast with an attrition rate below 3%, and the diversity of their workforce exceeds member representation. It is important to note, they never focused on diversity first, and their focus remains on inclusion as the core of their organizational culture.

Through the Diversity Lens: A 2020+ Snapshot

Here is a snapshot of where we are on workplace diversity in the business climate here in the United States. Remember to keep in mind that the dominant (yet misguided) focus within the workplace is diversity, not inclusion.

Statistics are a great way to examine trends with an organization or demographic. Here are some interesting figures from the US General Census:

- White, non-Hispanic in the United States population is declining (from 63.7% in 2010 to 57% in 2020).[9]
- In 2019, the US workforce was comprised of the following ethnic percentages: White = 78%, Black and African American = 13%, Hispanic or Latinx = 18% and Asian = 6%
- Note: This is a workforce number, not a census number.
- By 2044, groups formerly seen as "minorities" will reach majority status as a collective.[10]
- By 2065, the US population will not have any single ethnic or racial majorities, according to the Pew Research Center.[11]

Trends in Talent

It appears that unemployment among veterans, the disabled, and people of color rose in 2020. Organizations were unable to retain these largely untapped talent groups. (numbers?)

- Women are expected to make up 47.2% of the workforce by 2024. We have a long way to go and this says nothing about equity, leadership roles and the C-suite.[12]
- Women have more higher education degrees compared to men, driving the competitive workplace landscape—yet only 8% (41 women) of Fortune 500 CEOs are women,[13] and only 4% are women of color.[14]
- As of 2021, there were only 4 Black CEOs of Fortune 500 companies.[15]
- According to Glassdoor, 76% of potential employees evaluate an organization based on diversity and 80% based on culture.[16]
- Over half of organizational employees feel their organization needs to improve diversity, but they are at a loss as to how.
- In 2021, 82% of organizations that started a diversity initiative as a response to an event found those initiatives fell short or failed.

In reviewing the latest and greatest diversity trends, it is pretty obvious where organizations are focused: gender and people of color. However, those are only two affinities out of many. Moreover, there are many affinities that are completely left out (more on this in Chapter 2).

When I ask if an organization is diverse, it is not surprising that I often hear, "Absolutely, my company is diverse" or "I have no idea." Think about it this way. If an organization is only looking to add one or two affinities, they may be diverse in that affinity; however, the workforce is not diverse. So, when I hear the first comment, I always ask the person to explain: "What do you mean by diverse—how do you know? And through that diversity, what is the impact?" I often get the deer-in-the-headlights look in answer to that the last question.

Workplace Diversity Is Broken

> *"Diversity, or the state of being different, isn't the same as inclusion. One is a description of what is, while the other describes a style of interaction essential to effective teams and organizations."*
> — *Bill Crawford*

The concept of workplace diversity is not new, and while there has been great movement here and there, we still have a long way to go. Society's perspective on diversity has also shifted, as in the 1970s diversity was equated with minority advancement and today diversity has become a business case followed by blame.[17] You'll often find in organizations that diversity training and diversity initiatives have left some feeling the burden of blame, i.e., "it is not my fault we lack women in leadership." Research also has demonstrated that diversity initiatives may leave some questioning the skills of a minority affinity group when they advance within the organization. (You've probably heard some variation on "She was only promoted because she's a woman.")

Even though it is the wrong one, diversity has become the needle that we in business and society are focusing on to determine business success. Let's think about the definition: **Workforce diversity** *refers to the individual affinities employees have that make them unique. These characteristics can include gender, race, ethnicity, religion, age, sexual orientation, sexual identification, veteran status, disabilities, physical abilities, and ideologies.* Diversity allows us to separate employees into affinity groups and measure them.

The US has been measuring affinities since 1961 with the legislative body of work known as Affirmative Action. A simple lens on a confusing action, **Affirmative Action** *is a set of procedures that are specific to business and/or governmental agencies (to include public universities) where special rights of hiring or advancement for protected classes are designed to eliminate unlawful discrimination among applicants, remedy the results of such prior discrimination, and prevent such discrimination in the future.*[18]

Furthermore, diagnostics are in place within an organization that then measure the percentage of minorities/protected classes. Although this body of legislation really helped advance minorities in the workplace, research has shown that this benefit really slowed to a stop in the 1980s due to political forces.[19] Today, affirmative action is primarily focused on organizations that have federal contracts. There are pros and cons to affirmative action, and I am not here to argue either. However, I will share that I do see this body of work as helping to tarnish the word "diversity" as it separated the workforce into affinity boxes, and some argue those boxes do not receive equal treatment.[20]

Today, the Equal Employment Opportunity Commission requires organizations to share their EEO-1 report. *This report is a mandatory annual data collection that requires all private sector employers with 100 or more employees, and federal contractors with 50 or more employees meeting certain criteria, to submit demographic workforce data, including data by race/ethnicity, sex and job categories.*[21]

The Securities and Exchange Commission (SEC) is also requiring companies to submit their Human Capital Disclosure, a new mandatory diversity reporting tool (as of August 2020) for organizations that are publicly traded on the stock market—with the goal of providing diversity transparency. This reporting requires a company to describe its human capital resources *"to the extent material to the understanding of that registrant's business taken as a whole."* Specifically, the human capital disclosure must include *"the number of persons employed by the registrant, and any human capital measures or objectives that the registrant focuses on in managing the business (such as, depending on the nature of the registrant's business and workforce, measures or objectives that address the development, attraction, and retention of personnel)."*[22]

From the top down, all this focus on affinity numbers further serves to reinforce the misguided notion that diversity needs to come first. I argue that the result of "diversity first" is costly to organizations as they are missing the foundation of inclusion. Furthermore, organizations are hiring diversity managers and directors to manage initiatives, without the strong foundation. This leads to a situation where everybody's an expert in diversity, yet they're lacking the true practitioner's knowledge, skills, and abilities (KSA) for inclusion & diversity.

Please let me reaffirm, diversity initiatives are not one-size-fits-all and may often alienate many of those in the room. Diversity is not sensitivity training and blaming. We need to shift our lens and pivot to seeing diversity for what it truly is. It is an affinity that drives diversity of thought and life perspectives. It is a measurable metric in the workplace. However, employees have more than one affinity, meaning there is quite a bit of intersectionality, so at best it remains difficult to see what those numbers really mean if we "count" just one affinity.

For example, how does your workplace diversity coordinator "count" or categorize an affluent woman of color who holds an MBA and is a lesbian? Diversity is a label that separates employees into groups. In that regard, I argue that the word "diversity" does more harm than good in the workplace, and the research backs me up. Separate a bag of Skittles candy by colors, then count how many of each color you have—that is diversity. So, what does that tell you about the bag of Skittles? That there are four different colors and the numbers of each color. What that doesn't tell you is how they interact with each other, the outcome of the bag, and potentially the risks of indulging in that much sugar.

The Risks of Focusing on Diversity Initiatives

During my research, I discovered that the current literature has determined the risks and return on investments when an organization attains diversity. Research has often shown that diversity initiatives 1) are done incorrectly, 2) are done without a defined goal, 3) have the wrong person leading the change, 4) lack full leadership buy-in, and 5) may have the right goal but the wrong initiative. These five points can have a detrimental impact on your workplace and its culture.[23] Add to that the normal human resistance to change, and if there are any difficult organizational traits to overcome in diversity, then diversity is already set up to struggle. When diversity programs fail, organizations can find themselves facing employees who feel alienated, singled out, blamed, and excluded.[24]

Unfortunately, once these attitudes set into an organization, it is hard to reset and move forward. It is no wonder we are now seeing a rise in alienation and diversity fatigue, and an increase in trust issues, especially affecting the human resource manager and those held accountable for diversity. The word "diversity" has morphed itself into the be-all word, encompassing diversity, inclusion, equity, belonging, and in some instances, racial differences, leaving little room for error.

Alienation and Exclusion

One risk of diversity initiatives has been shown to be alienation and exclusion. This risk can happen with diversity initiatives and training for a variety of reasons, from poorly communicated material and lack of transparency to measuring the wrong outcomes and goals of the program. Alienation of employees happens when one protected group (the out-group) is the focus of the diversity program and thus allows blame or perception of blame to be placed on others for their overall lack of equality.

Furthermore, exclusion creates the us-versus-them workforce atmosphere that damages the construct of diversity. Blame then in turn promotes resistance to any changes. One example is Lipman's (2018) research on gender-focused diversity training and its effect on men. The study demonstrated that men who left a gender-diversity training program reported feeling alienated. Lipman further concluded that this may have promoted an atmosphere of resistance toward change and the other gender (women).

Diversity Fatigue

Another risk organizations must be aware of is diversity fatigue. Diversity fatigue happens when those who work in the diversity field become exhausted from trying to change the organization.[25] Diversity fatigue is seen in the workplace when those entrusted with driving diversity become burnt out due to lack of change and progress in the organization. This occurs when diversity initiatives and programs become more "check the box" than focused on shifting attitudes and behaviors. Those in the diversity and inclusion field may feel isolated when the organization mandates diversity shifts and initiatives.

I am waiting to hear the term "inclusion fatigue," as organizations are slowly slipping into using this newly trendy word, even while they are still wrongly focused on diversity first instead of inclusion. Diversity fatigue is caused by ineffective training and diversity initiatives that result in harming the organization's inclusion.[26] Poorly planned initiatives that must be restarted again and again increase the risk of diversity fatigue, even for the organization's employees. It also refers to the time and energy spent on diversity while seeing no improvement.

Employees also can suffer diversity fatigue. This occurs when action plans fall apart, there is repeated training on the same concepts of diversity, and when the focus is on one affinity group, such as gender. This all leads to employees feeling more marginalized and an overwhelming fatigue towards diversity training due to the lack of results.

Take the case of Wanda, for example, a senior human resource vice president who was put in charge of DE&I at her organization in 2014, in response to the Black Lives Matter movement. In 2016 she hired me for coaching. She was exhausted, frustrated, angry, and a bit lost. Her expertise was total rewards/compensation and operations, not DE&I, but she was a person of color (one reason her company gave her for the assignment). In the two years she was in this role, her health declined, she gained 30 pounds, stopped working out, was put on hypertension medication, and her husband and friends shared she was just no fun anymore. Wanda was putting in 50 hours a week at work, hitting her head against the wall to create programs and initiatives that had limited results or could not produce measurement metrics. She felt her overall value to the organization was falling short as she could not succeed in driving diversity companywide.

Does this sound familiar to you? Wanda was in the wrong role, playing to her KSA deficits rather than to her strengths. No matter how many times she expressed her concerns about this, she felt unheard (a sign the culture is lacking inclusion). This is a severe case of diversity fatigue with only one solution. Upon going through coaching with me, she left the organization to pursue a more fitting opportunity. I am happy to say Wanda found a better fit elsewhere, at an organization where her talents and strengths were appreciated. She is now healthier and much happier.

When it comes to diversity initiatives, we need to go back to the foundation for every new idea or program. What problem are we trying to solve in the organization; what will improving diversity solve? That's a tough question, but we need to ask it and then gather data to support the desired need for a solution. Please remember that we do *not* need to start from scratch every time we "hear" about diversity and inclusion or now, "belonging." Ask these five questions before you spring for a new diversity initiative or program:

- What are we trying to solve in the organization; what problem will improving diversity solve?
- Does this initiative align with the organization's business strategy?
- Does this initiative have senior leadership support?
- How will this change be rolled out to the organization?
- How will we measure the outcome?

Lost Trust

Perhaps the greatest risk of diversity initiatives that are done poorly is lost trust. Diversity is not affirmative action or filling quotas, even though some organizations approach it that way. They desire to see an actual percentage of diversity in the working ranks and leadership, so they create programs that target that population. However, let me ask you this: Is there full transparency to the employees about the program? Does the organization openly share its goal to improve diversity of gender in senior leadership and why doing so is important? Does the initiative become focused on a select few and leave everyone else in the cold? How does intersectionality fit in?

Remember, our employees have more than one affinity. As employees are not defined by one affinity, the perception of "fairness" in the workplace appears to be skewed as many employees are quickly becoming skeptical of the return on investment from diversity programs and initiatives. The end result is a risk to trust, and that leads to a hit on employee retention.

Sustainability

Is the work you're doing in this space sustainable? Can the processes be repeatable? Are your metrics demonstrating sustainability (continuous growth)? Sustainability of inclusion and diversity is so important, because no one wants to recreate the wheel every time an organization needs to be reactive instead of proactive. In many cases, organizations jump onto the diversity bandwagon without fully understanding what they are looking for or focusing on. Diversity is not a solution to a problem and diversity alone is not sustainable. The lack of inclusion and diversity sustainability can drive all the risks mentioned above, as organizations burn through one initiative after another without ever wondering about or defining the actual change they want to see. All these programs cost money. This also leads to diversity burnout for everyone. Do your employees cringe when you mention diversity?

Inclusion and diversity work is more than just checking off the box, and that includes training. When I was working with Covidien in the early 2000s, the training department introduced a new sales model every year. In the three years I was with them, we launched SPIN Selling, Miller Heiman, Consultative Sales, and the Challenger Sales Model. The end goal was to create better sales agents out of their people, many of whom were already quite successful in selling. The cost to Covidien for *each* project ranged in the $100,000s market space. I struggled to find overwhelming evidence that any of these programs actually would work within this organization. Covidien sells medical devices, not hammers, yet one training program focused on tools. (Cue forehead smack!) The end result was that employees stopped listening to or trusting the organization, hindering the sustainability of this new shift or change. Every year, training was met with the proverbial eyeroll.

Another factor that hinders sustainability is that the diversity space is becoming saturated with consulting companies that offer to solve your diversity issue, yet prospective client organizations are lacking the foundation, focusing on the wrong training or initiatives, or are unclear on what they need, so they purchase a Band-Aid to stop the hemorrhaging. As inclusion and diversity practitioners, executives, and leaders, we need to be focused on transparency and accountability, uncovering the real issue and digging in to solve it.

The industry also appears to link diversity programs and initiatives to training and expect the same outcomes. To clear up the confusion, diversity and inclusion initiatives help organizations create a more diverse, inclusive, and equitable workforce through the utilization of programs and policies. The end goal is focused on building and maintaining a workforce culture where all are treated without bias and have equal opportunities for advancement or hiring. Diversity training, on the other hand, augments those programs and initiatives to *increase knowledge*.

The solution to all these risks is creating an inclusive culture. Inclusion is sustainable as the organizational culture will adapt with the changing times and will remain inclusive—thus driving employee job satisfaction, innovation (which is critical to sustainable trends in new product development and solutions) and employee retention (as employees are heard). The research does demonstrate strong benefits to workplace inclusion (we will hit all of those benefits in Chapter 4). Yet, with all this data and the overwhelming lack of results, today we are still focused on diversity in the workplace.

Focused on the Wrong Needle

Companies often latch onto the newest ID&E buzzwords in part because it is easier than admitting, "Hey, our diversity efforts have not worked." What was the end outcome? Diversity was the buzzword in the workplace until the mid-2000s, when "inclusion" caught on. And while the word changed, the focus did not. Often an organization uses "inclusion" when they really mean "diversity" and base their initiatives on diversity drivers rather than on inclusion drivers.

We need to have the strength to *speak truth to power*. To openly have conversations with senior leadership around the impact the word "diversity" has and the process itself. We need to stop being afraid to have these conversations in the workplace. As a leader, if you fear saying the wrong thing, please do not just leave it on the table—pull up your big girl/boy pants and have the conversation anyway. Here is what I have seen work when leaders struggle to speak truth to power. I encourage you to identify the elephant in the room: "I am not sure how to say this as it may be seen as offensive, so let me start off by saying my goal is not to be offensive. However, I need to speak truth to power."

While this work is not easy, the results are extremely rewarding. We as practitioners need to demand better for the workforce and understand the full implications of our work. We need to hold leadership and the C-suite accountable for the work that needs to be done. Diversity in the workplace is not a one-person role, it is a companywide mission, if you desire for it to take hold. So take hold of inclusion and move diversity forward; what are we waiting for?

As I mentioned before, there's $8 billion a year thrown at diversity training that isn't necessarily doing what it's supposed to. According to the Massachusetts Institute of Technology, this number is growing annually. There must be an equation in many corporate heads that says: "Diversity Training = Diversity, Right?" Wrong! While training increases awareness, it does not actually increase diversity.

Let me stop the guesswork right now: **If you are looking to improve organizational diversity for diversity of thought, it is the organizational culture of inclusion that drives success.** Think about that for a minute. What does each affinity group bring to the table besides the affinity? If we were talking brown eyes and blue eyes, they bring nothing to the table other than eye color. However, we're not talking about eye color or hair color, we're talking about diversity affinities that directly shape a person's perspective or thoughts on life. And that, my friend, is the moneymaker: Organizations want diversity of thought and diversity of perspectives, which is what drives productivity, conflict resolution, communication, job satisfaction, and more. To enjoy these benefits, your workforce needs to be open to sharing their diversity of thoughts and perspectives. The organizational culture must support the workforce in doing this.

The greater the amount of variance within an organization's affinity scale or diversity scale, the more diverse perspectives we'll have when we're in a room together. However, if the organization is not inclusive, no one is going to hear the diverse perspectives. And that's why we truly need to focus on building an inclusive organization before we try to build a diverse one.

I have provided you with a look into DE&I's past and present state. I've demonstrated the business case is missing for diversity alone. And, we've taken a look at how affirmative action, risky diversity initiatives, and a misplaced focus on diversity have all damaged an already damaged system.

There is still a bit more on diversity affinities we need to understand as well as level setting the diversity frames. Let us dig deeper into what diversity is—what the protected classes are AND where organizations are missing the boat on recruiting amazing talent.

2

The Lenses of Diversity Are More than Gender and Color

Every employee has a unique set of affinities and lived experiences. We as practitioners need to embrace that uniqueness rather than slotting our employees in a box for counting.

With diversity, the temptation is to default to the "typical" notions, put employees into boxes so we can count and label them, and call it a day. Yet as one contributor notes later in this chapter, putting people in boxes with labels can feel patronizing—and does nothing to improve inclusion or help diversity stick.

Typical Lenses of Diversity

There is no typical lens of diversity. Yes, we currently have eight protected classes, but diversity itself is untypical in large part due to intersectionality (see Chapter 4). Diversity is more than gender or color—although these may be the first categories that come to mind when you're asked about diversity. There's also cultural diversity, physical diversity (increased hiring of candidates with physical disabilities, for example), generational diversity, neural diversity/neurodiversity, and intersectionality. Then, of course, we need to examine the diversity we find within an organization. Every individual has a unique set of affinities and lived experiences. We as practitioners need to embrace that uniqueness rather than slotting our employees in a box for counting.

As inclusion and diversity practitioners we need to focus on what is evident versus what is political, what is evidence based and proven, utilizing critical thinking. We need to review ID&E with an open mind and a clear lens before jumping right in.

At first, diversity in the workplace focused on markers associated with what we call "protected classes." According to the Thomson Reuters Practical Law website, a protected class is *"a group of people with a common/similar characteristic and affinities who are legally protected from employment discrimination based on that characteristic. Protected classes are created by both federal and state law."* The US Equal Employment Opportunity Commission (EEOC) website lists these protected classes:

- Race/Ethnicity
- Color
- Religion or creed
- National origin or ancestry
- Sex (including gender, pregnancy, sexual orientation, and gender identity)
- Age (40 or older)
- Physical, mental, and learning disability
- Veteran status
- Genetic information
- Citizenship

Under the EEOC, applicants, employees and former employees are also protected from retaliation (punishment) for filing a charge or complaint of discrimination, participating in a discrimination investigation or lawsuit, or opposing discrimination (for example, threatening to file a charge or complaint of discrimination). The EEOC was established and laws were passed to correct a history of unfavorable treatment of women and minority group members, yet I sit back and ask—what about today?

How does the EEOC become more proactive rather than reactive to issues? From the protected class lens, are not we all protected within the organization? Yet today more so than ever, the protected class lens is constantly under political siege. One only has to turn on the TV to see where politicians flip-flop. We are in a business world where equality is a political question or debate. Utilizing a critical lens, I ask, is the EEOC list up to date? What about sexual orientation and gender identification (SOGI)? Race and color really need to be updated; does not ethnicity cover both? Genetic information is fairly new, and legal is still catching up; where are the gaps? How do new state laws protect or discriminate against protected classes?

As inclusion and diversity practitioners, our role goes beyond the workplace as we should be reviewing and suggesting changes in the EEOC and its legislative body to be more inclusive. Yes, we need to become beacons of change, rather than sitting on the sidelines, and our organizations should support that change and our actions.

Ethnicity vs. Race

We can't have an informed discussion about diversity without looking at a few loaded terms. I prefer to use "ethnicity," not "race," because race is a sociopolitical construct that is very confusing. Remember, we are focused here on improving workplace diversity and inclusion—not on solving wider societal problems such as racism.

To put it simply, race is a person's physical qualities that make them fit into distinct groups. Groups of people who share similar physical and/or cultural beliefs and characteristics, like the color of their skin, are grouped together in racial categories. Yet, people belong to many different cultures that shape their perspective (not one culture) and there is quite a bit of intersectionality in culture. Moreover, is the utilization of race healthy? Race thinking polarizes individuals. There is no "race chromosome" in our DNA. We also should not be defined by one affinity, either. For example, are all Caucasians from England? No. To add to the confusion, race is ever-changing based on the political environment. For example, in the US, people from Mexico have been sometimes counted as "white" and other times not, and at one point in US history, the definition of "Black" varied from state to state.[27]

Furthermore, **while we have been trained to think that race was biologically determined, science has now proven that race is a social** construct.[28] Scientists have argued for phasing out racial terminology in the biological sciences, "as racial categories are weak proxies for genetic diversity." The researchers do acknowledge that using race as a political or social category to study racism is still necessary, to understand "how structural inequities and discrimination produce health disparities between groups." In 2020, the American Medical Association came out with a statement along similar lines, recognizing race as a social, rather than a biological, construct.[29]

But what does that mean, exactly? Well, at one point people thought that when you were of a certain race, you were significantly biologically different from people of other races. This was often used as a means to oppress people or treat one group of people worse than others. For instance, one of the justifications for American slavery was that Black people were inherently genetically inferior to white people, making the latter the "superior" race. Recent science has shown that race is actually something developed and assigned by society. **That is, scientists have discovered that a person's race doesn't make them significantly genetically different than anyone else.**[30] Race has been a way for societies to differentiate people based on common physically expressed traits.

Want more evidence that race is a social construct? The Human Genome Project proved humans are 99.9% alike in genome structure. There is no one skin color; we say "black," yet there are unlimited shades of "black" as there are many shades of "white." Did you know even Crayola, the crayon company, now has a color pack called "Colors of the world" with 24 shades of skin tone AND white and black are NOT in the box of colors.

To add to the confusion, census forms frequently ask about our ethnicity, yet there are also questions on race and color. Are you White or European American; Black or African American; Asian American; American Indian/Alaska Native; and/or Native Hawaiian/Pacific Islander? You can identify as "white" AND be two or more ethnicities. What about Asian Mexicans? How do they define? Choose two or more categories? To add more confusion, any time we apply for a job we get asked to define our race and/or ethnicity and in that selection, we have ethnicity and color noted. Color is not a race.

The workplace lens needs to remove color and race from its construct on self-identifying questions, and maybe provide more defined descriptions as well as the reason for why are we asking this question. As inclusion and diversity practitioners, we need to help remove some of the confusion around ethnicity and race. To that point, the US Census recognizes six ethnic categories: white, black, Asian, Amerindian/Alaska native, native Hawaiian/Pacific Islander, and mixed ethnicity. Yet in many other regions, such as Africa and Asia, there are literally hundreds of distinct ethnic groups within various national borders.

Taken directly from the US Census Bureau, the table below shows what each ethnicity category includes.[31]

Table 2-1 US Ethnicity Categories

Ethnicity or Color	Defined
White	• Origins in any of the original peoples of Europe, the Middle East, or North Africa. • Includes people who indicate their race as "White" • Entries such as Irish, German, Italian, Lebanese, Arab, Moroccan, or Caucasian.
Asian	• Origins in any of the original peoples of the Far East, Southeast Asia, or the Indian subcontinent • Includes Cambodia, China, India, Japan, Korea, Malaysia, Pakistan, the Philippine Islands, Thailand, and Vietnam.
Amerindian/ Alaska native	• Origins in any of the original peoples of North and South America (including Central America) and who maintains tribal affiliation or community attachment. • Includes people who indicate their race as "American Indian or Alaska Native" • Entries such as Navajo, Blackfeet, Inupiat, Yup'ik, or Central American Indian groups or South American Indian groups.

Native Hawaiian/ Pacific Islander	• Origins in any of the original peoples of Hawaii, Guam, Samoa, or other Pacific Islands. • Includes people who reported their race as "Fijian," "Guamanian or Chamorro," "Marshallese," "Native Hawaiian," "Samoan," "Tongan," and "Other Pacific Islander" or provide other detailed Pacific Islander responses.
Mixed Ethnicity / 2 or More	• People may choose to provide two or more races either by checking two or more race response check boxes, by providing multiple responses, or by some combination of check boxes and other responses. • For data product purposes, "Two or More Races" refers to combinations of two or more of the following race categories: "White," "Black or African American," American Indian or Alaska Native," "Asian," Native Hawaiian or Other Pacific Islander," or "Some Other Race

Read this table—does it confuse you? Pakistan is in South Asia and may align with some cultural traditions, however some see Pakistan as being part of the "Greater Middle East," so someone with Pakistani heritage could identify as white OR mixed ethnicity. The Middle East is considered "white," according to the US Census. Mixed ethnicity is a bit more confusing as it is rare to just be one ethnicity. What about being white in skin color yet being from Africa? Does that person identify as black or white, and why by color? Do our employees know this? Are we all on the same page when self-identifying? I'm thinking probably not. You know what they say about data: bad data in creates bad data out.

Beyond reporting ethnicity in the workplace to the government, what is the goal or purpose of self-identifying our ethnicity in the workplace? I have pondered this question quite a bit, and the evidence demonstrates the purpose is just to measure the different protected class affinities. Yes, some may say it's to better the workplace or highlight barriers or to understand different cultural backgrounds; however, there is zero evidence that demonstrates this is the goal or the goal is met. Furthermore, take a look at the classifications: there are way too many different cultural nuances in each block. Hofstede's work on national culture (see Chapter 10) is not in alignment with the ethnic/color classification in the workplace. So, we self-identify for reporting reasons—alone.

Let me try to shed a bit more light on ethnicity in the United States. Figure 2-1 is a graph from the US Census Bureau.[32] While organizations are focusing on diversity in the workplace, often they target one race, "promote people of color (POC) into leadership, increasing POC diversity at 3%." If your organization is in the state of New Hampshire, for example, you are already setting yourself up for failure, as I often argue the state does not have the infrastructure to attract and retain diverse ethnicity which includes POC.

Figure 2-1 Racial and Ethnic Diversity Index by State: 2020

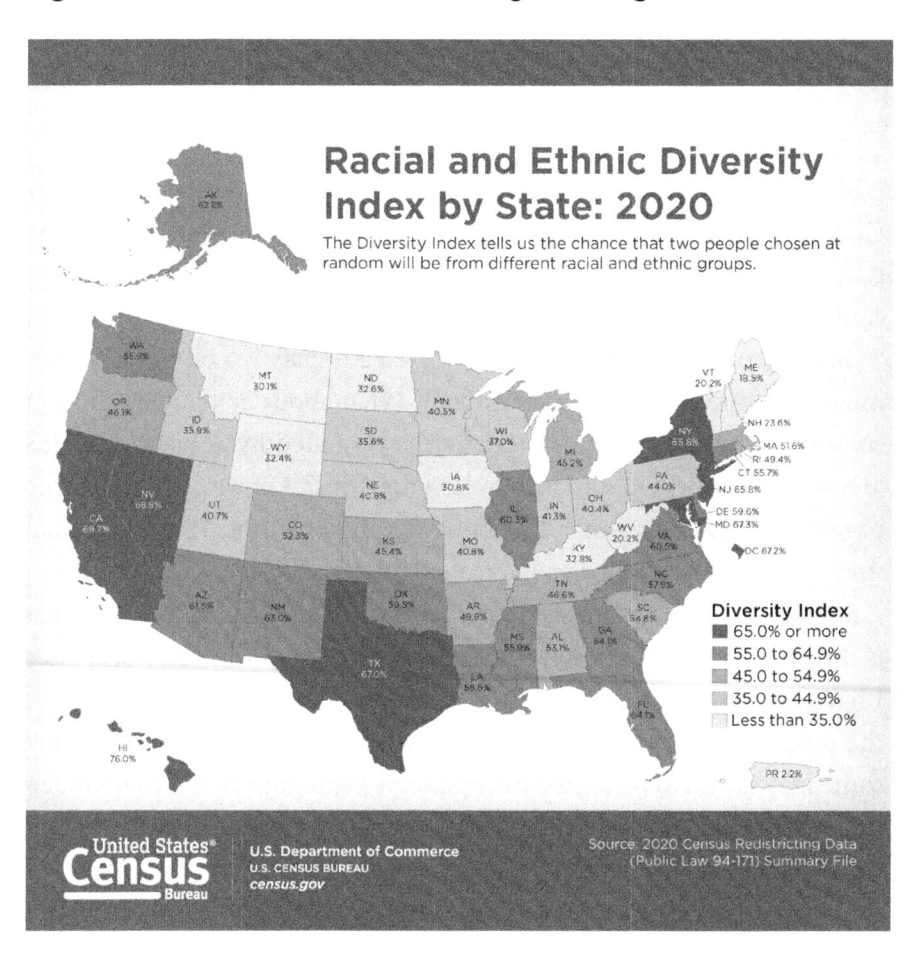

Racial and Ethnic Diversity Index by State: 2020

The Diversity Index tells us the chance that two people chosen at random will be from different racial and ethnic groups.

AK 62.8%
WA 55.9%
OR 46.1%
MT 30.1%
ND 32.6%
MN 40.5%
ID 35.9%
SD 35.6%
WI 37.0%
MI 45.2%
VT 20.2%
ME 18.5%
NH 23.6%
NY 65.8%
MA 51.6%
RI 49.4%
CT 55.7%
WY 32.4%
NE 40.8%
IA 30.8%
PA 44.0%
NJ 65.8%
NV 68.5%
CA 69.7%
UT 40.7%
CO 52.3%
KS 45.4%
MO 40.8%
IL 60.3%
IN 41.3%
OH 40.4%
WV 20.2%
VA 60.5%
DE 59.6%
MD 67.3%
DC 67.2%
AZ 61.5%
NM 63.0%
OK 50.5%
AR 49.8%
KY 32.8%
TN 46.6%
NC 57.9%
SC 54.8%
MS 55.9%
AL 53.1%
GA 64.3%
TX 67.0%
LA 58.6%
FL 64.1%
HI 76.0%
PR 2.2%

Diversity Index
- 65.0% or more
- 55.0 to 64.9%
- 45.0 to 54.9%
- 35.0 to 44.9%
- Less than 35.0%

United States Census Bureau
U.S. Department of Commerce
U.S. CENSUS BUREAU
census.gov

Source: 2020 Census Redistricting Data (Public Law 94-171) Summary File

EVIDENCE BASED INCLUSION

From here on out in this book, we will utilize the term "ethnicity" instead of "race."

The Multigenerational Workforce

We need to explore and embrace the ever-changing multigenerational workplace we now find ourselves in. This is a very unique lens as for the first time we have five generations working together, with very different lived experiences. Each has its own strengths and areas of development, and through inclusion we can all benefit from the knowledge brought to the table.

So What Defines a Generation?

Historically, we see a 30-year time period where there is a 20-year window of defining activity for each grouping based on birth years and aptitude. This is the period where a person is old enough to understand the world around them and its impact as well as their own footprint in the sand. Researchers call this period the *formative years* and they are fluid.

Sounds simple … nonetheless, one of the main struggles with defining who falls into which generation is there is no single set timeline for each generation. Look at Generation I or Z—whichever name you prefer. Some definitions place these individuals as born from 1997–2010 and others (me included) prefer to use the 2001–2015 range. So, be aware that this can only add to the confusion if we go around "labeling" employees. That said, there is some utility to understanding what makes each generation in the workplace tick, and that's why I'm tackling this topic here.

Events, culture, society, and music are some of the factors that shape each generation. During the formative years, we can also see the name of a generation shifting. For example, some call Millennials Gen Ys while others call them Gen Zs and then we see Generation I being called Generation Internet or Gen Zs as their formative years are still rolling. Generational nicknames can also harm a generation by creating self-fulfilling prophecies, as seen with Gen Y, also known as the Entitled Generation.

Beware of the Self-Fulfilling Prophecy

Case in point: Millennials. Here we have a generation of people who, when they feel they are not being included, are in fact empowered enough to take their talent and go elsewhere. And guess what? They *are* wanted elsewhere. It is the organization's loss when they lose talented members of any generation, especially when it is due to the lack of organizational inclusion.

For the sake of this book, the generations are broken out as follows in Table 2-2, because much like diversity, there are several different definition dates for each generation.

Table 2-2 Generational Workforce

Baby Boomers	**Generation X**	**Millennials**	**Generation Z**
• Born 1946–1964	• Born 1965–1976	• Born 1977–1995	• Born 1996–2010
• Formative years 1950–1969	• Cuspers 1975–1980	• Cuspers 1996–2000	• Cuspers 2010–2015
	• Formative years 1970–1989	• Formative years 1990–2009	• Formative years 2010–2029

Today our workspace has up to five different generations, including the Silent Generation (born between 1928-45). *Generational Cuspers* tend to be at the beginning or tail end of the year ranges noted and can take on traits of both their generation and the nearest adjacent one. These individuals fall between two generations as their formative years will blend the two. They have a unique vantage point on each population segment and often share dual traits. However, note that anyone can take on the values of any generation if it speaks to them.

A generation's worth is not measured in time. I would argue we truly cannot label a generation's worth due to the simple fact that greatness can happen at any given point in one's life. There is no set expiration date on success. For example, today we see Baby Boomers who are just starting to reach their full potential and members of Generation X are looking to see where they will leave their own mark. The Millennials are still too new to the workforce to even begin to comprehend what greatness they will leave as their legacy. Yet within each grouping, some have already peaked and shown sparkle. Therefore, rather than label someone based on when they were born and think we can understand them, we need awareness.

Things All Generations Have in Common:

- All have a similar motivational framework from extrinsic, to individual to intrinsic.[33]
- We are all unique and thus hate to be put in a box and labeled.
- Managers need to focus less on generational differences and look at the root of a given issue.[34]
- While some generations scream they want to be part of something bigger, it is in fact a need for all individuals to be engaged and accepted.
- "Job-hopping" is not a generational trait.[35]
- All generations are equally independent and crave autonomy.
- Job satisfaction is equal amongst all generations.
- All generations value security and professional growth equally.
- Strong leadership: each generation creates a different pattern in leadership that meets the demand of the business world at that time.
- Great leadership is NOT a generational phenomenal.
- We need each other to learn and grow.
- All are equally motivated and desire for success.
- All have shared work ethic values.[36]

Again, we have more in common with each other than not; however, each person's lived experience is the golden nugget of perspective. While I would love to do a deep dive on each generation, this book is focused on inclusion. Fear not, on the book website is a white paper highlighting what you need to know.

Generational Inclusion
Generational inclusion begins with the knowledge of a generation's

strengths, what makes them stand out, their struggles and fears. We then need to add in the individual factor around their own mindset, or as I refer to it, the generational mindset. This is the values they place on their perspective of the world around them, and how their own upbringing reflects on the personal outcomes that shape their vantage point. When you add understanding a generation to its individual mindset, you come to awareness.

U+M=A

Example: I was born in 1968—thus I am a Gen Xer, but what resonates more with me personally is Millennial thinking.

In the end I believe we have to look at what each individual brings to the table in regard to their strengths and areas of development versus when they were born. We have all heard the negative stereotypes about Millennials: *They are entitled, lazy, arrogant, spoiled, win a medal for everything, would rather talk to you through social media than face-to-face.* Yet have you ever asked yourself what is true in those stereotypes? Or asked what they are based on? Just one personal example? Ask a Traditionalist how they saw Generation X in the workplace, and you will be surprised. When Generation X entered the realm of employment they were seen as money hungry, overly driven and self-centered. Factor women into that generation and there was even a comment that women should not enter the workforce because they were not smart enough for the demands.

I, as the author, ask you to toss out what you think you know about the generations and to start pivoting your thoughts to the strengths the generations provide. There is a lot of talent in each generation, but you just might miss it if you are closed off. Organizations need to build a strong foundation of sharing perspectives and communicate openly around the need for inclusion. Inclusion does not just happen. Employees need to spend time together and value what the other brings to the table. In the end, respect for all is paramount for inclusion to succeed. Here's the kicker: it takes time, trust, and strong leadership, as inclusion cannot simply be demanded.

Hiring Untapped Potential

Today organizations are facing serious talent gaps. These gaps in both employees and leadership have been predicted in the last 20 years—yes, many of us knew the Great Resignation would happen and that there would be a large gap between available talent and the jobs that need to be filled. It also became quite apparent way back in 2000, with the birthrates declining compared to the increased number of people retiring, we would also face a large leadership crisis as there is a gap in filling those current positions with experienced individuals.

In today's business climate, it is essential that companies have a healthy organizational culture. One part of the solution to finding highly talented individuals is creating an organizational culture where all employees will thrive. A second part of the solution is uncovering highly skilled talent pools that have yet to be tapped and/or retained. These talent pools are made up of those who are veterans, disabled, and neurodivergent.

In bringing these employees forward, the organization must be both inclusive and accessible. Mentorship goes a long way in bridging any gaps in inclusion, awareness, and accessibility. You will hear me state this again and again: this all starts at the top of the house. Leadership must embrace inclusion and hiring the untapped potential.

Not only will hiring those who are veterans, disabled, and neurodivergent fill your talent gaps with skilled individuals for organizations outside the nonprofit arena, those companies that are listed on the NASDQ will benefit in improved numbers on the Human Capital Report. In August 2021, the SEC approved Nasdaq Stock Market LLC's rule changes[37] related to board diversity and disclosure, which will require each Nasdaq-listed company (subject to certain exceptions) to have at least two diverse board members, or to explain why it does not.[38] All publicly traded companies are required to disclose what their human capital (employees) looks like. Think of it this way: we know that companies with an inclusive culture hire and retain top talent that is diverse. That diversity in turn drives organizational success. So why would I as an investor support an organization that is not inclusive and continuously loses their top talent resulting in decreased profits when I have other companies to invest in with better talent retention and profits?

Veterans

In the last three years, organizations have demonstrated the struggle to retain employees who are veterans of the armed forces. This is a federal affinity group, yet it gets very little attention. In 2020, 18.5 million men and women were veterans, and veteran job seekers are 15.6% more likely to be underemployed than nonveteran job seekers.[39] I look at veterans as a specialty affinity group, meaning I must ensure there are workplace programs in place to support many veterans. If an organization has the intent to hire more veterans, it must be ready with senior leadership buy-in and support, a clear sense of what specific needs are in place (i.e., strong mental health programs), and ensuring that job postings and resume reviews include veteran-friendly language.

Job descriptions and military positions need alignment. Recruit Military has a complimentary e-book that aligns job functions with Military Occupational Specialty (MOS) as they understand the military-to-civilian language.[40] There are many tools online that can help your recruiters align veterans by career choice. I suggest having a specialist on your team who is a veteran advocate to work with potential veteran candidates and have them active on LinkedIn with veteran recruitment and with continuing education for veterans. There are small nuances when comparing civilians and veterans, and we need to appreciate both groups. Keep in mind that once you hire a veteran, the support needs to continue, as the civilian business world is very different than the military world. However, the benefits of hiring a veteran are outstanding.

The benefits of hiring veterans include leadership and management excellence, loyalty, goal orientation, team building, work ethic, and more.[41] This diversity of thought has many facets from performance and strategy to processes and innovation. Furthermore, your organization may be eligible for a work opportunity tax credit. The IRS has specific guidelines on this (see https://www.irs.gov/businesses/small-businesses-self-employed/work-opportunity-tax-credit#targeted).

Individuals with Disabilities

Think about this: According to Survey of Income and Program Participation

(SIPP) data, approximately 54 million Americans have a disability. Of that number, 5.4 million are unemployed yet are ready and looking for work. That's a lot of untapped potential. A critical factor in employing those with disabilities is accessibility, followed by awareness.

The workplace culture must be safe for employees to disclose their disability and employees should be celebrated for their perspectives. There is a need to destigmatize disabilities and mental illness; by doing so, you make it easier for people in your workplace to self-identify and/or disclose if they have a disability. Individuals with disabilities is an affinity group that has demonstrated a strong return on investment upon hiring. Yet again, your organization needs to ensure it has a disability policy AND a realistic Accommodation Policy (see the book's website for more information on these). This group is full of untapped potential and may come with tax benefits depending upon which state your workplace is located in.[42] Disabilities include but are not limited to:

- Learning disorders
- Medical disability
- Psychological disability
- Hearing impairment
- Mobility impairment
- Temporary disability condition
- Neurodiversity / Neurodivergent

Once again, we see the benefits through diversity of thought when hiring someone with disabilities. Individuals with disabilities are just as motivated for excellence and advancement, plus they tend to be creative, talented, and loyal, and see the world through a very different lens.

When we add the lens of intersectionality, you may find many of your current employees have undisclosed disabilities. When I examine workplace culture, disclosure of a disability sheds a light on how inclusive the culture is. Remember, inclusion is feeling you fit within the company—that the company values you and wants to know how best to support you. It is no wonder companies listed on DiversityInc's "Top Companies for People with Disability" are thriving in today's market.[43] Companies such as Eli Lilly and Company, TD Bank, Mastercard, and Hilton value and support all their employees, regardless of disability; however, they go above and beyond supporting those with disabilities.

A significant subset of disability hires falls to neurodivergence, including hiring employees who may have a learning disorder (ADD, dyslexia, etc.) or those on the autism spectrum. These are brilliant employees, with an affinity that makes them unique.

Neurodiversity

People who are neurodivergent may have autism, ADD, ADHD, sensory processing disorder, dyslexia, dyscalculia, dysgraphia, epilepsy, PTSD, Tourette's syndrome, mental illness, alexithymia, or Asperger's syndrome, to name a few.

Figure 2-2 Neurodiverse Brain

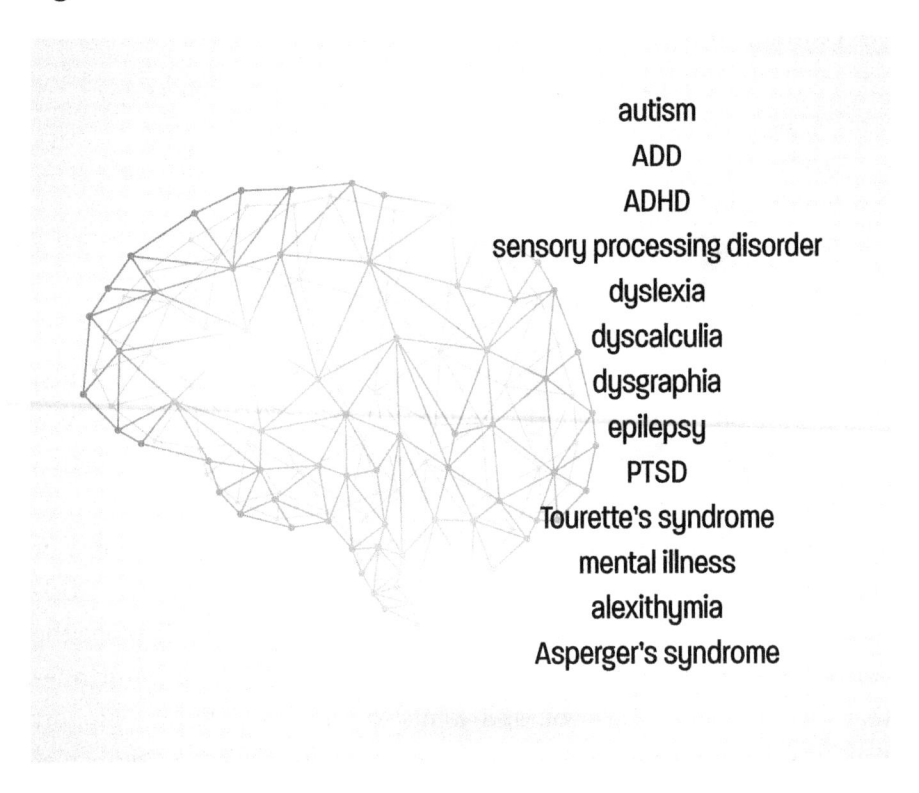

autism
ADD
ADHD
sensory processing disorder
dyslexia
dyscalculia
dysgraphia
epilepsy
PTSD
Tourette's syndrome
mental illness
alexithymia
Asperger's syndrome

Being neurodivergent myself (I am dyslexic), I would like to provide a bit more background on the neurodivergent workforce. It should not be surprising that currently, when an organization looks at neurodiversity, it finds that many of its employees are neurodivergent. However, we often find that employees with neurological differences tend to stay silent. They do not report or check the box for having a disability, often due to lack of knowledge that they fall under a disability and/or feelings of shame. For this section, I reached out to Susan Fitzell, MEd, CSP, president at Susan Fitzell & Associates, to gain more perspective.

Susan Fitzell, MEd, CSP, Author, Speaker and Consultant, works with organization leaders, and employees embracing neurodivergence into the workplace. For more information, visit Susan's website at www.susanfitzell.com.

Let's begin with a few definitions:

- **Neurodiversity** is the diversity of human minds, the infinite variation in neurocognitive functioning within our species.
- **Neurodivergent**, sometimes abbreviated as ND, means having a brain that functions in ways that diverge significantly from the dominant societal standards of "normal."
- **Neurotypical**, often abbreviated as NT, means having a style of neurocognitive functioning that falls within the dominant societal standards of "normal."
- **Neurominority** refers to any group, such as people with autism, which differs from the majority of a population in terms of behavioral traits and brain function.

Neurodivergent Thinkers

What can employees with dyslexia, autism or dyspraxia, or who are differently abled bring to a company? People whose brains process information differently than the majority of us (the neurotypical humans) are considered neurodivergent. Adding divergent thinkers to teams in the workplace may be the best investment a company can make to increase its competitive advantage. Neurodivergent employees think in ways that bring a different level of talent and skill to the problem-solving process. For example, a person with dyslexia can be an advantage to a company that needs someone skilled in pattern recognition. "Many people with these disorders have higher-than-average abilities; research shows that some conditions, including autism and dyslexia, can bestow special skills in pattern recognition, memory, or mathematics. Yet those affected often struggle to fit the profiles sought by prospective employers," said Robert D. Austin and Gary P. Pisano in a *Harvard Business Review* article.[44]

Neurodivergent team members challenge groupthink and the status quo, which can help a company because this brings a new perspective to process improvement, problem-solving, and innovation. These team members can see value and opportunity in areas that may be otherwise overlooked or put aside.

The Business Case of Neurodiversity

Some companies are leveraging divergent thinkers' powerful skill sets. At companies like SAP—one of the first companies to develop a neurodiversity program—as well as Google, Microsoft, IBM, Hewlett Packard Enterprise, Ford and others, divergent thinkers have helped to drive innovation and find radical solutions to tough problems. Accommodating the preferences of neurodiverse teams can drive positive changes across the workforce. In fact, "paying attention to the comfort of your diverse employees, especially neurodiverse ones, will make your working environment better for your staff," writes Celia Daniels in a Daivergent blog post.[45] At SAP, including divergent thinkers on teams had an immediate effect. "SAP teams who have colleagues with autism report a rise in patent applications, innovations in products, and an increase in management skills and empathy," said SAP's chief executive Christian Klein, according to a report on The Conversation.[46] Keep in mind, inclusion is the foundation for neurodiversity.

Research shows that neurodivergent employees can help boost profits because their contribution increases the opportunity to discover better solutions.[47] There's so much to be gained. However, if we don't do the groundwork first, the initiative may fail. It may turn into a poor experience for the team, and worse, a bad experience for the neurodivergent employee. As with all other diversity initiatives, the repercussions of this failed initiative can be devastating because divergent thinkers have often experienced years of unemployment, underemployment, being let go from a company, or not even getting in the door because they don't interview well. Their confidence levels may not be very high to begin with and to have a bad experience on top of that can have a tremendously detrimental effect.

How to Lay the Groundwork for Neurodiversity in the Workplace

Why would an initiative designed to support neurodivergent employees end up failing some of them? There's been much research about the competitive advantage of diversity in regard to ethnicity, gender, sexual orientation, and socioeconomic status. Diversity among our brains is another kind of diversity. The interest in building capacity for neurodiversity in the workplace is based on evidence that neurodiversity also gives companies a large competitive advantage. And while that is true, the benefits only appear when the neurodiversity program is done right. The risk of course, is that when such a program is done wrong, it could be a complete failure, leaving damaging fallout (the human kind) in its wake.

The reality is this is often how diversity initiatives are brought into our organizations. The idea is brought to the table and is developed into an initiative. Then, somewhere between conception and implementation, the process for hiring and supporting a diverse workforce fails. If we're going to do this work, we need to do it right. We need to proceed thoughtfully and with sensitivity. We need to leave our ego behind and listen to divergent thinkers' concerns. When we include people in our workplace who cognitively process information in a different way, the benefit to the company and to coworkers can be immense if implemented thoughtfully.[48]

Recruiting and Hiring Neurodivergence

It's easy to see that customary hiring practices will almost always miss neurodivergent talent. Trying to change this by hunting for more variety in candidates has been shown not to work. The *Harvard Business Review* article noted, "Many have taken that approach: Their managers still work top down from strategies to capabilities needed, translating those into organizational roles, job descriptions, and recruiting checklists. But two big problems cause them to miss neurodiverse talent."[49] Those two problems are traditional interviewing approaches and a desire for conformity. These are trouble spots, especially for those on the autism spectrum. At recruitment, accommodation or support is often poor. Not out of desire, but often because staff have few reference points. There are often few sources for guidance beyond rigid standard policies.

Many people on the autism spectrum do not interview well. They may have trouble making eye contact or take the conversation off on a tangent. Worse, their confidence may be low due to poor interview experiences in their past. The traditional interview is not a good way to assess their capabilities. Companies recruiting neurodivergent talent are adjusting their interview and selection process to be more inclusive.

Once employed, there's often a gap in support, and often that support needs to be in place before new hire onboarding. Support may include technical equipment, mentor partners, or sensory tools, for example. Awareness training on neurodiversity also goes a long way in providing inclusion for all employees. Once again, if you are looking to include neurodiversity within your workplace—and you should—intent is critical for success.

Remember to take care not to put neurodivergent individuals in a box with a label. It feels patronizing to some of them. Celebrate their divergent thinking without labeling their giftedness. Create a safe space where employees can share their neurodiversity—I am dyslexic and openly share that with anyone and everyone. My thinking and learning pattern are different than others; however, it is not a label that defines me. Susan Fitzell suggests the following best practices; please note that these best practices also work very well for other affinities, too:

- **New ways of communicating with each other can be promoted.**[50]
Employees can become more aware of how they speak to or email each

other. Managers can approach employees from a more empathetic standpoint and discard the old "my way or the highway" attitude that practically defined the corporate workplace just a couple of decades ago.
- **Make a cultural shift in the workplace.** As we move forward with neurodiversity, employees and managers must be given the opportunity and training that causes a shift in their perspective. That shift can't be forced. It must come from the lens that there is much to be gained, personally and professionally, from embracing neurodiverse teams in the workplace.
- **Create a work space that is psychologically safe for neurodivergent employees.**[51] In fact, all employees will be more effective when the workplace culture fosters safety: safety for the open expression of ideas, for differences in work styles, for different learning and communication preferences, and for diversity.
- **Pivotally level set your organizational language** so there is a clearly defined meaning to neurodiversity. It takes away the fear and neutralizes unconscious biases.
- **Ensure the inclusion of divergent thinkers at the table.** This is critical. The table must be safe for different thinkers. Without thoughtful implementation of safety, the results can be devastating for both companies and individuals. Some neurodivergent employees have already been casualties of good intentions in companies that have not carefully implemented these initiatives. The reality is that most companies already have neurodivergent thinkers in their ranks. The overwhelming majority of those employees are in hiding. They are invisible, unknown and unrecognized.
- **Avoid stigma and labeling of neurodivergent employees.** It follows that true inclusivity is not achieved through a "one-size-fits-all" approach. Rather than consider a job prospect's specialization and skills, employers are often quick to dismiss their candidacy because of their social challenges. Neurodivergent thinkers are often labeled as "disabled" when, in fact, their abilities are only limited in certain areas. A better term might be "differently abled."

It is essential to create a psychologically safe environment for neurodiversity to flourish. It is possible for organizations to promote neurodiversity and inclusivity if they recognize and address the negative impact of stigma, labeling, and discrimination when these issues occur. Accommodating differences, celebrating abilities, and enhancing diversified teams is key to achieving collective success.

Lenses of Workplace Affinities

Figure 2-3 Organizational Diversity Wheel

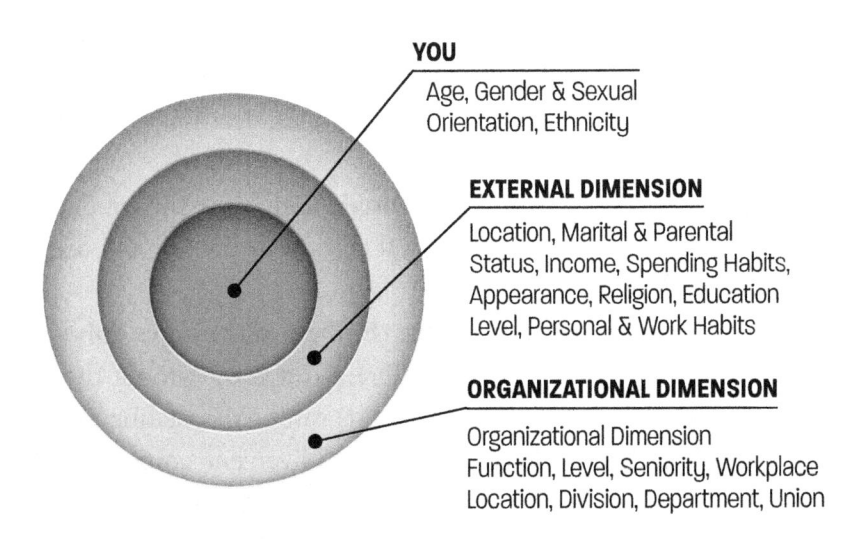

YOU
Age, Gender & Sexual Orientation, Ethnicity

EXTERNAL DIMENSION
Location, Marital & Parental Status, Income, Spending Habits, Appearance, Religion, Education Level, Personal & Work Habits

ORGANIZATIONAL DIMENSION
Organizational Dimension Function, Level, Seniority, Workplace Location, Division, Department, Union

Does this wheel in Figure 2-3 look familiar? It should, as it provides a look at how much diversity an organization holds. An organization is both an open and closed system where diversity flows and changes based on the employees in it. Remember, an open system is one where a company functions while becoming increasingly mixed and complex due to its growing relationship with its environment. The closed systems that reside in this open system are the internal sub-units of the organization (i.e., organizational development and learning, assembly lines, specialized information technology) that do not interact or interface with the external environment or consumer.

There are quite a few lenses to examine within the workplace. At the heart of how we are different is personality. Did you know personality clashes are the number one cause of workplace conflict, often resulting in conflict management (where we place a Band-Aid on the issue) rather than conflict resolution? (And that is a whole other book of solutions!) The question I often get asked is "Can we change our personality?" and of course my response is this: through emotional intelligence, you can soften some of those harder edges.

The second ring in the Organizational Diversity Wheel is your internal affinities, and some may change over time. One example is age. This is followed by the third ring—external affinities, which are life experiences. The final outermost ring is organizational—which is how and where we show up in the organization.

So here we have yet another way to explore workplace diversity; however, this is more than diversity. In each ring a person can find barriers to their own success. Here is why is we bring the Organizational Diversity Wheel into this book: This wheel is also bringing the conversation to intersectionality (more on this in Chapter 4), where we acknowledge we are all unique and bring many different affinities to work, shaping our unique perspective and thoughts.

Diversity Is More than a Social Movement

ID&E are business constructs or ideologies, compared to a political/social paradigm. I prefer to note this early, as often programs, goals, initiatives, and measurement are business focused, not personal. Knowing this, ID&E should not be emotional or personal. It is not directly about you; it is about a strategic business focus or imperative driving a healthy organizational culture.

It is also worth noting that workplace diversity is not anti-racism. Think about this: the workplace should never be racist, thus anti-racism is not a focal point. I have had employees argue that their organization needs to make an anti-racism statement, such as "Company X is anti-racism."[52] What the employees do not recognize is that *"to be anti-racist is to acknowledge the permanence of racism through organizations, industries and communities, and to recognize that racism is a system of disproportionate opportunity and penalties based on skin color,"* says Laura Morgan Roberts, a University of Virginia professor.[53] Organizations are not in the habit of taking political stances and more often than not (hopefully), the organization has in place a structure within its culture to eliminate workplace racism. Yes, my friends, this only adds more confusion and is still in the infancy stage in theory.

However, there is a separation; we understand that today's workforce is unique in its attitude to Corporate Social Responsibility (CSR), Environmental, Social, Governance (ESG), and sustainability. Employees want to work with organizations that have a strong focus on and ties to CSR/ESG, as these social movements impact the workplace. However, there is little to no benefit for an organization taking a political stance on social movements. In fact, data supports the idea that doing so can hurt an organization. One study examined the overall impact of this and found organizations that took a pollical stance on a social movement demonstrated a significant decrease in work product quality and productivity, and discovered relationships were at risk, thus leading to more conflict, challenging interpersonal relationships, and business decisions that were poorly made.[54]

A great example is Exxon Mobil flipping its stance on Pride and the company's Employee Resource Groups.[55] Here we find an organization which, in the past, openly flew the Pride flag during Pride month outside their corporate offices in Texas and has now banned the flying of this flag outside its office. Exxon has taken a pollical stance on Pride due to the state's (Texas) political stance on Pride, and Exxon's employees are up in arms. Exxon should have become Switzerland—neutral—and continued as they always have. Unfortunately, that was the path they did not choose, and they will see and feel the negative effects of this stance in spades. When all the dust settles, I have to ask, who does the Exxon stance benefit and hurt?

So let me address this now: 70% of today's employees feel organizations can and should make a large impact on social issues[56] and this number is steadily growing. Addressing racial disparities, injustices and inequalities within the workplace is one way organizations can help combat societal racism. Employee Resource Groups (ERGs) often provide a safe space to sound off or have crucial conversations on such political and social topics, while allowing the organization to remain Switzerland on the issue—and still have a very important impact on those movements. ERGs also directly affect the "S" in ESG; they are the social impact on our employees and clients.

This is a wonderful opportunity for education. LinkedIn Learning has many educational programs vetted and geared towards the role of the workplace in addressing racism. Done correctly, training on microaggressions and unconscious biases can educate employees and hopefully, through that education, your employees will begin to identify and correct those behaviors in themselves and others. Your organization may also see a shift in hiring practices, where removing barriers to employment and hiring talent also addresses racial issues. So, within the organization we can bring attention, education, and conversation to social movements, without the organization itself taking a pollical stance. Organizations should be a safe space to work regardless of your ideals; however, your personal values should be aligned.

At this point, I hope you agree with me that the workplace needs more than gender and ethnicity to be diverse. Focusing on just two affinities will not provide the diversity of thought the organization needs to thrive. In fact, just the opposite. In working with organizations, I try to remove the word "diversity" from the discussion and focus on "affinities." This opens the dialogue to advance to intersectionality, which leads to better inclusion. Having a stronger knowledge foundation in diversity, we can now begin to make the move towards inclusion; that's what we'll cover next in Chapter 3. We will explore inclusion, the real business case, ESGs and more in Section 2.

SECTION 2

Evidence-Based Inclusion

*If there is no evidence or proven outcome,
how do you know you had an impact?
Inclusion is evidence based and measurable.*

3

It All Starts with Culture

Inclusion is NOT a human resource imperative;
it is a company-wide imperative that is led by leadership.

Organizational culture is a hot topic today, due in large part to the dynamic shift towards remote work. Much like inclusion & diversity, culture has some variation in definition (see Table 3-1). However, we need to remember that culture is fluid and ever changing due to many factors. In the end, it is the employee's commitment to the organization's culture and values that matters when we are talking about inclusion. This chapter is not intended to function as the be-all and end-all of culture, but it should provide you with a solid framework when adding the value of inclusion into the culture.

Table 3-1 Selected Definitions of Organizational Culture[57]

GLOBE	• Project the shared motives, values, beliefs, identities, and interpretations or meanings of significant events that result from common experiences of members of collectives that are transmitted across generations.
S.P. Robbins	• The system of meanings that are assumed by the members of an organization; it distinguishes that organization from other organizations; this system of common beliefs is a set of basic characteristics appreciated by the organization.

A. Brown	• The pattern of beliefs, values and learned ways of coping with experience that have developed during the course of an organization's history, and which tend to be manifested in its material arrangements and in the behaviors of its members.
O. Lundy, A. Cowling	• Basic values, ideologies, and principles that influence the behavior of an individual and organization and shape them; they manifest in more measurable aspects, such as legends, rituals, language, decoration, office design, or dress code.

Organizational Culture

Organizational culture is the heart of the company. It's the collective shared values, expectations, and standards for how to reside within the company that guide the actions of ALL employees. Organizational culture is the embodiment of the organization's values and the beliefs that drive organizational outcomes. It is how the company functions within itself (when healthy). The business case for a healthy organizational culture reinforces both culture and talent brand, positive recruitment and retention of talented employees, strong organizational performance and job satisfaction numbers, and a strategic competitive advantage. This is not new information. Culture has been examined and reexamined over and over with the same conclusion on results.

Here is a new issue: how do we embed inclusion into an already full plate of values? Let me ask you this, do your employees represent your organizational values or are you finding silos and struggling with communication? How are you recruiting—are you changing up your AI algorithm's search terms or are you leaving "values" on the floor? Would it surprise you to learn that *Forbes* reported in 2021 that trust is a direct factor in a healthy culture, and when the culture is unhealthy, research has demonstrated 46% of employees lose trust in human resources, the chief executive officer, and leadership?[58] Never mind the lost revenues associated with employee turnover.

Culture is important. How important? Let us look at some of the numbers that paint a picture of culture's importance:[59]

- According to the Society of Human Resource Management (SHRM), in the last five years, the cost of turnover due to workplace culture has totaled $223 billion dollars.
- Company culture is an important factor for 81%% of job seekers (Jobvite).
- Healthy organizational culture that engages its employees can lead to a 202% increase in performance (Deloitte).
- 94% of executives and 88% of employees feel culture is instrumental in organizational success (Deloitte).
- Unhealthy organizational culture is the number one reason employees leave an organization—the lack of fitting in (lack of inclusion), according to Randstad.
- Fifty-eight percent (58%!) of employees would jump ship to a competitor if they had a better organizational culture (Speakap).
- Over 73% of executives would leave their organization for a better culture (Robert Walters).
- SHRM reports over 85% of US workers who say their company has a strong workplace culture admit to talking positively about it outside of work, compared to only 57% of those who say their company has an average culture

An employee's experience of culture starts when they apply for the job, continues through onboarding, development, and training, and ends months after they leave the organization. A healthy, positive culture that enables your employees to thrive through the organizational values receives the same amount of press time as an unhealthy or toxic culture.

I have mentioned that culture is fluid, and if an organization is looking to add diversity to its culture, it is time to shift the culture to support that business decision. Culture changes along with the business, political and social environment. Employees also shape the organizational culture—and they are the living, breathing result of that culture. Give the organization permission to change or shift its culture towards inclusion. If the organization's culture does not adapt to and change with the times and needs of its employees, the culture becomes stale and potentially toxic.

What Does Your Current Culture Look Like?

This is one of the first questions I usually ask when either interviewing or doing research on a company. I ask people to please describe their organizational culture and provide evidence that supports their description. Your organizational culture should be part of the organization's value statement. One only needs to go to the Johnson & Johnson website to see what their values are. (See https://www.jnj.com/living-our-values.) The organization's culture sets an important tone for the entire company. Gaining awareness around your organization's culture requires asking a lot of questions.

So, what are your organization's cultural values? How many do you have? How many is too many? It is better to be strong in three cultural values than to be weak in seven cultural values. Some organizations are stuck in the "more is better mentality"—let's have more values and we won't miss any. Oh, and how do we add inclusion and diversity into our values—let's make them an entirely separate value system under culture. Here comes the confusion again!

In breaking down workplace culture, I first look at the organization's overarching theme: Where is your business focus when it comes to employees? Is your culture focused on people, outcomes, or teams? Is your business value focus on innovation, collaboration, competition, stability, or aggressiveness? Now look at the cultural values and ask: Is inclusion one of the values? If it's not, what would we remove to place inclusion into the culture? Now, define the cultural values and share them throughout the organization.

Personally, I like to have the organization create a word cloud of their culture, where employees are surveyed to list 3 to 5 words that best define their culture. This is a great way to do a culture check, too—and the resulting word cloud makes a wonderful visual to share with the whole organization. (See an example in Figure 3-1.)

Figure 3-1 Culture Themes

Overarching Theme—People focused and collaborative

Core Cultural Values—Pick no more than 3

INCLUSION   INNOVATION   STEWARDSHIP   INTEGRITY   COMMUNITY

Define what the cultural values mean to the organization

Cultural Sub-Values—choose no more than 5

INCLUSION	STEWARDSHIP	COMMUNITY
DIVERSITY	INTEGRITY	PARTNERSHIP
EQUITY	EXCELLENCE	HONESTY
INNOVATION	COMPASSION	DIGNITY

But Our Culture Is Built on Meritocracy

I'll admit I struggled with where to place this topic in the book, as it is becoming a topic of concern within the workplace, and it is a system found within an organization's culture. There is quite a bit of noise around inclusion and diversity. There are arguments that a merit-based system around workplace advancement and salary can lead to pay and advancement disparities for marginalized employees, arguments that meritocracy is in conflict with inclusion, and arguments that meritocracy is a failed system in business as it drives workplace inequities.[60] Before I go any further, let me say this: meritocracy is an important business function in the workplace. Yes, there is research that claims meritocracy leads to workplace inequities; however it is simply an argument, as it has yet to be proven. Deloitte did a large research study on this exact topic and the findings showed that with meritocracy there is a high level of bias towards rewards and gender (male), a lower rate of salary increases for minority affinity groups, and it may decrease transparency and accountability.[61] The caveats: this research was done in an academic center, the population was students, and biases were NOT monitored. I believe this is the study most in the field are currently referring to. Let me provide you with their findings:

> *So should organizations back-track from pursuing meritocracy? Clearly not. What this research argues is that while meritocracy is a worthy goal, embedding a meritocracy is hard. To help leaders ensure that their organizations are meritocratic, systems and processes should be reviewed, and perhaps enhanced, to identify if they are unintentionally leading to biased outcomes.*[110]

There are too many factors that would need to be shaken out to draw an actual causation to this statement. I am not going to say meritocracy does not have a role in workplace inequities, as every leader has unconscious biases and those biases can play a role. **But wait!** It's the leaders' biases that lead to workplace inequities, and there is evidence for this. And it is the system of meritocracy that allows for leadership and management to advance or pay for performance. They are the decision makers. Still, there is no correlating data that identifies meritocracy resulting in inequities. So, please, let me level set meritocracy.

Workplace meritocracy is an organizational performance management system built into the organizational culture, in which employees advance into positions of success, power, and influence based on their demonstrated abilities and merit. It is focused on performance as a driver for advancement, salary and external/internal motivation.

I love this example: Meritocratic: We could consider getting a job due to higher qualifications as a sign of meritocracy working. In this instance, you'd get the job purely based on your ability to outdo your competitors and not based on factors like nepotism or politicking.[62]

I would argue in the United States the system of meritocracy is somewhere in place for every business entity. Because the opposite of meritocracy is everyone gets a medal regardless of how you played the game. Furthermore, would you want to work in an organization that is based on hereditary aristocracy, where your job function, salary and field are determined by the lottery of birth? Meritocracy often provides the motivation to do well, to be competitive and to innovate.

How does this relate to inclusion and diversity? Researchers at Delta Alpha Psi Services Ltd. highlight the following myth busters and argue that the notion that meritocracy is derailing an organization's inclusion and diversity initiative is just a smokescreen:

Myth: You can't have it all... Meritocracy, inclusion and diversity are values that are "at odds" with one another and cannot be achieved simultaneously

The notion that meritocracy and diversity cannot go hand in hand suggests that in order to increase diversity some degree of sacrifice on performance or suitability must be made to accommodate this. The message that is delivered is one that those not in the powerful majority are "lowering the bar." To counter this, we offer the logic that a Board or workforce that is unrepresentative and non-diverse serves as evidence that the organization is not operating a meritocracy, and that in order for an organization to be a truly meritocratic it would be representative by its nature.

Myth: Underrepresentation of certain sociodemographic groups must be due to innate differences between these groups and those who are in the powerful majority

This myth asserts that if organizations prioritize merit in appointments and some sociodemographic groups remain unrepresented, there must be some innate differences between sociodemographic groups that warrant certain groups unsuitable for appointment. Alternatively, and more accurately, the overrepresentation of certain sociodemographic groups at Board level and in leadership positions can be attributed to an advantage afforded to those in the powerful majority who fit a narrow leader archetype, have greater access to social capital and are sponsored into positions of power. Thus societal, systemic, and institutional factors (and chance of birth) are the cause of disparate outcomes.[63]

The advantages of meritocracy include potentially removing biases, as performance is the key performance indicator (KPI) for advancement, salary increases, bonuses, and other rewards. It also can engage employees as they may learn from more skilled coworkers, thereby leading to self-development. From the inclusion and diversity lens, meritocracy provides an equal ground for all employees regardless of their background or lived life experience and may even go to reward those with different lived experiences. **CAUTION!** I am not saying go off and make your organization merit based only, just that it is one system for improved performance. Yes, it is okay to have meritocracy within the workplace—providing a few things. (It is never just an easy application.)

According to the Massachusetts Institute of Technology (MIT), the key to implementing a meritocratic system falls to organizational accountability AND transparency. This is critical for processes and criteria for advancement and rewards, organizational outcomes and allowing the employees to be part of the discussion. I like to call that inclusion. Leadership and management play a key role in the system of meritocracy, therefore it is advantageous to have deep understanding around one's biases, where they come from and how to keep them in check. Look at meritocracy as a people management tool, as it focuses on both the organization's and the employee's goals and performance.

Please do not toss the baby out with the bath water; in the workplace it is important to adjust. All the more reason to have inclusion as an instrumental part of your organizational culture.

The Cultural Misalignment

Often, I am brought in to examine organizational culture, and you would be surprised how often the organization has it wrong. They describe their culture as open, inclusive, and welcoming of differences, only for me to find leadership is hierarchical, employees do not feel heard, and different perspectives are not valued. Fixing a situation like this will take more than an employee engagement survey.

Let me give you an example. One such organization felt they had such an amazing culture, they refused to change. Their culture was about having beer in the fridge so you could just sit down with your boss and share a cold one. People could wear whatever they wanted (including flip-flops and workout gear). Every Friday afternoon from 3:30 to 5 p.m., the company hosted a mandatory social with beer and wine. Yet, leadership was true to the top-down model, and at these socials you could see the "lunchroom effect" (where the room siloed based on ethnicity and job level). The company's retention rate was in the high 70s, and while that is not too bad, it did show that turnover was highest among the most experienced employees, those in the Generation X and Traditionalist cohorts. This was a technology firm, so employee experience is critical. While their stated main concern was hiring and retaining experienced employees, their culture did not support those hires. Unfortunately, they did not want to work on culture, so the company was sold two years later.

Here's another example: I had the CEO of a rather large financial company tell me he did not need to hire more women or people of color for his workforce because they were doing all right with what they had. What they had was a workforce of highly skilled white men and very high profit margins. I like to think of this as a 1970s and 1980s school of thought, in part because the state of business during that time was transactional, lacked an emphasis on globalization, and did not have workforce diversity in the mindset. I had to bring awareness to this CEO of where the money resided in the US, who held the purse strings, the future of business, and changes in employee transparency and investing. In order to be willing to make a change, he had to first see the value of an inclusive culture and how diversity within the culture will drive business outcomes.

If an inclusive foundation is missing in your organization—as I suspect, it is—now is the time to act. In working with organizations, often I will have employees ask me for referrals for coaching to "fix" themselves. One employee was told in her performance review she had an accent that made her hard to understand when doing presentations. She was willing to pay a vocal coach thousands of dollars to help her try to get rid of her accent. This is a great example of an organization that is lacking inclusion. I reminded her there's nothing wrong with her accent, and to make herself more comfortable in presentations she could simply talk slower rather than try to hide her accent. Authenticity or the ability to be authentically you in the workspace is so important. Your organization needs to be a safe space where each employee can bring their authentic professional self to work.

Can you imagine working for a company that would not allow your hairstyle? One of my close friends was told he had to cut all his braids off if he wanted to work at a certain company. What? And it is not just the workforce—we can find similar stories in youth sports. **So please let me say this clearly to job hunters: If the organization you are looking to work for is trying to "sterilize" ethnicity and authenticity, pass on that organization.** Today, due to the "great job migration of employees," the number of open employment opportunities is higher than the number of talented employees to fill them. Thus, it is imperative that your organizational culture has inclusion as a key cultural value.

Measuring Culture

Creating and maintaining an inclusive organizational culture all starts with awareness. What does your current culture look like? What are your employee values? When did you last do a culture survey? Keep in mind a culture survey examines your employees' perceptions of the everyday working flow, the organization's values, expectations, internal structures, and skills that influence organizational behavior. Compare that to an employee engagement survey, which looks at how employees feel about their value to the organization. Often when organizational surveys are rolled out, they focus on employee engagement and only have a few culture questions. Why not do both? Wouldn't it be useful to have an employee survey that not only measures the employee's perception of their value within the organization but also how they see the organization's culture? If you're looking to have an inclusive culture with diversity, then you need to be able to measure it.

Here's how to have the best of both worlds: In Appendix F, you'll find a Culture / Engagement Survey that is open source (meaning go ahead and use it freely). You can also find this on the book's web page. This survey has validity and is adaptable to your organization. There is also an interpretation guide for your review. I encourage you to use this survey the next time your organization wants to examine culture and engagement (usually annually). The best part is you can load this survey into most survey platforms (such as Survey Monkey) with little to no trouble.

Once you understand what your current organizational culture looks like and how it's embraced by employees, you can strategically adapt that culture. **Caution!** A few notes: 1) do not over-survey your organization and 2) be sure to act on the survey results. Nothing is more frustrating when employees take the time to share their view on the organization only to then have it ignored. This is where leadership needs to practice workplace humility.

The Inclusive Culture Value

It may be time for your organization to update the employee value proposition and statement if inclusion is not currently a part of it. And that is okay. Did you know? Organizations with inclusive cultures are:

- Two times more likely to exceed financial targets,
- Three times more likely to be high performing,
- Six times more likely to be innovative and agile, and
- Eight times more likely to achieve business outcomes.[64]

Culture drives the organization, innovation, communication, and leadership. An inclusive organizational culture tends to have high retention rates, because employees do not want to leave, and the time it takes to fill an open position is short. The work is rewarding, and employees feel a strong sense of pride in their workplace and their own work because they feel it matters and has an impact. Change is welcomed and even encouraged, as new ways to move forward are discussed. Leadership is more than a title; it is a shared value. There is a high amount of productive collaboration, where the organization is not siloed. Accountability is a key pillar to engagement and work.

The Roadblock

Yet when it comes to inclusion followed by diversity, often the focus is not on culture but rather affinities, as highlighted by British businesswoman Inga Beale, former CEO of Lloyds's of London:

Many conversations about diversity and inclusion do not happen in the boardroom because people are embarrassed at using unfamiliar words or afraid of saying the wrong thing—yet this is the very place we need to be talking about it. The business case speaks for itself—diverse teams are more innovative and successful in going after new markets.

Caution! Often when a discussion around ID&E happens, it is a knee-jerk reaction to something, like the George Floyd case and the nationwide protests that sprang up in response. If that's the case in your organization, slow your roll here and breathe. Evaluate your current organizational culture. Do your employees feel heard? Are there bigger issues at play, such as misalignment between the organization's values and employee values? Or is this a reaction to the broader political climate? What does an inclusive culture look like? How do we infuse inclusion to build diversity within the workplace?

Employees can tell knee-jerk reactions from proactive action, and in the case of knee-jerk reactions, we are all well aware that the shiny object loses its luster after a time.

Today's employees are smart and resourceful. They are more aware politically and socially than any workforce in the past. They want their work to matter.

Please be aware of this—do not doubt or misjudge your employees. Trust me, they have the bandwidth to change the organizational culture for the better, AND if change does not happen—if they feel the organizational culture is lacking inclusion—they will leave.

An Inclusive Culture Is Collaborative

Having an inclusive culture does not necessarily mean we sit and have coffee once a week as a collaborative check-in. Collaborate with intent, and be intent on finding different perspectives. Take a second look at the Organizational Diversity Wheel in Chapter 2 and utilize this wheel when you're working on a project to drive intentional collaboration. Such collaboration will help you advance inclusion within your teams and the organization.

When it comes to advancing inclusion, I strongly recommend that a diverse collaborative team is needed. I look cross functionally, and yes, I'm a fan of the RACI chart when assigning roles. (RACI stands for Responsible, Accountable, Consulted, and Informed.) The clearer you are at the beginning, the less resistance you face down the road.

In intentional collaboration, you must ask yourself:
1. What is the purpose or intent of this change? Get as clear as possible; you may need to collaborate with another person to really shake out the purpose. What do you want to achieve or accomplish?
2. What are the outcomes? Start a running list of potential outcomes—be sure some can be measured. This list will grow once you create your collaboration team.
3. Who can drive or influence this project, program or initiative? Make a complete list and begin to reach out.
4. Who has a diverse perspective? What is missing—what are we not seeing?

Within the collaboration, we must ask:
1. How does intersectionality fit with this change? Who am I missing? How is everyone impacted?
2. What is the benefit for our employees—business and personal?
3. Reexamine your purpose.
4. Be open to hearing each other. We must learn to listen. Understand that being welcomed is what feeds that workplace curiosity.
5. We must understand what it means to be accountable.

A collaboration team can be two to six people. Keep your teams small so you are focusing on those individuals who have influence and are in the need-to-know group. However, remember to be transparent about your purpose and outcomes within the entire organization.

Inclusion Is Built on Transparent Communication
Communication is one of the greatest skill gaps found in today's work-

place (regardless of the new normal of hybrid and remote workers). Five different generations, multiple ethnic groups, gender differences and confusion, oh my! The first step in communication is listening. For inclusion and diversity work, listening comes first, followed by your own authenticity with self-awareness and courage. To that end, your audience must listen. Let's have an honest moment here—we know that the minute you say "diversity" we stop listening. Say what you mean, not what you think you should say. Language is in a state of constant change, and we must change with it. Every time you broad stroke an inclusion initiative or diversity training with the words "diversity" or "DE&I," you lose 27% of your audience as they immediately feel excluded from the conversation.[65] Another great reason to level set the organization.

Transparent communication is information that is shared openly. In the end, it removes the guessing game of why. It should also answer these questions: Why are we doing this, what are we looking to change, how does this affect me, and how can I help—what is my role?

Leadership Drives Inclusion, Not Human Resources

Leadership needs to be held accountable for the organization's culture, and must be held accountable for creating an inclusive culture. **Inclusion is NOT a human resources imperative; it is a company-wide imperative that is led by the organization's leadership.** Human resources professionals and/or your inclusion and diversity practitioner are the stewards of inclusion and diversity. If the organization is looking to increase diversity, then inclusion is one of the organization's foundational pillars.

Leadership must have buy-in, and yes, I understand we are all very busy in today's business world. However, if inclusion and diversity are not a business imperative, your organization will sink to just surviving. I used this saying in the mid-2000s regarding the generational workforce: *if your organization is not embracing a multigenerational workforce, it will be only surviving in ten years, not thriving*. And wasn't that the truth? Organizations that did not focus on embracing Millennials in the mid-2000s are struggling today, as 55% of millennials are reporting they feel disengaged within their organization.[66]

Getting Leadership's Attention

So how does one go about getting leadership's attention on inclusion and diversity, in an already noisy workplace? First, we need to focus on one area at a time—are you focused on inclusion followed by diversity?

- **Demonstrate the business case for inclusion.** Have that conversation and dig into your own organizational numbers. Look at turnover trends, notice who is leaving. Make the business case personal as well. Remember, your employees are people, not numbers. How will inclusion followed by diversity benefit your organization? Be sure to include the risk of *not* talking about inclusion and diversity. How will the lack of inclusion followed by diversity hurt the company (or is it already hurting the company)? Create a human resources dashboard to track changes in the workplace. Look for gaps in hiring, advancement, and retention.
- **Create the organization's narrative on inclusion and diversity.** Allow leadership to take the active role of creating the organization's narrative (purpose, values, and story) on inclusion followed by diversity. This goes beyond inclusion and diversity statements. This is the company's story, or, as I like to call it, the 60-second pitch. When someone asks, "How does your company embrace ID&E," the answer is your 60-second narrative. It must be personal. Share it company-wide. I am also a fan of individual leadership stories on inclusion and diversity—why inclusion followed by diversity matters to me.
- **Demonstrate the employee impact for inclusion.** Again, get personal and speak truth to power. What will inclusion look like for the company's employees? What are the clear employee benefits? How will you support inclusion followed by diversity within the team? What are the team benefits? Be sure to share measurable results, too.
- **Create an opportunity for leadership advocacy.** Where can the organization's leadership be an advocate for different affinity groups? (Hint: ERGs, inclusion followed by diversity councils, and community outreach—see Chapter 7.)

- **Pivot from inclusion and diversity trainings to adding leadership development coaching.** This is my personal favorite and apparently the *Harvard Business Review* agrees. Inclusion and diversity are wonderful coaching topics for leadership development. Rather than tell leadership why inclusion followed by diversity is important, coach them into seeing it for themselves. Hey, coaching creates lasting impact, so why not use it?
- **Allow leadership to lead the change.** This is often the biggest hiccup in inclusion and diversity work. Inclusion change is led by leadership and embraced by all, yet often only a few people take charge of change. Create leadership "work teams" (or as my wonderful SVP calls them, strike teams) and inclusion and diversity steering committees to manage the change.

Unfortunately, when the inclusive cultural foundation has a crack in it, you've got to fix it quickly or run the risk of alienating people and having employees leave. It's not a quick fix. Once you build the inclusive foundation, and continue to follow that, then your diversity of thought candidates will find you, hence a meaning of inclusion followed by diversity. When an organization is strong on inclusion, it trickles out into the community. There are social responsibility benefits. I have seen that happen. For example, once word gets out that affinity groups are doing community service because they WANT to, not because it's expected, the action attracts other likeminded individuals, thanks to social media and sharing of photos.

As with any change or adaptation, a culture shift needs to start with leadership and awareness. Please do not keep this change quiet. Celebrate your awareness! I love when organizations are transparent with change. Be strategic in building an inclusive culture (on top of what you already have). In the next chapter, we take a closer look at why intersectionality is a critical lens for examining what an inclusive workplace looks like.

4

Inclusion Is More Than a Trend— It Is a Must

Inclusivity means not just "we're allowed to be there," but we are valued. I've always said: smart teams will do amazing things, but truly diverse teams will do impossible things.   —Claudia Brind-Woody

An inclusive organizational culture is a must if you want your company to thrive, not just survive. To dig deeper into inclusion, we'll look at the difference between transactional diversity and transformational diversity, and how intersectionality is a useful and critical lens for looking at inclusion in the workplace.

What Has Happened to Our Workplace?

Looking around today's workspace, we are seeing yet another shift in the how, the where, and who shows up. I like to think of today's business environment as a transformational windstorm that is shaking many who have soft organizational cultures and workplace processes. We are faced with supply chain disruption, government policy shifts, ever-changing customer demographics, the ability to further globalize or pull back, a focus on Environmental, Social and Governance (ESG) issues by both stakeholders and employees, public health concerns, and a whole new diverse employee base looking to the organization and often human resources to help them adjust and develop.

Add to that the local issues of hybrid, remote or in-person work, five generations in the workplace and employees (Baby Boomers) retiring and/

or leaving the workforce to become entrepreneurs (Gen Xers) and losing leadership talent, leaving companies with a very small amount of bench strength. Organizations that have a strong foundation in inclusion will outperform those that do not by 42 percent.[67] You may be tilting your head and saying, "I do not understand. Why does inclusion matter so much when we want diversity of thought?"

Here is the all-important pivot: When organizations focus on diversity first, no matter how many diverse candidates walk in the door, they won't stay, because inclusion isn't the foundation of the organizational culture. Without inclusion, organizations lose their innovation maker—diversity of thought. Money walks right out the door. The current research supports emphasizing inclusion first with diversity; the business case has been strongly made for inclusion first—and this is not a new trend, as this research, when read correctly, goes back 20 years.

Yet, only 23% of executives demonstrate a strong understanding of ID&E.[68] According to HR Dive, 98% of organizations focused on ID&E remain focused on the "D" of diversity.[69] The thought process focuses on diversity, especially around one or two affinities. And this becomes the rabbit hole where you are chasing diversity. Remember, employees leave an organization based on its culture and their direct manager; they leave culture and people first. Organizations may have diversity initiatives and programs, but they are lacking an inclusion process.

Some organizations have turnover of 30%—that translates to a ton of money spent on rehiring. There's the cost to attract a new employee, and the loss to the organization during that time you're trying to replace someone. The new employees that companies are bringing in for diversity will leave if the organization isn't inclusive, and we typically see that happen within seven months. It's very expensive, given the cost of hiring and turnover. The Society for Human Resource Management (SHRM) has data on this and a spreadsheet for calculating the cost of employee turnover.[70] The cost to hire and the cost to replace an employee is often 50–60% of that employee's salary, with overall costs ranging from 90% to 200% of a salary. It's ludicrous that it costs $30K–$45K to replace an employee whose salary is $60K. And it costs the company $54K–$150K overall to do that replacement.

Here's an example: *A medical company I worked with had a 44% turnover rate. They were losing an employee almost every day by termination or employees quitting. They were profitable, making millions, but the question is, how much **more** profitable would they have been without those enormous turnover costs? The cost of those turnovers equated to over $142,000 per employee. That's correct; every time an employee was terminated or left the company, it would cost said company over $142,000 to replace that employee—and that was their entry-level employee. Are you focused on the math? I am! That equates to $6,915,499.00 of loss for that year. OUCH!*

Here's the kicker: leadership did not want to change their culture or their leadership style. Their own organizational culture was based solely on meritocracy—without the inclusion lens. To further reinforce their own poor culture and leadership style, they were listed as best in their state for women hires, yet they didn't want to create an organizational culture of inclusion that supported any affinity.

Today, six years later, they are still in business, but competition is fierce for employees, and their current turnover rate is 68%—SUPER OUCH! Their customers are not happy, as they never know who their account manager is, due to turnover. Their employees constantly leave and go to competitors that are now outperforming them (surprise!). When your employees leave, the new employer benefits from all the training you gave your former employees. Your company is part of their perspective, and they take that with them when they leave and go to a new employer. I will admit I only lasted four months as an outside consultant to this company due to the culture's toxicity. That's not surprising, because they lacked an inclusive organizational culture and did not build on their diversity.

Let me provide a reframe: business today is very different than it was 20 years ago. If we add in the COVID-19 pandemic and the workplace changes, I can honestly say business today is very different from even just four years ago. Twenty years ago, business was transactional. Today it's transformational. Five years ago, there was very little flexibility in work schedules and placement, but today hybrid and remote work appear to be here to stay. How DE&I was done 20 or even five years ago is different, and most importantly, if you stay in that old mindset, you may cost your organization money.

Today ID&E must be flexible yet sustainable with intent and strategy.

The Role of ESG in Inclusion and Diversity

The roles of ESG in inclusion and diversity are significant. While I thought I would stay away from this topic, I felt I needed to add a bit of a foundation around ESG, noting that inclusion & diversity primarily focuses on the "S" of social impact. Here's the business case for ESG: Organizations with an active focus on ESG out-recruit, out-retain and outperform those without ESG initiatives. Why? It's because 84% of job seekers look for ESG responsibilities and 50% of your consumers also feel ESG engagement is a benefit, as they want to purchase from companies that are socially responsible. According to the *Financial Times*, data supports the statement that companies with a strong ESG track record outperform those without one.

Figure 4-1 What Is ESG?

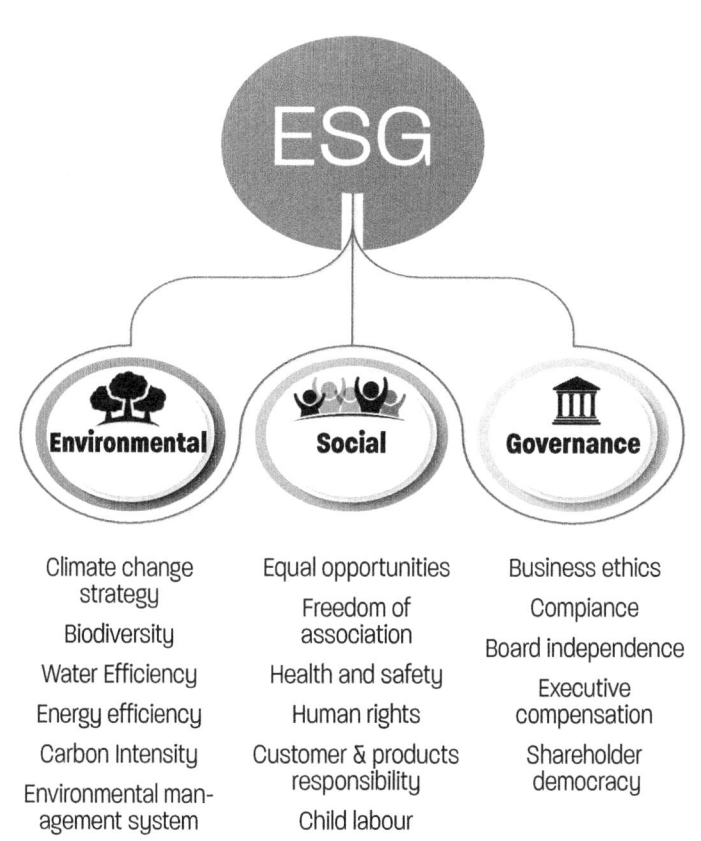

Environmental	Social	Governance
Climate change strategy	Equal opportunities	Business ethics
Biodiversity	Freedom of association	Compiance
Water Efficiency	Health and safety	Board independence
Energy efficiency	Human rights	Executive compensation
Carbon Intensity	Customer & products responsibility	Shareholder democracy
Environmental management system	Child labour	

ESG initiatives are a great way to measure inclusion and diversity as well as employee engagement by focusing again on the S (social). Your Employee Resource Groups (ERGs) have a significant and active role in driving the organization's social impact. Where is the organization making its mark? Are you active in creating equal opportunities for all? How about human rights? Where are your employees volunteering?

Intent is the word that comes to mind with ESG—there needs to be an open intent about where the organization will focus and who will be your change agent.

Transactional vs. Transformational Diversity

Today's global business world is transformational, yet when we began this journey on diversity in the 1960s through the 1990s, the business world was transactional. As business changes, so must the lens we utilize to examine and create business solutions. And yes, even diversity and inclusion have tentacles here as well. "Transformational diversity" is a hot topic today. Unfortunately, it would seem many organizations are stuck in *transactional* diversity. You give us this, we'll give you that.

Affirmative action fit in well during the transactional business period, as the focus was on quota attainment. We were talking percentages and bonus points. If you meet the quota, we will give you a break on your taxes, for example. In 1995, with the focus and force of globalization, it became much more transformational. We need this because the transaction is gone. Today, we're looking at a much broader **diversity spectrum.**

In the simplest of definitions, **transactional diversity** is without inclusion and equity, because the focus is on quota attainment and numbers, employees are labeled, and initiatives are focused on "this is done so now we have that" and check-the-box affirmations. When an organization is stuck in transactional diversity, I often hear statements like these:

- "We need to increase our people of color by 4% in management or leadership."
- "When hiring, we must review 25 diverse candidates for the following roles …"

- "Our goal is to have our board of directors be 25% women by 2025."

I hope you know what follows these statements: Yes, it is "or we will not meet our goal of …" It is all transactional—do this, get that. Not only are such statements and intentions transactional, they are also focused on only one or two affinities, based on the belief that those affinities will further drive the business case and results of diversity in the workplace. We will be focusing on the business case of inclusion further in this chapter.

Transformational diversity/inclusion is a pivotal, intentional shift within the workplace where inclusion is the foundation upon which you build diversity. In utilizing transformational diversity/inclusion in the workplace as the lens and approach, practitioners and leadership alike will see the complexity and intersectionality of diversity in every approach, as we have the ability to see and respond to intersectional complexity. When we embrace and utilize this approach, we take inclusion and diversity to a higher level.

Simply put, transformational diversity or as I will now refer to it, *transformational inclusion*, ensures that individuals are more than a singular affinity. They are seen for all their affinities, and their thoughts and ideas are embraced, creating an organizational environment that is sustainably able to thrive in any economic state.

There is a level of complexity with transformational inclusion. Unconscious filters or biases need to be continually challenged. Practitioners and leaders must examine how cultural, leadership and management competencies are measured, and utilize intersectionality when considering work product. As we see our employees and teammates through a more inclusive lens, their output takes on a new impact. Employees bring different skills and perspectives that are unique, and cross-pollination and collaboration is strongly encouraged.

Moreover, the pivot to transformational inclusion is strategic. There is intent with measurable goals. As the business world is transformational, so must one's organizational culture be. To create a transformational culture, the organization must focus on having and/or building a solid foundation of inclusion, a strategic pathway that will shift and change the organization's culture from top to bottom. In the third section of this book, I introduce **The Inclusion Paradigm.**® This model provides a strategic framework (not a holy grail) for inclusion, leading to diversity and equity. Best of all, it is evidence based, and it works. It's a journey and a process. Here is a peek at the model.

Figure 4-2 Inclusion Paradigm®

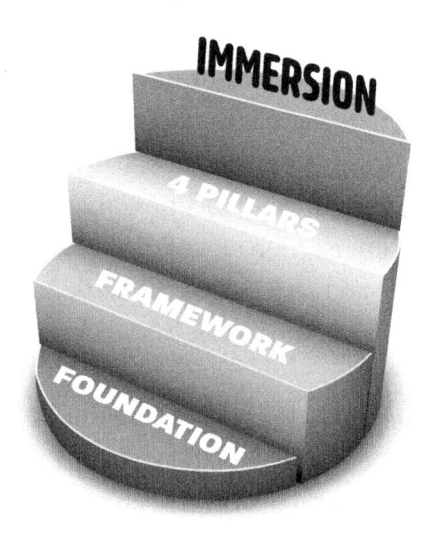

The Damage of Quota Attainment

Organizations have been exploring the notion of workforce diversity since the 1970s, in large part thanks to an out-of-date affirmative action policy.[71] According to Cornell Law School, *affirmative action "is a set of procedures designed to eliminate unlawful discrimination among applicants, remedy the results of such prior discrimination, and prevent such discrimination in the future. Applicants may be seeking admission to an educational program or looking for professional employment. In modern American jurisprudence, it typically imposes remedies against discrimination on the basis of, at the very least, race, creed, color, and national origin."*[72]

I note this is out of date due to the lack of inclusion of affinities and the underlying continuance of quota attainment based on affinities (which is also illegal). Affirmative action has not changed with the business times. It is out of date, and I argue it may lead to litigation in the workplace as reverse discrimination. Think about this—does your organization have affinity attainment goals? If yes, that could be seen and has been seen as reverse discrimination. In 2021, the case of *Duvall v. Novant Health, Inc.* demonstrated the damages of reverse discrimination when the plaintiff, Duvall, was awarded a $10 million settlement based on reverse discrimination based on his color and gender.[73]

Companies bought into diversity in the workplace, based on misinformation on diversity and the business case, and followed it up with strong and often unachievable quota attainment. Today more than fifty years later, I am still hearing from my colleagues, organizations and the media a focus on quota attainment for boards of directors and C-suite and leadership roles. I am still seeing organizations focus their human resources dashboards on gender and/or people of color as affinity outliers for attraction, retention, and advancement. I have to ask: What has that focus done for us for the past 50 years? In the 1980s there was a focus on hiring and integration of people of color (although the term "people of color" was coined in the early 2000s) through quota attainment. In the early 2000s there was a campaign called 25% by 2025, referring to the goal that women would make up 25% of the board of director seats for an organization by the year 2025. To what end? Yes, quota attainment leads to tokenism—and tokenism will destroy an organization's culture, credibility and reputation.

Please stop quota insanity, because what you'll get is women being put on the board just to be the token females, and those voices aren't really being heard because you don't have true inclusion. This insanity also further alienates employees from each other. Quota attainment is NOT inclusion, it is NOT diversity, it is just a percentage of an affinity goal. Intersectionality is not even part of this equation.

To add to the confusion, most of the research on diversity measures affinities, but the outcome is from the combination of diversity and inclusion. Diversity is a measurement tool for difference in affinities, within these studies. It cannot measure impact because there is no way to remove an organization's culture from the equation. More importantly, if an inclusive organizational culture is not present, such companies are excluded from diversity research.

Intersectionality: A Critical Lens in the Workplace

Figure 4-3 The Critical Lens of Intersectionality

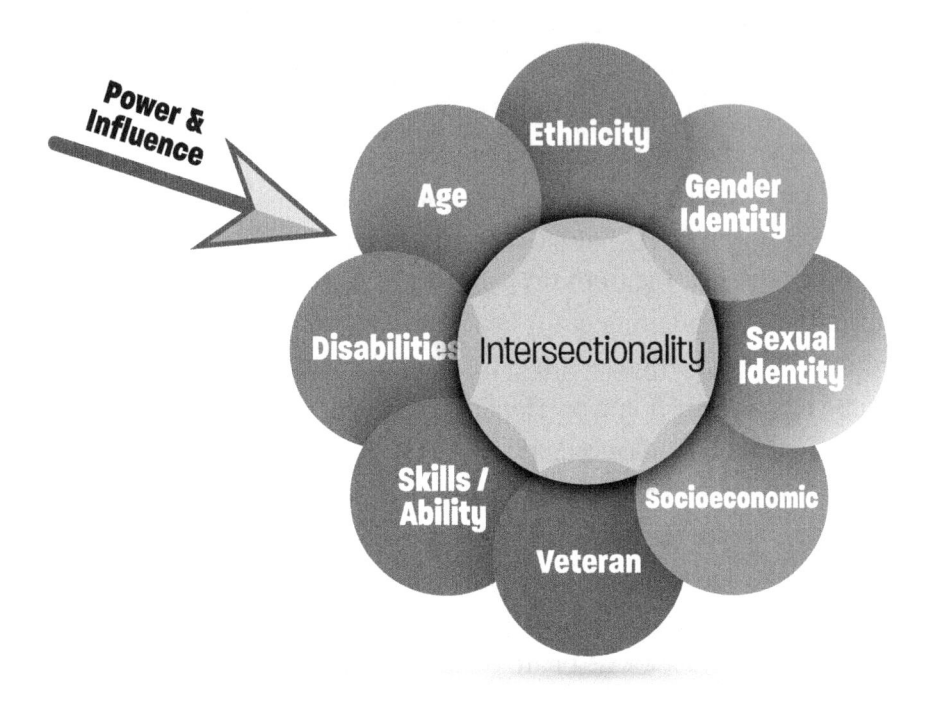

Power & Influence

- Ethnicity
- Age
- Gender Identity
- Disabilities
- Intersectionality
- Sexual Identity
- Skills / Ability
- Socioeconomic
- Veteran

The discussion of intersectionality within the workplace is more important today than ever before. To build a truly sustainable inclusive organizational culture, we as practitioners must see diversity through the lens of intersectionality. The term "intersectionality" was coined and introduced by Kimberlé Crenshaw to reference the unique oppression faced by Black women, who not only experience race and gender discrimination by themselves, but also experience the combined effects of both forms of discrimination.[74] Today the term encompasses how various affinity identities, including ethnicity, gender, sexual orientation, age, and disability status, intersect to influence experiences of discrimination. That said, it is easy to get lost in intersectionality as the qualitative construct of intersectionality is not clear and not simple. This is yet another area where confusion comes into play, and there's a real need for organizations to set the definition of intersectionality for their employees. Simply put, **workplace intersectionality** refers to the fact that employees have more than one affinity and those affinities combine to shape that employee's perspective.

Crenshaw states, "Intersectionality is a lens through which you can see where power comes and collides, where it interlocks and intersects." She adds, "It's not simply that there's a race problem here, a gender problem here, and a class or LBGTQ problem there. Many times, that framework erases what happens to people who are subject to all of these things."[75]

One organization I worked with refused to use the lens of intersectionality due to several leaders getting hung up on critical race theory (Professor Crenshaw is the leading scholar on this topic, by the way). Intersectionality may, at least in theory, support critical race theory; however, it is so much more than feminism, oppression, discrimination, and privilege. It can be an analytical framework used to understand oppression through social and political identities. **In the workforce, intersectionality is a lens to better see and understand our employees' needs and wants. It allows us to better provide support and advancement for ALL employees.**

> *If I'm a black woman, I have some disadvantages because I'm a woman and some disadvantages because I'm black. But I also have some disadvantages specifically because I'm [a] black woman, which neither black men nor white women have to deal with. That's intersectionality; race, gender, and every other way to be disadvantaged interact with each other. –Reddit user Amarkov[76]*

Every time I hear that an organization's goals are focused on specific affinities (i.e., gender or person of color), I think, "Here we go again!" They are lacking the intersectionality lens and it is going to be costly and waste a lot of time. How many times have we heard that the organization wants us to bring our whole self to work, while it creates initiatives and programs focused on just one affinity? Intersectionality is the secret sauce that drives inclusion to diversity and equity.

Research has shown that organizations that practice inclusion & diversity without the lens of intersectionality have a higher rate of salary inequality, have a gap in development programs, are unfortunately at a greater risk of discrimination and sexual harassment of employees and in hiring, and have higher turnover rates than those organizations that embrace and understand intersectionality.[77] Furthermore, there are gaps in recruitment, leadership bench strength, employee engagement, and decision-making. I would argue that any organization not utilizing the lens of intersectionality when examining its culture, workforce, development, and engagement programs is essentially throwing the program at the wall and seeing what sticks with their employees. If that is not enough of a business case, imagine your impact on your clients and customers if you utilized that same lens in sales, marketing, and research and development.

One example of lacking intersectionality is leadership development programs focused on women. In creating a development program that is affinity focused, I have to ask: Is this program focused on the needs of all women? Does it include women who may be ethnically different—does it include those perspectives? How about women who are veterans, or transgender, or who have a disability?

Shifting your lens, think about an ERG in your organization. The Women's and Allies ERG would like to support the local breast cancer walk. The intersectionality lens allows us to see that there may be women who are disabled within the group, and therefore allow this ERG to put in place accommodations for those individuals to still attend this event and be part of this effort to support a local fundraising activity.

Another example is management development training. Suppose an organization is looking to improve its management bench strength. Using the lens of intersectionality, we might find women and men who have a disadvantaged socioeconomic background, so college was not an option for them. In understanding that, we can remove the college barrier and create a training program that includes foundational coursework to advance those individuals who are high performers with an affinity towards management, regardless of what degree they do or do not hold.

Intersectionality helps to drive organizational inclusion, not diversity, yet when the lens is applied, diversity and equity increase. This is a lens that truly needs to come from the top down. Leadership needs to be educated on what workplace intersectionality is and how to use the lens. This then trickles down the organization. I will say it again: intersectionality is imperative for sustainable inclusion. However, be sure you have clearly defined this term for your employees so there is no confusion as to which lens you are utilizing.

Intersectionality should be part of your recruitment and development strategy. Encourage discussions and feedback on intersectionality of employees, as it is part of their identity. Leaders, get comfortable with uncomfortable, as uncomfortable leads to personal growth. Look at barriers for your employees that come from intersectionality (i.e., labeling employees or placing them into a diversity box). Be accountable for examining programs with an intersectionality lens—ask, who does this benefit? Define your intersectionality. Build up your own empathy. Intersectionality is a critical lens you should employ now rather than waiting. And yes, you will need to educate leadership as to the why and the business case. I apply this lens to every program, project, collaboration, training, and strategy. For more, see the Intersectionality Exercise in Appendix E.

Getting Your Supports Ready

Are you ready to pivot to inclusion as the driver of diversity? As the driver of workplace culture? Are you alone in this thinking or do you have your team of believers? Have I presented enough evidence for you to switch? Do you have questions? Know that with this book, I am in your corner. You can always email me to ask questions.

Here's the bigger question: Is your leadership team ready? I put together an open-source PowerPoint presentation that will help (it's available on the book's website). This is a look at the business case for inclusion—it's what I like to call the company WIFM (What's In It For Me). Share this and more with your team. While inclusion starts with an "i," it is not just one single person's job. This is a change for the organization and one that cannot be completed alone. There is more evidence to come—as I will make the business case for inclusion in the next chapter.

Ready to Pivot….

5

Pivoting to an Inclusive Organizational Culture

Pivoting is not looking back—it is looking forward without rose-colored glasses and moving forward with intent and evidence.

Far too many companies are looking for a quick fix to diversity, inclusion, and equity. In my work, I've observed that they are looking for that fix that will hit all three. But as you now know, diversity, inclusion, and equity mean three very different things and are measured differently. Furthermore, they have three different mindsets. All these corporate attempts at quick fixes have helped the word "diversity" become cringeworthy. The focus was all diversity, diversity, diversity. Now, it's all inclusion, inclusion, inclusion. Tomorrow it might be equity and belonging. Yet again, no matter what you call your ID&E initiatives and programs, the foundation lies with inclusion.

Is Your Organization Ready to Pivot?

You might say, "We have an inclusive organization." But how do you *know* you have an inclusive organization? Have you defined it? Have you done the measurements? Are you seeing the benefits? Have you applied the intersectionality lens to all best practices?

In the companies I've worked with, no one has sat down and said, "This is what an inclusive organization means to my company." Instead, they end up broad stroking with the definition: "Inclusion is a place of or a sense of belonging." I'll ask, "How do you measure a sense of belonging?" When it comes to diversity and inclusion, so many "experts" are lacking that practitioner lens of understanding that inclusion, diversity, and equity make up a business paradigm that has inclusion as its pillar for the business case. It's a business model that starts from the attraction, recruitment, and retention of employees and then hits every department within the organization. It's the employees' lifecycle and experience.

Best yet, inclusion is not one-size-fits-all, just as no one organization is the same as another. So, there is no one solution for creating an inclusive organizational culture. There is, however, a clear pathway to create and drive an inclusive culture that will then attract diversity and create equity. The Inclusion Paradigm® is a framework strategy for building an inclusive organizational culture, but please understand that what fills in each of those channels is different based on what the organization's needs are.

Evidence

As I mentioned in a previous chapter, in 2020 I compiled a 10-year comparative review of over 150 organizations that actively hired consultants to create diversity solutions to address low workplace diversity numbers. The second criteria for my review were that the consultant had both pre- and post-employee engagement survey numbers, and an organizational culture survey (most organizations do these annually). I found that for 92% of those organizations that hired a consultant, the symptom was low diversity, but the actual problem was the lack of an inclusive organizational culture (based on the correlation of turnover, employee engagement and the organizational culture survey). More to the point, these organizations, while focused on diversity solutions, demonstrated an **increase** in turnover, and a **decrease** in employee engagement results at year-end. What is more problematic, of the 92% that lacked an inclusive culture, only 22% actually wanted to work on inclusion.

Looking at the 22% of companies (68 of them) that decided to work on inclusion, I created a complimentary custom Inclusion Paradigm® Blueprint. Each custom Inclusion Paradigm® Blueprint was based on the following: a company's submitted culture and employee engagement surveys, their retention rates, leadership bench strength, a history of past initiatives, and a completed Inclusion Paradigm demographic report.

Here are the results, as the organizations that participated resubmitted all their data as of January 2022: On average, the 48 organizations that implemented their custom Inclusion Paradigm® Blueprint increased employee engagement by 29%, retention by 37%, leadership bench strength by 19%, attraction of diverse employees by 43%, and job satisfaction by 37 percent. Several of them even won awards for being best places to work and received other types of recognition. If you would like a copy of my research article, which has been submitted for publication in the Winter 2023 issue of *Emerald Publishing's international journal, Equality, Diversity, and Inclusion*, please email me at Lauran@DrLauranstar.com. Once it is published, I will send you a complimentary copy.

Pain Points

You may be ready to start making the pivot to an inclusive culture if your organizational pain points include any of the following:

- a lack of diversity within leadership,
- lack of diversity in recruitment,
- organizational diversity that does not look like your client base,
- diverse employees lack representation on important decisions and projects,
- employees fail to or are afraid to speak up,
- employee engagement surveys reveal low levels of engagement,
- turnover above 10%,
- organization appears to be high conflict,
- low in innovation, and/or
- legal claims in the realm of harassment, hostile workplace, EEOC.

Is your organization ready to recognize the true value of diversity, which is diversity of thought? Once we have a sturdy foundation for an inclusive culture—and I say "foundation" because "inclusive culture" is never a box you can check off and be done with it—you're always going to be working on it as your employee base changes, as your industry changes, as society changes, and so on.

Once you have the foundation for inclusion, and you are ready to pivot, ask these questions:

- Do we have a diversity of thought in the workplace?
- Is our workplace openly rewarding and recognizing and advancing this?

Inclusion: More Than a Trend, It's the Foundation

Inclusion is a cultural mindset. It's having your voice being heard and not being afraid to share your insight or your perspective and experiences, and having it be respected when you do share it. The benefits of inclusion open the door to diversity of affinities, which gives you diversity of thought. Inclusion plus diversity leads to equity. When everyone is valued and included, equity naturally follows.

Workplace inclusion refers to creating a work environment where all people are truly welcomed, valued, and respected, for all of who they are, regardless of differences. It's the feeling of being accepted, being understood, and being valued in a group or team of individuals in the workplace; being of value based on other factors than diversity

Think of it this way:

Inclusion is the cake with Diversity being the flavor of the cake.

Inclusion Drives Diversity, Which May Result in Equity / Equality

Belonging

At this point, I'd like to offer some commentary on the misguided notion around the word "belonging." Seems this is the trendy new ID&E word, the notion that employees want to belong to their organization or that the organization must have a sense of belonging. Really? As belonging is part of the definition of inclusion, why focus on it? You "belong" to a family, a tribe, a house of worship. But organizations, especially businesses, aren't families (no matter how much they insist they are). Belonging implies a permanency. The term itself seems to only be relevant here in terms of the fact that when you've got an inclusive workplace, the people in it feel like they belong there, that they aren't outsiders. However, let me make this very clear: **Inclusion DOES NOT EQUAL Belonging.**

Inclusion is a business term, a business initiative, a goal for a business culture. It does have the word "belonging" in its definition. Belonging, on the other hand, is a social construct for family and friends. You belong to your family, to your friend group. And in that friend group or family group, the behavioral constraints are generally light. It may be appropriate or acceptable to drop the F-bomb without getting in trouble. (This is generally not the case in a business context.) With inclusion, you can share your perspective openly and as part of the organization. But there's a definite set of parameters or constraints around your behavior in that organization.

You may be thinking, "Well, there are lots of articles about belonging in the workplace, why don't you agree with that term?" My answer is this: Belonging is just the next buzzword because we've milked "diversity" and "equity" dry. Don't fall for it. Belonging has an ownership implication—but does your company OWN you? No, it does not. That would be very constrictive. And belonging is not changeable. I'll always have my bachelor's degree from the University of Massachusetts, and I will always be a member of the alumni group; however, I can take my degree and go where I wish. Moreover, midway through my degree process, I could have taken my credits and gone elsewhere (oh wait, I did that too). Same with the workplace—you can take your skills gained and go to another company if you so choose and if your organization is not inclusive, I encourage you to do so.

Back to inclusion. Inclusion feels like you have an impact on the company's outcomes. It's known, it trickles out into social responsibility, and is contagious. Your employees get excited, they become the problem-solvers. Inclusion opens our eyes to different world perspectives and allows us to look at things in a different way to solve problems.

What Inclusion Looks Like

Very well, you may be thinking, but what does inclusion actually look like? How can we recognize it? Here are five signs that an organization has an inclusive culture.

- There is a level playing field for all, opportunities for advancement are openly shared and are inclusive in nature. This means HR has removed specific barriers that may hold one back or has brought in development to elevate those who may have a barrier (such as offering a management development program instead of demanding a college degree). Think of the job posting as listing only the must-haves instead of listing everything. What must the candidate have to advance into this position?
- The decision-making process is inclusive not exclusive—all voices are heard. However, the employee must recognize that while their voice is heard, it may or may not be acted upon due to project constraints. Collaboration is an intrinsic part of the decision-making process. Opportunities for expression and exploration of ideas is a value in the decision-making process.
- Employees feel that they can comfortably and safely share concerns or issues. Remember the old open-door policy? An inclusive culture is similar to that, however, now it encompasses how the employee feels in relationship to the organization's culture, decision-making process, advancement and so on, in respect to their affinities. That said, be sure you have boundaries in place. If an employee comes to you with a problem, concern, or issue, be sure they know to come with at least two solutions to bounce around. Here is where self-awareness, empathy and problem-solving come together and are must-haves, skill-wise. Remember, one goal of leadership is developing their people, so yes, develop them.
- Employees feel part of the community. How do you know? They enjoy coming to work—you can directly ask them about that. They are involved where it is more than just a job, they take fewer sick days, they engage cross functionally. Community volunteering goes up, sick days decrease, engagement within the company increases. ERGs thrive.
- Diverse supply chain/customers. This is now trendy, where supply chain and procurement functions manage who they do business with. They may openly look for companies that have affinity specialization attached to them. Just like your workforce, your supplier base should represent your customer base.

When your organization is inclusive, it trickles out to your customers and the community. Your culture brand will include inclusion. An inclusive organizational culture supports diversity of thought, where employees are being seen and heard for their uniqueness and their unique perspective, regardless of gender, disability, or other factors. Innovation comes from diversity of thought and perspective. Nobody can argue with that. And we all know that innovation drives organizational success. To go back to basics, an organization that is failing often lacks innovation, and that's an organization that's forgotten (or refused to acknowledge) that diversity of perspective and thought drives innovation, and inclusion is the foundation.

The Business Case for Inclusion

The argument for an inclusive organizational culture, to pivot away from the diversity metric and focus on employee inclusion, is the easiest to make. I have found the more proficient one is at making the business case for inclusion, the simpler the change process.

Today's business thinking goes like this: If you have a diverse organization, you'll have more job satisfaction, innovation, problem-solving … all the benefits of inclusion. But that statement is only partially correct. Yes, those are indeed the benefits of inclusion, but if you have a diverse organization, you just have a diverse organization. Think again of that bag of Skittles candy. When you dump out the bag on the table, you have a mixture of colors. To understand how diverse that bag is, you sort the candies into color groupings. Now you know the bag's diversity. You do not have an idea how they will all taste together, because you have not created an inclusive handful to taste.

There is a giant misnomer and misconception when it comes to business case and inclusion versus diversity. After reviewing well over 500 research articles on the business case for diversity and inclusion (notice how diversity and inclusion tend to be linked together), I found that every company or classroom had one thing in common: an inclusive culture. Part of the research inclusion/exclusion criteria for all 500 articles noted that culture had to be inclusive in order for an organization to be included in the study—so what are they measuring? It is difficult to measure the impact diversity has on an organization without inclusion. Remember, diversity is the measurement of affinities; however, 🌀 *workplace inclusion* refers to creating a work environment where all people are truly welcomed, valued and respected, for all of who they are, regardless of differences.

Caution! Inclusion is not the same as tolerance. This word should be banned in ID&E work. It's not about putting up with people who are "different" in some way, but rather is about full acceptance. I'm talking about the feeling of acceptance, understanding, and being valued in a group or team of individuals in the workplace; being of value based on other factors than diversity.[78]

To put it simply, business outcomes found within DE&I studies (the majority) do not demonstrate the benefits of diversity, they demonstrate diversity affinity measurements. The organizations within the study are already enjoying the benefits of having an inclusive organizational culture.

Although, one could argue that the diversity measure demonstrates attraction and retention of diverse employee, and I agree. Again, we need to know what we are measuring and the why. 🌀 The benefits of having a workplace culture of inclusion which embraces diversity of thought are many. Figure 5-1 shows just a few improvements companies have observed:

Figure 5-1 Inclusive Value Proposition

Increased/improved
- conflict resolution
- talent brand
- problem-solving
- decreased sick days and employee stress
- diverse workforce
- organizational flexibility
- job satisfaction
- team cohesion
- organizational reputation
- employee morale
- employee engagement
- interpersonal connections
- creativity
- culture brand

Do you want more evidence? In a recent article, Vijay Eswaran cited numerous research studies that found when you had an inclusive organizational culture that embraces diversity of thought, the following can be seen.[79]

Companies
- Demonstrate 1.7 times more innovation, creativity, and problem-solving
- Indicate over 1.4 times increase in revenue
- Are 120% more likely to hit financial goals
- Find 57% of employees believe their companies should improve
- Are seeing a 15-fold increase in sales revenue
- Established an increase of 2.3 times in cash flow per employee

Workplaces
- 78% of employees see D&I as offering a competitive advantage
- 70% of executives argue D&I is an important facet of or focus for business
- 85% of CEOs with strong inclusive cultures notice increased profits
- Are 87% better at making decisions, innovation, and problem-solving
- 67% of jobseekers search out inclusive companies
- Diverse/inclusive boards see an increase of 43% higher profits

It is imperative that the organization's top leadership understands the business case for inclusion and that inclusion is critical in keeping their talented employees and is part of their culture brand. Further, they must also embrace and lead with inclusion. The business case for inclusion must be customized to the organization. This way you know what you are trying to do and how to measure it. For example, if you have a diverse employee pool, look at retention rather than attraction—as you appear to already have that. How is the organization's leadership bench strength—do you have diversity in the leadership ranks? Is this something you wish to improve? Then show leadership the data on inclusion and increasing affinities in the leadership ranks. This is the value proposition of inclusion for your organization.

Diversity is critical to an organization's success. Diversity of thought drives innovation and problem-solving; however, if your organization is not inclusive, that diversity of thought is wasted because it is not valued, heard, shared, or asked for. The research supports the idea that if you do not have the most diverse workforce, you still have some benefits when the culture is inclusive; however, if you do not have an inclusive culture, you have no benefits.

The Pivot

An inclusive culture drives the attraction and retention of diverse employees resulting in diversity of thought, leading to the organization enjoying the full benefits of inclusion and diversity. More research is needed to understand how equity/equality fit in this business paradigm.

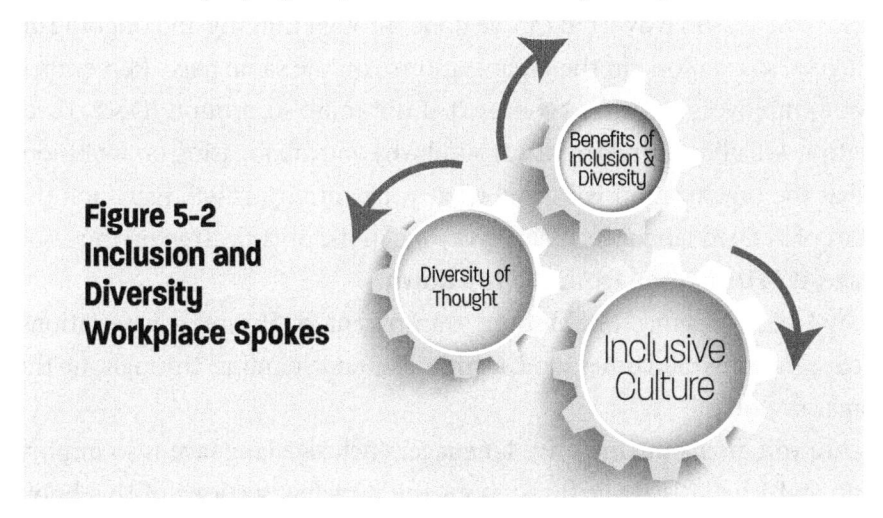

**Figure 5-2
Inclusion and
Diversity
Workplace Spokes**

Being an inclusion and diversity practitioner allows you to ask the difficult questions. You should be seen as the expert within the organization. Now that you are ready, the organization has to recognize whether it is ready to shift out of a diversity mindset and refocus on inclusion. If you're not ready to recognize that inclusion is the solution, you're still stuck in the fundamentals of understanding the role of inclusion in relation to diversity and equity. Sometimes coaching is needed to help a senior leader be ready to pivot the focus to inclusion. Utilize the business case to move the needle. However, remember you can bring the horse to water, but the horse has to choose to drink it. And this is a difficult concept to convey.

You alone cannot make leadership embrace inclusion; all you can do is influence how they see inclusion and its benefits and then they must decide to act.

Signs That Your Organization Is Ready
What does it look like when your company is ready to pivot? The organization is level set on inclusion. They understand the difference between inclusion and diversity. There is an air of excitement for change. Honestly, this is one of my favorite phases in the journey. This is a journey that starts with the organization being in the awareness phase. They become aware of both inclusion and diversity and their role in each. They level set the organization as to how inclusion and diversity fits and the business case—the reason why. That can be done through training and ongoing dialogues, so everyone in the organization is on the same page. Remember, your employees are just as confused, if not more so, around ID&E. Level setting will allow transparency around why you are focusing on inclusion, what the organization will gain, what your employees will gain, and the start of defined language. It gets everyone in the organization on the same page; **it MUST come from the top down.**

Level setting: Establishing transparent definitions, expectations, goals, business outcomes, and a mutual understanding throughout the organization.

Are you discussing inclusive language? Inclusive language is so important, and I will discuss it throughout the next few sections of this book. For example, instead of "ladies and gentlemen," use "everyone." At Walt Disney World, the greeting has changed from "ladies and gentlemen" to "dreamers of all ages." Use more "we" instead of "I" and "you."

Leadership influences the organizational environment—without them, nothing will change. Does your executive leadership support this pivot? Executives and senior leadership must recognize that having an inclusive organization is important and must be willing to invest in it. Is your organization ready to put its money where its mouth is? I might go into a company that says it's ready and say, "Here are several initiatives you could implement, and it will cost $80K," and the answer is "nope." They're not ready. Leadership needs to be aware that inclusion, diversity, and equity is a strategic process. Right now, your organization may be at Level 1: Awareness, the start of the journey (see Figure 5-3).

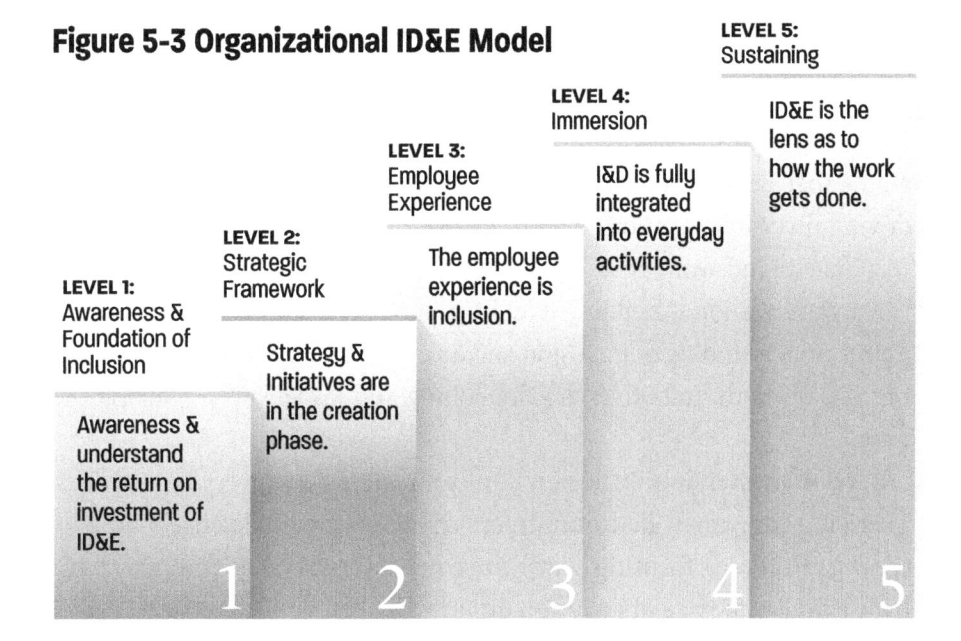

Figure 5-3 Organizational ID&E Model

LEVEL 1: Awareness & Foundation of Inclusion — Awareness & understand the return on investment of ID&E.

LEVEL 2: Strategic Framework — Strategy & Initiatives are in the creation phase.

LEVEL 3: Employee Experience — The employee experience is inclusion.

LEVEL 4: Immersion — I&D is fully integrated into everyday activities.

LEVEL 5: Sustaining — ID&E is the lens as to how the work gets done.

Organizational ID&E Maturity Model

Level 1: Awareness & Foundation of Inclusion: Awareness of and understanding the return on investment of inclusion and diversity. Diversity of thought (not diversity) is recognized as an innovating business benefit; however, it is understood that inclusion is the foundation.

Most organizations will find themselves at Level 1: Awareness & Foundation of Inclusion. This is where level setting happens. It is understanding the business case of inclusion, understanding what the diversity landscape of the organization looks like, why diversity matters—it's diversity of thought, survey measurements around employee engagement and culture, and the start of understanding why your organization is focusing on inclusion and diversity.

Level 2: Strategic Framework: Strategy and initiatives are in the creation phase. Leadership embraces inclusion as a critical foundation for success, the business case has been made. It is time for the creation of inclusion and diversity strategies that are designed to focus on creating an inclusive workplace.

Moving into Level 2 is strategic. The organization has teams in place to drive inclusion. The strategic mission and vision of inclusion and diversity are created and shared within the organization.

Level 3: Employee Experience: The employee experience is inclusion. Leadership and management are focused on inclusion and diversity programs that drive communication and inclusion. The inclusive culture is driving diversity retention and attraction through the talent, culture and corporate brand awareness.

The organization is building its culture and talent brand. Employees have a clear understanding of inclusion and diversity as well as the organization's mission on both. Initiatives are flourishing and leadership is walking the walk.

Level 4: Immersion: Inclusion is fully integrated into everyday activities. There is a companywide commitment to inclusion and diversity and now the organization is focusing heavily on equity / equality. The company has a high brand awareness of inclusion driving diversity.

The organization's branding on culture and talent is part of the fabric of the organization. Once in immersion, the organization can move on to equality versus equity, in terms of which one they will focus on (see Chapter 10).

Level 5: Sustaining: ID&E (be it equality or equity) are the lenses as to how the work gets done. ID&E clearly impacts performance and outcomes and is part of the performance process.

Seven Inclusion Themes

Gartner Research, an independent survey and research organization, examined the issue of measuring inclusion within the workplace. They surmised there were seven inclusion themes and questions that needed to be reviewed when assessing organizational inclusion, thus coining The Gartner Inclusion Index. These themes are reinforced within academia and business, resulting in the means to measure inclusion (level of workplace inclusion) by utilizing the Gartner Inclusion Index questions.

Those seven themes are:

- fair treatment,
- integrating differences,
- influence on decision-making,
- psychological safety,
- trust,
- acceptance/kinship, and
- recognizing and advancing of diversity.

To measure your inclusive culture, utilize a 5-point Likert scale (Strongly Agree, Somewhat Agree, Neither Agree nor Disagree, Somewhat Disagree, Strongly Disagree). The greater the degree to which employees agree with the statements below, the more inclusive the organization.

These are the statements that form the basis of the Gartner Inclusion Index:[80]

- Fair treatment: Employees at my organization who help the organization achieve its strategic objectives are rewarded and recognized fairly.
- Integrating differences: Employees at my organization respect and value each other's opinions.
- Decision-making: Members of my team fairly consider ideas and suggestions offered by other team members.
- Psychological safety: I feel welcome to express my true feelings at work.
- Trust: Communication we receive from the organization is honest and open.
- Belonging: People in my organization care about me.
- Diversity: Managers at my organization are as diverse as the broader workforce.

The Gartner Inclusion Index is the foundation for your questions and has **proven validity** in measuring workplace inclusion.

Figure 5-4 Themes of Inclusion

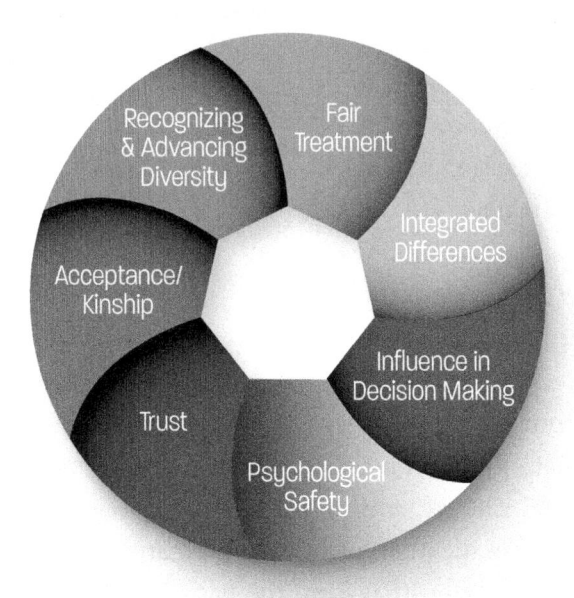

Themes shown in circular diagram:
- Recognizing & Advancing Diversity
- Fair Treatment
- Integrated Differences
- Influence in Decision Making
- Psychological Safety
- Trust
- Acceptance/Kinship

When you are creating an inclusive culture, these seven themes should be part of the discussion and strategic pathway to inclusion. Let's take a quick look at what each of these means.

- **Fair treatment**: Employees at my organization who help the organization achieve its strategic objectives are rewarded and recognized fairly. Advancement at my organization is based on knowledge, skills, and abilities (KSAs). Initiatives should focus on removing barriers for advancement, understanding of equality (yes, equality rather than equity), a holistic look at recruitment and leadership bench strength.
- **Integrating differences**: Employees at my organization respect and value each other's opinions. I am comfortable being myself in the workspace. I feel I am heard even when I have an opinion that conflicts with the general opinion. Cross functional collaboration is a cornerstone of business, and a strong sense of respect for differences is part of collaboration foundation.
- **Influence on decision-making:** Members of my team fairly consider

ideas and suggestions offered by other team members. My input is valued and sought out when decisions are made. Leadership needs to have intent in asking for different thought processes.
- **Psychological safety**: I feel welcome to express my true feelings at work, without repercussions. Leaders in my organization value and care about me. This truly is top-down—yes, you can feel psychologically safe within your department, thanks to amazing management. The bigger lens is company-wide psychological safety. Does my CEO have intent for all employees to feel psychologically safe? There are quite a few resources on how to create psychological safety in the workplace. Check out the book's website for more information.
- **Trust**: Communication we receive from the organization is transparent, honest, and open. Leadership is transparent and open to new ideas.
- **Acceptance**: People I am working with care about me as a person. I can bring my whole self to work, and I am empowered to be myself.
- **Recognizing and advancing diversity**: Leaders and managers at my organization are as diverse as the broader workforce. Leadership is focused on inclusion and is transparent around strategies and direction.

Measuring Inclusion

The simplest means to measure inclusion is through surveys and small focus groups. Inclusion is the foundation of any thriving organizational culture. When was the last time your organization did a culture survey? I am not asking about employee engagement, but instead specifically looking at organizational culture. Yes, engagement is part of culture, but it's often the case that engagement surveys do not measure or ask specific culture questions.

According to Deloitte, culture is a system of values, beliefs, and behaviors that shapes how actual work gets done—"the way things work around here." In contrast, engagement is about employees' level of commitment to the organization and their work—"how people feel about the way things work around here." Both are critical to business performance, hiring, retention, and innovation.[81]

To understand the organizational culture, practitioners need to examine both culture and engagement surveys. Table 5-1 summarizes the variety of available tools to help you do this.

Other Measurement Tools

Tool	What It Measures	Strength	Weakness
Workplace Representation	Diversity of Affinities	Easy to Identify underrepresented groups	Can create a bias related to role or function. This is just one lens; more need to be applied to truly understand gaps, trends and biases
Retention	Diversity of Affinities Trends in retention of affinities	Can identify trends around affinity groups that may be less satisfied with the workplace	Identifies trends not reasons Involuntary attrition needs to be heavily examined for unconscious biases
Recruitment	Diversity of Affinities Where gaps are in recruitment based on all affinities	Identifies barrier for entry, pipeline issues and recruitment biases based on affinity.	Does not identify why some affinities may apply and others do not Focus groups may provide more insight
Promotion Advancement	Bench Strength	Identifies biases in assessment and selection	Does not share if affinities are self-selecting out of promotion opportunities.
Pay & Benefits	Equity	Identifies biases in compensation	Like-for-like pay equality (equal pay for an equal role) obscures inequality in opportunity.
Employee Engagement	Engagement Culture	Must compare affinity groups rather than overall company-wide	Engagement surveys do not focus on inclusion

Employee Focus Groups	Culture	Complements workforce analytics and is qualitative	Disenfranchised employees may keep quiet or not volunteer for focus groups—psychological safety issues
Exit Interviews	Lived Experience	Lived Experience	Biased based on whom the information is gathered from—may be reactive
Customer Diversity, Experience, and Loyalty	Brand Awareness on Talent and Culture	Can help identify the consumer segments' needs	May be reactive
Supplier Diversity	Dollar Spend	Measures the company's commitment to diversity through spend dollars	Dollars spend—may be slightly higher depending on the company.

There are additional ways to measure inclusion, and this should be part of both the company and leadership scorecards. Pay careful attention to the questions you use. Don't ask, "What is your diversity ratio, how many women do we have compared to men?" Instead, ask, "What does your sick day ratio look like among all affinity groups? Are people using all their sick time or leaving it on the table?" (Some companies don't divide paid time off into categories like sick, vacation, etc.). Employee engagement and culture surveys also allow you to measure inclusion. **Caution!** Be sure you ask the same questions year after year to reinforce growth.

If you are planning to focus on demographics alone, investigate retention, hiring and promotions by all affinities. Look at performance reviews to see if inclusion is part of a person's performance measurement tool. You could ask things like, "Of your ten departmental employees, what percentage are in a developmental process?" Look at team functionality. Ask for specific examples. Do not accept "Oh, we function well as a team." Pull out the "how." Is there a lot of conflict on the team? If there's a lot of conflict, you don't have cohesion. If there's an imbalance of power, people are not being heard.

You'll likely be looking at a mix of qualitative and quantitative data as you assess how inclusive your organizational culture is.

Barriers to Inclusion

As we've seen, creating an inclusive organizational culture is an ongoing process, and it takes some work. You may find you run into some barriers along the way. Lack of role models within leadership is one of the greatest barriers that needs to be overcome for inclusion to happen. This will always be a barrier until we have more depth in diversity within leadership. Organizations need to build up their diverse bench strength utilizing the lens of intersectionality. Otherwise, this lack of role models inhibits productive mentoring.

If your leadership team does not have a good role model or mentor, go outside to a professional organization. I am a fan of creating an association forum within an organization. This means building a relationship with professional associations within the area that can help the organization and its employees understand and adapt to challenges or barriers that affinity may face. Pulling from my ERG, the organization sponsors two or three employees per association. This association also becomes a wonderful recruiting site. The goal is a true partnership with the association.

Another barrier is stereotyping and/or unconscious biases. It is the most common barrier, and the struggle of course is that the person is unaware of that bias. We can alleviate this barrier by creating training that focuses on how to navigate around biases and by building our own self-awareness around our biases. Knowledge and level setting are important—we need to become more aware of situations that drive that bias. Beware of this training *faux pas*: thinking that by providing training you have created a solution, when really all training does is increase knowledge.

Other barriers include lack of accountability when making a mistake, bullying, insensitivity, perceived underperformance based on an affinity, attitude, environment, culture, lack of participation, social barriers, and hiring barriers. Inclusion is not easy or quick—I'll say it again: building inclusion is a journey and is not one-size-fits-all.

There are a number of steps an organization can take to ensure that employees and teams feel included and not singled out based on a perceived difference.[82].

- **Be clear on why the organization values inclusion and diversity.** Do your key leaders have a true commitment to diversity? Are they walking the walk, every day? Have we shared this within the entire organization? Is it posted somewhere?
- **Inclusion must be a strategic imperative.** If not, it may get lost or diluted based on other hot spots within the organization. Inclusion must be in the forefront of the business practice.
- **Have constructive, honest debates, even if they're uncomfortable.** These discussions should be "mainstream not sidestream." Have open forum meetings, provide quarterly inclusion and diversity updates to all employees.
- **Be deliberate and intentional, lead with intent** in shaping the agenda for inclusion and diversity with goals and support actions.
- **The merit of someone's ideas is more important than where they are in the hierarchy.** Include and encourage people from different areas and backgrounds to speak up and share.
- **Identify and empower the right leaders and change agents to do the right things.** Are there leaders in your organization who are willing to challenge the status quo? Use them to encourage the diversity of thought that will, as Parakala puts it, "transform and future-proof" the organization.
- **Measure inclusion and diversity improvements** so you can monitor progress and take timely action.

As I was writing the first four chapters of this book, I thought to myself, *no wonder organizations focused on diversity first—there is quite a bit to unpack with inclusion and culture.* Inclusion and diversity have quite a few facets that need to be understood, examined, and embraced before implementation, from the business case to inclusion themes and understanding where your organization is today. Inclusion and diversity work is hard, intense at times, and you need to be patient, as it's a journey. Inclusion is where the real work begins and understanding one's organizational culture is the starting line. We tackle this in the next chapter.

We have covered quite a bit in the last two sections. The next section of this book focuses on a proven way to adapt your organizational culture, thus advancing inclusion. At this point I trust I have made the business case for moving toward inclusion, cleared up some confusion around each prong of inclusion and diversity, and reinforced the importance of culture and moving away from diversity as strategic imperatives. Let's focus now on the pathway to creating an inclusive culture that will drive diversity.

SECTION 3

The Inclusion Paradigm®

The Inclusion Paradigm® is a researched and application-proven workplace inclusion model that provides a clear pathway for creating an inclusive organizational culture. It's an innovative scaffolding of steps that have been strategically layered, resulting in sustainable success. This paradigm is based on research (on workplace culture, diversity, and inclusion) followed by real-world application with proven, measured results.

6

Driving Awareness: The Foundation

The act of awareness is built upon intent, the intent to see organizational gaps and the intent to elicit change. Inclusion and diversity start with awareness.

There are very few true inclusion and diversity practitioners. By that, I mean those who have a deep understanding of the nuances and rely on evidence rather than trends, those who are culture change agents focused on the organization's #1 expenditure: their people. Organizations can benefit tremendously from employees and practitioners with the knowledge and courage to stand up and speak truth to power; yet organizations are willing to put in place people who "do diversity." This is a trend that needs to change.

Organizations desperately need skilled inclusion and diversity practitioners who have the knowledge and the ability to effect change. Ongoing learning is a must. If you are in the role of an inclusion and diversity practitioner and are lacking knowledge or skills, please develop yourself. There are plenty of certificate programs focused on inclusion and diversity. You do not need a PhD to effectively make an impact within your company. Ask the organization to invest in your knowledge, and if they refuse, ask yourself if you really want to work there with one arm tied behind your back.

Inclusion and diversity work is hard, and often misunderstood. Change can be slow and frustrating. As practitioners we need to call out issues within the organization around inclusion and diversity, and to do so we must have resiliency and self-awareness in spades. We do not need to do this alone, so please be sure you take care of yourself. Create a mastermind group of other inclusion and diversity practitioners—I created mine straight from LinkedIn. I actively reached out to movers and shakers within the business world and put together a mastermind group that connects monthly. This is my support network and sounding board. We keep each other in check around evidence and research.

If you are at this section of the book and are thinking, "Great, now let us check the box," please go back to Chapter 1 and start reading again. The Inclusion Paradigm is not a check-the-box application, yet it does provide a clearly defined pathway to advancing inclusion within the organizational culture.

The Inclusion Paradigm®

The Inclusion Paradigm® is a researched and application-proven workplace inclusion model that provides a clear pathway for creating an inclusive organizational culture. It's an innovative scaffolding of steps that have been strategically layered, resulting in sustainable success. This model also recommends inclusion initiatives that have proven to have the desired impact of driving inclusion within the organization.

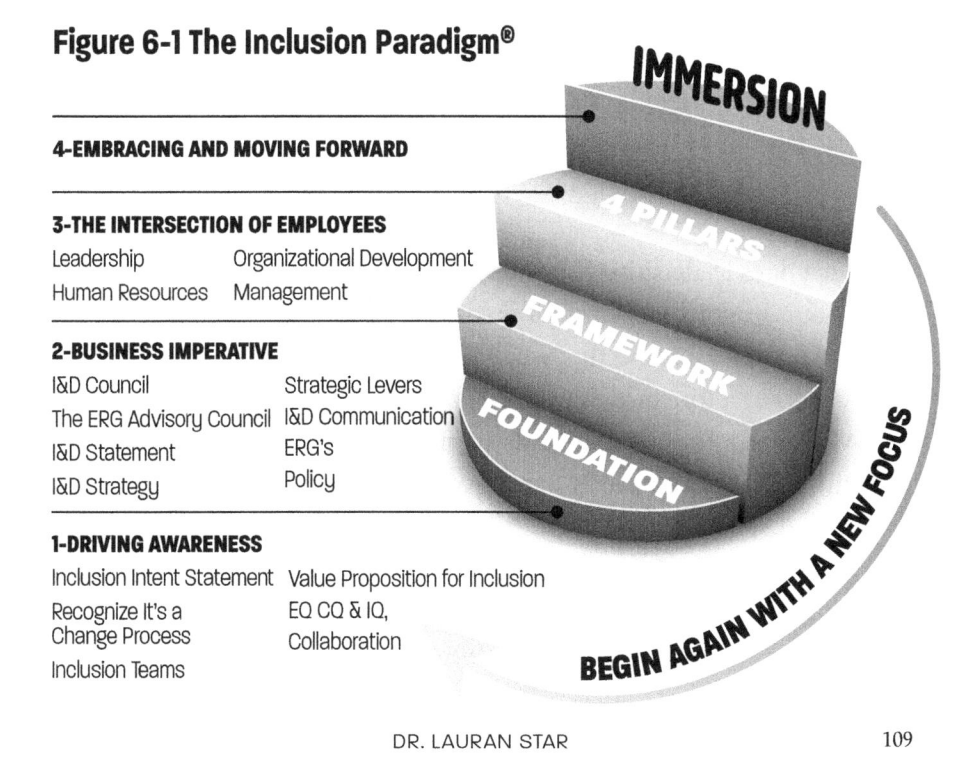

Figure 6-1 The Inclusion Paradigm®

4-EMBRACING AND MOVING FORWARD

3-THE INTERSECTION OF EMPLOYEES
Leadership   Organizational Development
Human Resources   Management

2-BUSINESS IMPERATIVE
I&D Council   Strategic Levers
The ERG Advisory Council   I&D Communication
I&D Statement   ERG's
I&D Strategy   Policy

1-DRIVING AWARENESS
Inclusion Intent Statement   Value Proposition for Inclusion
Recognize It's a   EQ CQ & IQ,
Change Process   Collaboration
Inclusion Teams

IMMERSION
4 PILLARS
FRAMEWORK
FOUNDATION
BEGIN AGAIN WITH A NEW FOCUS

This paradigm is based on research (on workplace culture, diversity, and inclusion) followed by real-world application with proven, measured results. This paradigm is evidence based.

The Foundation

The foundation is the first phase of the Inclusion Paradigm. A strong foundation builds an organization that is less resistant to the adaptation of inclusion, or the focal shift away from diversity and onto inclusion. This is not a labor-intensive phase; instead, it is the time to ensure everyone is on the same page with the same goals and outcomes.. Please do not rush this phase; use this time to truly establish the why (why are we focusing on inclusion?) and what (what exactly are we going to change?) The how will come later.

Awareness and inclusion start in the C-suite. That's right. Inclusiveness must start at the very top of the hierarchy, with your executive team, and then move downwards. Leadership must be on the same page and be part of the solution as well as understand and be in agreement on the following actions and ideas:

- Define the organization's return on investment for inclusion. What is the business case?
- The organization is starting to level set or define what inclusion and diversity looks like for the organization. Equity or equality comes much later.
- What does leadership wish to see from this change?
- What is leadership's role in this change?
- Transparency around the "why" is critical for change.
- What is in it for your employees?
- What is in it for leadership and management?
- Diversity is recognized as an innovation business benefit and is driven by inclusion.

Having gotten buy-in from leadership following the steps described in Chapter 5, we now take the narrative we created and begin to frame out the foundation based on goals and desired outcomes. What do we as an organization want to see? It is time to get organizationally focused on inclusion, since inclusion at Company A will be achieved slightly differently than at Company B. In creating the foundation, you are creating your own culture and your culture brand. Below is an outline of the six core elements for building a solid strategy to drive your inclusive pillar of culture.

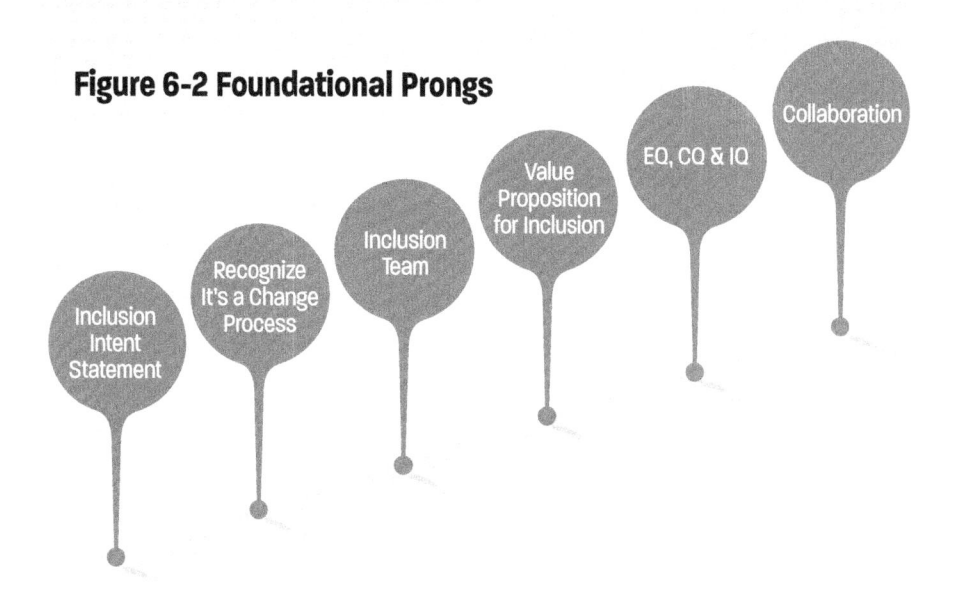

Figure 6-2 Foundational Prongs

- Inclusion Intent Statement
- Recognize It's a Change Process
- Inclusion Team
- Value Proposition for Inclusion
- EQ, CQ & IQ
- Collaboration

For the remainder of Section 3, I will be referring to all formal inclusion and diversity committees and statements as I&D. Please notice I am moving the E (equity or equality) out of the mix to reduce confusion, as we are focused on inclusion first, then diversity.

Inclusion Intent Statement

It's worth noting that inclusion and diversity success must be built on intent. Answering the questions above will help drive that intent. However, as you will see in the next chapter on the Framework, a strong strategic plan is an imperative. ***Lack of intent is often the first mistake organizations make when looking to improve diversity within the workforce.*** The statement leadership makes around increasing the percentage of one affinity over another can drive wedges within the workplace, since it can be seen as "us versus them." Improving the diversity of one affinity is not an intent. It may be a goal, albeit a narrow one.

Intent is the purpose of what your organization wants to change. Wait—am I saying improving diversity can't be the purpose? Yes, I am. Why? Because it's too narrow AND because diversity is the affinity measurement tool. Think of it this way: intent answers the "so what?" question. We want to improve diversity ... so what? Why? Now comes the intent. Here's what an Intent Statement might look like:

We are focused on advancing our inclusive organizational culture, resulting in / to drive attraction, retention, development, performance, and employee engagement while embracing / benefiting from our employees' diverse perspectives and thoughts. Inclusion is the core of our culture brand and diversity will be the core of our talent brand.

Wow, right? I will share that I always ask the companies I am working with, "What is the intent of this change?" It may take time to shake out. For example, I was contracted with an organization that first stated their intent this way:

We want to focus on diversity because our employees are starting their own grassroots diversity campaign due to the killing of George Floyd.

Again, where is the purpose? Diving into the statement above, what is the intent of the grassroots diversity campaign? What will it accomplish? Are there measurable goals? Creating a solid purpose/intent statement will help minimize resistance as the organization clearly understands the purpose of the change.

Practitioners, I suggest you look at **intent as a tool to build buy-in for an inclusive organization.** You can show the business case for inclusion to build intent. Intent is a critical frame created by and for executive leadership. As a practitioner I have sat with many executive leadership (C-suite) teams focused on creating an intent for the inclusion statement.

The intent statement is the return on investment—the business case as to why Company X is shifting towards an inclusive culture. It is imperative that the executive leadership creates this statement.

Recognize It's a Change Process

Before we begin to create the foundation for an inclusive organizational culture that drives diversity, we must first recognize this is a change process (and a strategic one, at that). As human resource practitioners and executives and senior leadership, we have all worked with change within an organization; however, this particular change is not linear. This change is multifaceted, hitting every nook and cranny of the organization. The focus of the change is on building an inclusive organization that drives diversity; therefore, every employee will be affected by this change.

Please know that this section of the book is not meant to be a Change Process 101 course. Instead, this is the highlights reel of things often forgotten and that are specific to changing an organization's culture. Based on my extensive research and work with organizations, here are a number of key things to think about in facilitating THIS change:

Know what you're changing before you change it. Understand the key aspects of your organization's culture and the employee experience. Then, and only then, should you move to promote inclusivity.[83]

Do not do this alone. Inclusion is company-wide, so you must create an Inclusion Team that looks like your organization. Be sure whoever is leading this team understands the business imperative of inclusion and diversity. Include leadership as well as managers (yes, be inclusive).

Create your communication matrix. Transparent communication is critical for the success of inclusion. The more transparent, the better. There also needs to be a communication matrix in place for information—we'll build upon this throughout the book because it's a HUGE factor in whether an inclusion pivot succeeds. (See Figures 6-3 and 6-4.)

Figure 6-3 Communication Exchange

Senior Leadership

Executive Leadership

Inclusion Teams

Employees

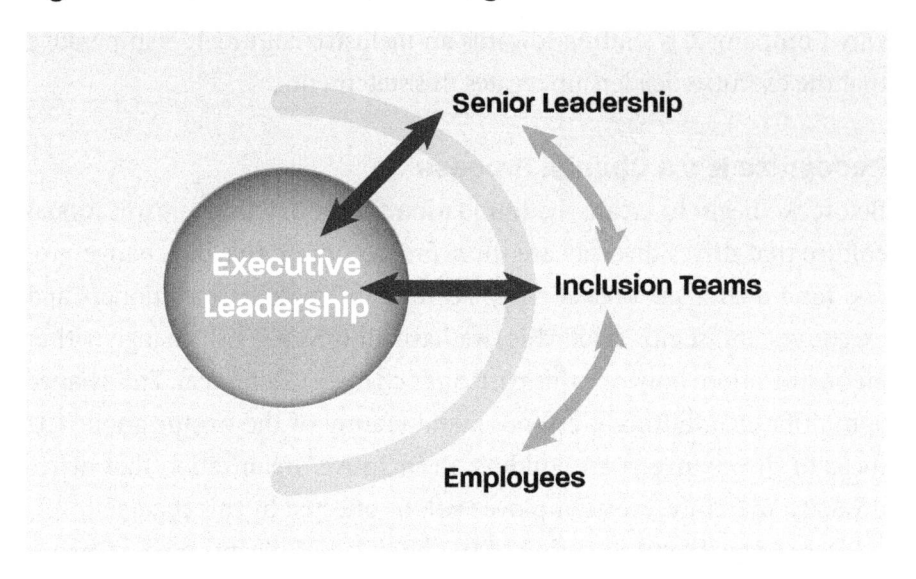

Figure 6.4 Communication Matrix

Information	Audience	Mode	Frequency	Responsible Sender	Outcome
ERG Events Update	All Employees	Newsletter	Monthly -	ERG Leadership	Measure engagement/ Attendance
Inclusion Council Update	Leadership Teams to share down	Inclusion Council Teams meeting	Quarterly	Inclusion Council Sponsor	Knowledge update/feedback from leadership

Be strategic! Why are we doing this? Why inclusion? What is the benefit of an inclusive organization to the employee, to the organization, to its clients? Why now? Think big and brainstorm. A solid, clear and concise inclusion and diversity statement will serve as your framework, so spend time creating it. In the next chapter, we will dive deeper into creating your inclusion and diversity statement.

Facilitating Change

Here are some proven tips for facilitating change.

Create a sense of urgency
- Often inclusion and diversity will lose momentum and leadership may begin to shift their focus onto a shiny new topic area. To keep momentum going, I like to link business outcomes to every program or initiative. Creating an employee demographic dashboard that notes promotions and attrition by ALL affinity groups allows you to continue to drive your inclusion and diversity business case.

Win top leadership support
- This is critical for inclusion and diversity. As soon as leadership steps back from inclusion and diversity, meaning they stop focusing and discussing, employees will follow suit. Please let me say this again (as it is often forgotten): Leadership drives the change, while human resources (or wherever your inclusion and diversity practitioner falls) is responsible for the inclusion and diversity stewardship.

Communicate *and* educate
- Inclusion and diversity is dependent on intent and transparency. The clearer the communication, the better. Add in educational trainings to level set the organization.

Why Is There Resistance?
- People typically resist a change that they believe conflicts with their self-interests. Fear of the unknown resides in resistance. The fear of personal loss is perhaps the biggest obstacle to organizational change.
- Employees often distrust the intentions behind a change or do not understand the intended purpose of a change. Provide them with a clear purpose.
- People who will be affected by a change or innovation may assess the situation differently than managers or promoters of a new idea do.

This change to an inclusive organizational culture needs to be transparent and garner everyone's support. I like to think of this change as 1) a strategic business plan (mission statement and what levers throughout the organization will need to be pulled), 2) level setting knowledge training, and 3) transparent marketing and programs that empower employees. The key word here is **STRATEGIC**—everything must have a reason and buy-in.

Inclusion Team: The Inclusion Drivers for Your Change

This is a change management initiative focused on creating an inclusive culture. Members of the Inclusion Team must be key influencers and be a diverse representation of the people in your organization (by gender, ethnicity, shift, orientation, workplace level, department silo). Participation should be voluntary and team members must be committed to creating an inclusive workplace. This is a great place to start utilizing a RACI chart (see Figure 6-5). The RACI approach clearly defines **who owns what** in a change process or in new initiatives. Inclusion takes everyone, so you need to be able to collaborate cross functionally. Know your RACI: Who is **R**esponsible for the task, who is **A**ccountable for the task, who are your **C**onsultants, and who needs to be **I**nformed?

Figure 6-5 RACI Chart

Responsible	Accountable	Consulted	Informed
Project Name:			
Decision/Tasks → Person/Department			Notes:

I have seen quite a few RACI charts, some of them very complicated. However, this does not need to be more complicated, so keep it simple. The RACI will help to keep the change process moving forward.

The Inclusion Team's role includes:

- Review and revise the Inclusion Intent Statement
- Develop the Change Vision—what does this change look like for the employees and the organization?
- Identify the barriers to asking questions.
- Identify the focus area of inclusion (gender, generation, ethnicity, etc.).
- Communicate / Be Transparent / WIFM (what's in it for me?) to get buy-in from all about the initiative.
- Identify resistance to the change to an inclusive culture.

The Inclusion Team should also have access to transparent data, as part of their overall responsibility is to report out on progress. The Inclusion Council will also need this data and will look to the inclusion and diversity practitioner to collect and decipher it.

- Collect data and feedback on an ongoing basis—ask, is this working?
  - Ask what is the next step: how do we add on to this?
  - Look at impact data.
  - Share the information.
  - Gather data from roundtable employee interviews.

Value Proposition for Inclusion
It is essential that leadership understands the business case for an inclusive organization, embraces the change, and sees the need for this change. They should be able to share this with their teams. Inclusion and diversity are strategic imperatives for an organization to thrive in today's business world. Here is even more data on the business case for inclusion.[84]

Talent & Employee Engagement:
- Improved retention of top-performing talent (63%): In an inclusive

organization, the culture brand of inclusion is palatable. Employee do not wish to leave as they are invested in the culture. They also enjoy working for the organization.
- Attraction of qualified diverse talent (67%): Inclusion becomes part of your talent brand. Potential employees will come to you.
- Maximized productivity of individual contributors because they want to be there.
- Decreased aggressive and discriminatory behaviors due to overall increased knowledge.
- Increased employee engagement and job satisfaction (29-42%).

Financial Performance
- More likely to hit financial goals (120%).
- See an increase in sales revenue (15-fold).
- Establish an increase of cash flow/performance per employee (2.3 X/employee).
- Increase overall revenue from innovative products and services (38%).

Innovation & Team Cohesiveness
- Increase in creativity, innovation, and openness in the healthcare marketplace (59.1%).
- Optimal member-driven solutions with a financial lens (44%).
- Decreased groupthink, leading to better decision-making and problem-solving (49%).
- Improved organizational cross functionalization, leading to improved solutions (62%).

Reputation
- Overall improvement of organization's reputation (57.8%).
- Better able to recognize the needs and interests of different stakeholder groups.

EQ, CQ and IQ
There are three types of intelligences found in the people within an

organization and it is important to bring all of these to bear in the change effort. It is possible to build a person's cultural intelligence (CQ) and emotional intelligence (EQ); however, someone's intelligence quotient (IQ) stays the same throughout life (with age comes stability of score). IQ measures several practical cognitive abilities, but it does not measure how skilled you are at your job or task, or how adaptable or curious you are.

Emotional intelligence is essential when an organization is pivoting toward inclusion. Having strong emotional intelligence allows for understanding and empathy with those whose affinities may be different than yours. Furthermore, research has demonstrated that having strong EQ also helps mitigate unconscious biases and microaggressions, improves mindfulness, and drives inclusion. Does that mean you have to master all EQ skills? No. However, I do recommend you focus on self-awareness, empathy, communication, and intentionality first—make it part of your awareness around your organization's Inclusion Campaign.

Self-Awareness Is the Foundation for EQ and CQ

In my first book, *LEIP Forward* (international best seller—Germany loves my work), I highlighted the need for the skill of self-awareness. Self-awareness is all about you and your own level of awareness and empowerment. It has little or nothing to do with others. This is where you gain the crucial awareness of self. Understanding your awareness and power level allows you to then work on how that embraces others.

Self-awareness is the ability to understand why we react the way we do in every situation. It also encompasses the skill of regulating the subsequent reactions to a situation to achieve the best results. **This is THE most important EQ proficiency, especially for inclusion and diversity.** No matter how strong we may be in this area, we need to keep working on it.

A note about self-awareness denial: If you are overconfident in your abilities within this competency, you may be in "development denial" regarding self-awareness. Consider the following example: Have you ever worked with a leader who thought they were an outstanding communicator, when in all actuality you felt they struggled to get the point across in a meeting?

Here is what self-awareness looks like...
- You know the "what and why" about your feelings.
- You understand where your biases come from and understand how to navigate around them.
- You understand what is driving the emotional/gut response.
- There is an overall understanding regarding the full ramifications of your actions.
- You are aware of yourself in different situations and adjust your behavior accordingly.
- You utilize your insights when a situation is causing havoc on your internal emotional system, to seek solutions and to gain strength.

Often it is easier to see when **self-awareness is lacking** as the person presenting the lack of self-awareness does so grossly. The lack of self-awareness often presents itself as stress or always being stressed out, even in calm climates. It's the blatant reactions to situations without thinking. I like to call this Foot in Mouth Syndrome (FIMS). Even more apparent, these individuals who are lacking self-awareness often can't get past the emotional stumbling blocks of life. Someone who lacks self-awareness will often revert to microaggression—being the aggressor. If their unconscious bias is rearing its ugly head, then the microaggression is the brain fart of the bias.

Developmental Tips for Self-Awareness

Journal, Journal, Journal.
Write down in your journal when you are feeling stressed, angry, frustrated, happy, giddy, or relaxed. When an unconscious bias become conscious, write it down, then write down where it came from and why you feel this way. Keep it simple, so you can look back on it and reflect upon your responses. Think about how to approach a similar experience next time. (I keep a little red book for my journal. I am amazed how I react sometimes!)
Did you know? Journaling (writing) activates your Reticular Activating System (RAS), providing a filter for what is important and then filing it

away. The RAS helps you filter true and false information when journaling, thus reinforcing behaviors towards the positive (if you are journaling for positive change). The RAS helps you set intent and focus as well as being responsible for your fight-or-flight response and your wakefulness.

Table 6-1 Journal Page

Situation	Your Response	Positive or Negative and Why	How to Improve
What took place?	What did you do, think, or say?	How did it affect you?	What should you have done differently?

As you are writing, label one column "situation." When you journal and see an inappropriate reaction or an action that left you a bit short of the desired result, think about how to change it and then write it down. I use a highlighter to help draw my attention back to it later.

- Journaling is you writing about you—how you feel, situations that went well, situations that went poorly, your strengths and areas of development, where you wish to be in the future, goals and more.
- Be honest with yourself and open yourself up to your fears and concerns. What keeps you up at night? Write it down—and you will fall back to sleep rather than wasting mental energy on the issue.
- Journaling is personal; share it only if you wish to share it.
- Find a quiet moment. You don't need an hour; if you have five minutes, write away. Create a five-minute window, which can be a coffee break or wine break, depending on the time of day. By writing something down, you purge it from your brain so you can reflect, embrace, and grow later.
- Reflect on what you wrote, a day or two later. This will provide you with solutions as well as insights into your behavior and situations.

Become Aware of How YOU React to Stress
When we are stressed, our brains can go into lizard mode, or the RAS

is activated, and you are in fight-or-flight mode. When this happens, we forget logic—and unconscious biases are waiting in the wings, unless they were neutralized by journaling.

Is your stress response physical? For example, your shoulders tighten, your jaw clenches, and you get a headache, or your heart rate increases. Is it emotional, presenting as yelling, crying, screaming or withdrawal? When you feel stressed, do a body check. Stress causes body issues you may not even be aware of, therefore your body is like a stress barometer for you. When you're feeling anxious or agitated, conduct a body check. Ask yourself: Are your shoulders tight, teeth clenched? Are you biting your lips? Do you have a headache? Ask yourself why you feel this way. Note what is causing the emotion—are you stressed, frustrated, angry, impatient, etc.? Then write it down! This will remind you when you clench your teeth that you're actually stressed out, and then you can identify the stressor.

Body Check: Do an emotional self-check throughout the day. How am I feeling right NOW? Note it and journal it! Finally, get to the nitty-gritty. Ask yourself, "Why am I feeling _____ and what can I do to change the behavior?"

Self-awareness is a skill set that always needs work—regardless of your score in this proficiency. Why, you may wonder? It's because your organizational, family, and personal dynamics are always changing. If you want to change with these situations, continue to work on self-awareness. It will serve you well both personally and in your professional efforts to help create an inclusive workplace.

Cultural Intelligence (CQ)

In the interests of transparency, I'll state here that I am aligned with the Cultural Intelligence Center (CIC). I have found that, in my opinion, CIC has the most adaptable and comprehensive frameworks for CQ. Cultural Intelligence is the ability of people, organizations, and businesses to relate and adapt their behavior in culturally diverse situations and work effectively/adapt to them.[85] CQ can also be a wonderful level setting training program. Please visit CIC's website for more information.

Collaboration

Many of us think we actually know how to collaborate, but are you collaborating with intent? Are you collaborating on the right project? And what is your added value? Collaboration is a co-creative team relationship in business where the focus is on one goal, and all have an impact. That sounds simple, right? If you want to have successful collaboration, there again must be a clear, definable purpose as to why you are collaborating. Again, as we've emphasized in previous chapters, the purpose or intent of this collaboration is to drive an inclusive organizational culture. Remember the Intent Statement?

> *We are focused on advancing our inclusive organizational culture, resulting in / to drive attraction, retention, development, performance, and employee engagement while embracing / benefiting from our employee's diverse perspectives / thoughts. Inclusion is the core of our culture brand and diversity will be the core of our talent brand.*

This is the purpose of your collaboration. However, this is a very big purpose, so we must break down the initiatives into bite-sized pieces (goals) so we can specialize and focus our collaboration.

For example, one initiative may be to bring in neurodivergent employees. In working with one technology firm, the above intent statement was set, and one goal was to hire more neurodivergent employees. The collaboration team was comprised of talent acquisition, occupational health, organizational development and learning, and the pilot department in information technology. The success of any collaboration depends on a clear purpose and the right people. So, people were included who were decision-makers and those who would have an impact on or be impacted by the change.

I have also seen collaboration fall completely apart, either by including the wrong people or due to a lack of purpose. When that happens, the negative effects linger, as those around you are less likely to collaborate with you in the future.

If you want to collaborate effectively, the clearer the purpose, the better your outcomes will be. It also takes focusing on the right people to collaborate with. Use your RACI chart in collaborations and do repeated check-ins as follow-ups.

The first four elements of the strategy for building a solid foundation for an inclusive organization speak to your inclusion intent statement. Interweave these elements. The last two elements should be part of all employee development. Inclusion and diversity take intent and yes, work. If you find you have a gap in these elements, dig in and fill that gap. There are plenty of learning tools on LinkedIn Learning, as well as books and online articles.

Moving Forward with Inclusion

Building your foundation for inclusion is focused largely on awareness while intently focusing on change stability. A strong foundation is paramount for inclusion success; however, today's inclusion and diversity practitioners and organizations tend to spend the least amount of time here. This is due in part to the lack of measurable results available for this phase, yet, without the awareness of inclusion, the value of inclusion and the intent of inclusion, the other phases are met with resistance and unclear goals. Take time to build your foundation, be sure you have the right people's attention and buy-in as to why inclusion, and remember, this is not a race—it's a journey. A strong foundation will drive the framework.

To ensure you have not missed anything, set up a SharePoint and/or Teams Channel file titled inclusion and diversity (or opt for whatever business platform your organization utilizes) to share and update information. The goal is to have a file with all information available to executive leadership (C-suite), leadership, the inclusion team, and the inclusion and diversity council. Use technology to keep all this simple.

Files to include (but don't be limited just these):

- Inclusion Intent Statement
- Value Proposition for Inclusion

- RACI Excel file
- Inclusion & Diversity, Value Statement
- Inclusion & Diversity Strategy

See templates and examples on the book's website.

I stated earlier that building the foundation is not as much heavy lifting as it is alignment. It is important we spend the time securing alignment from leadership on down. The Inclusion Paradigm® is a stool with four legs, so if one leg is missing or weak, the stool will remain wobbly rather than solid. Take the time needed to understand your current organizational culture and the change of adding another pillar (inclusion) to your culture, then dive into the framework that's explained in the next chapter.

7

The Business Imperative: The Framework

Nothing ever 'just happens' in a thriving business—it takes intent and a solid framework to create a sustainable business imperative.

Thinking back to Chapter 5, is your organization still in awareness (Level 1) or moving to Level 2 (creating a strategic framework)? There is no rush to move from one level to another. If you're still in the awareness phase, that's okay. When you recognize that your organization's leadership **embraces inclusion as a critical foundation and driver for success**, it's time to create the organization's Inclusion and Diversity Statement.

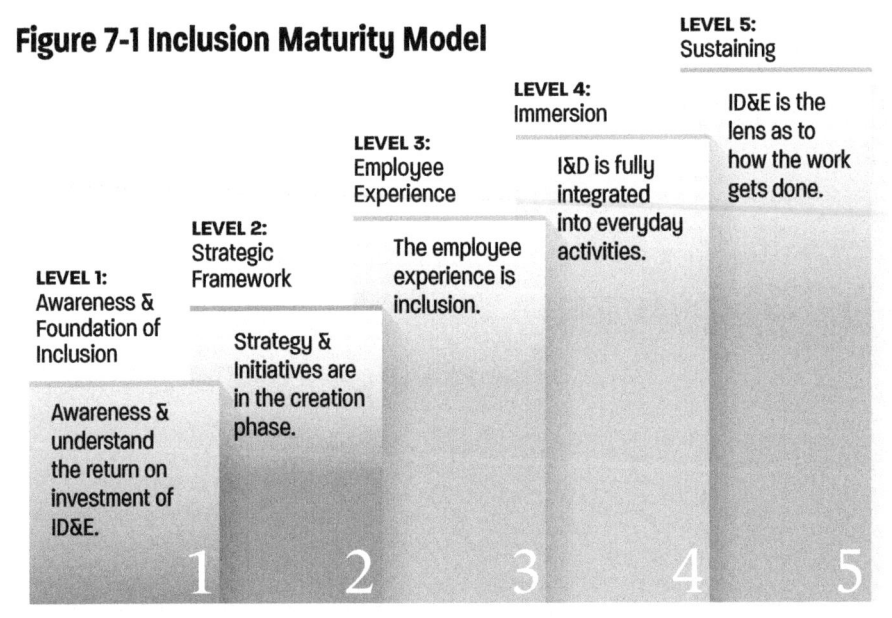

Figure 7-1 Inclusion Maturity Model

LEVEL 1: Awareness & Foundation of Inclusion
- Awareness & understand the return on investment of ID&E.

LEVEL 2: Strategic Framework
- Strategy & Initiatives are in the creation phase.

LEVEL 3: Employee Experience
- The employee experience is inclusion.

LEVEL 4: Immersion
- I&D is fully integrated into everyday activities.

LEVEL 5: Sustaining
- ID&E is the lens as to how the work gets done.

126   EVIDENCE BASED INCLUSION

Moving forward to the Framework, this chapter will highlight what must be in place at a minimum and then acted upon within this stage. We first need to understand how inclusion can be advanced within the organization. Being evidence based, the Shore Model of Inclusion clearly demonstrates the role and impact of leadership and management throughout this change. Trust in the process is critical, and transparent communication and evidence-based initiatives and models build trust.

Shore Model of Inclusion

Believe it or not, there is a model of inclusion for you to use, and it is simple. Lynn Shore and colleagues developed this model, and it works (see Figure 7-2). This model intersects inclusion and uniqueness. Being process driven based on proven evidence, I follow the Shore Model of Inclusion.[86] Simply put, an organization's leadership makes a commitment to inclusion and diversity. They are the drivers—or, if you're looking at a RACI chart, they are the ones who are R (responsible) and A (accountable). Leadership understands and drives the seven inclusion themes (covered in Chapter 5). This drives the inclusive culture in tandem with compliance and policy reviews. Leadership empowers management to embrace and drive inclusion to their teams. This model reinforces the critical role leadership plays in creating an inclusive culture.

Figure 7-2 Shore Model of Inclusion in Organizations

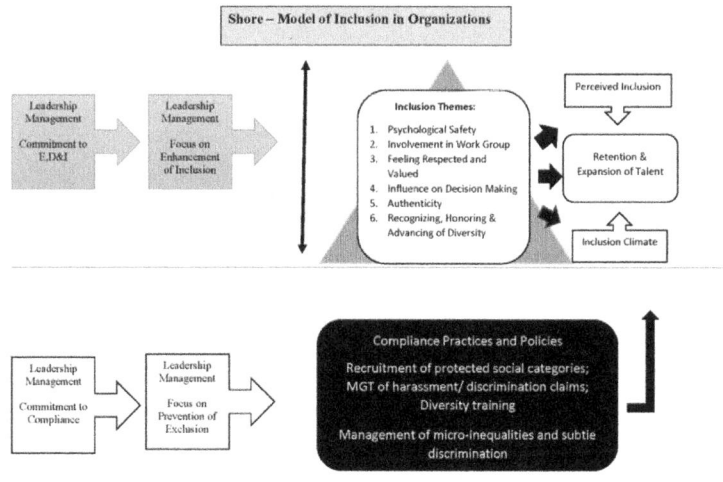

Source: Shore et al., "Inclusive Workplaces: A Review and Model," *Human Resource Management Review*, 28(2): 2018, https://doi.org/10.1016/j.hrmr.2017.07.003.

When using Shore's model, you'll find that the inclusion and diversity council is imperative for culture success. This is evident based on who is responsible and accountable for this change.

The Framework

The Framework has eight spokes as you can see in Figure 7-3. They are described in more detail below.

Figure 7-3 The 8-Spoke Framework

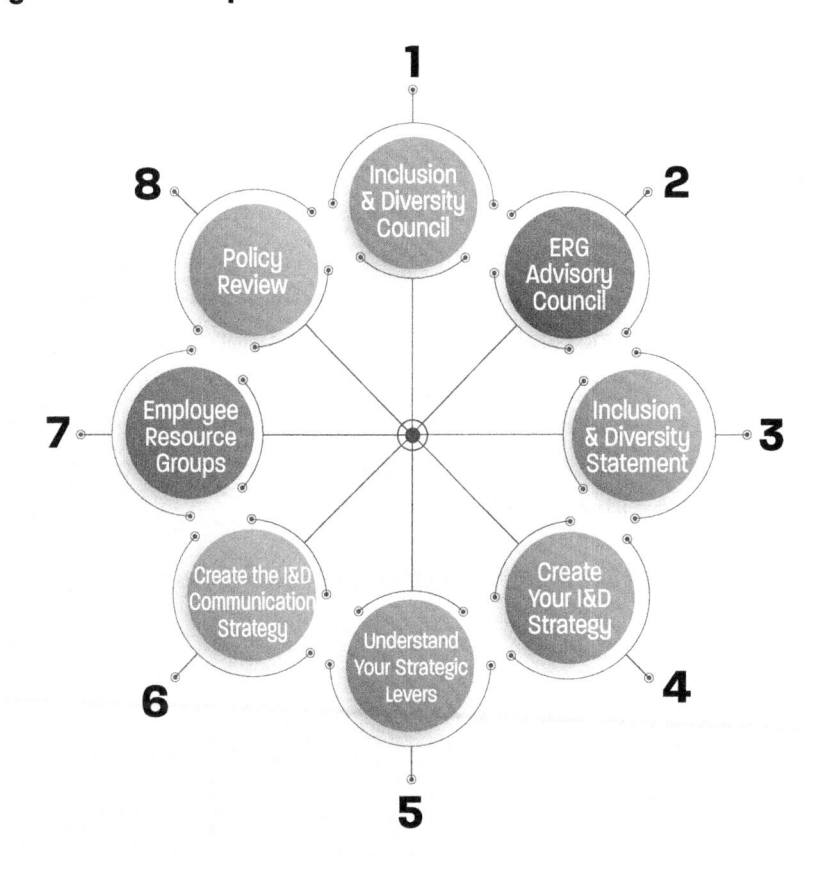

Spoke 1 - *The Inclusion & Diversity Council (I&D Council)*
Statistically speaking, 78% of diversity councils in organizations fail, according to the Society for Human Resource Management (SHRM). Well, no wonder they fail. Nobody's comes out and said, "Here's the evidence

and a workplace inclusion model that shows how if you create an inclusion and diversity council in this framework, you will drive inclusion and diversity." Until now.

When I was working with a large healthcare organization in 2017, they shared with me their structure for a DE&I council. They failed to define what they wanted their diversity council to achieve—they didn't define their outcomes and goals, nor did they define what they needed to work on or the status of their current culture.

The first words out of my mouth were: "This isn't going to work." And as you might imagine, the organization was not happy to hear that. Furthermore, I was told by their diversity professional this had worked in a prior company, so "why not here?"

If you don't define first, then you have no idea what type of council you want to put together. Yes, they disagreed with me. I stepped back from the contract and planned to check back in eight months to see their progress. Not surprisingly, I was called back to the company in just six months. Now they were ready to let me put together a diversity council that was going to fit, based on their needs.

Inclusion and diversity is not a one-size-fits-all change, initiative, or program, and I think that's part of the problem. We've gotten so used to the pre-packaged, one-size-fits-all solutions that may work for some issues that we fail to recognize that with inclusion and diversity, this is a culture shift and pre-packaged won't work. Grab your Inclusion Intent Statement, which was created by your executive leadership during the foundation phase. It is time to build upon it and begin thinking about your Inclusion & Diversity Council and strategy.

I&D Councils are today's critical driver in creating and fostering sustainable organizational change that is focused on inclusion and then diversity strategic imperatives. **Caution!** Do not lump inclusion and diversity together when it comes to goals and outcomes. The councils also oversee and assess inclusion and diversity programs, initiatives, and metrics, and they engage when a course correction is needed. An I&D Council is the governing body that creates strategic missions and plans as well as initiatives around inclusion and diversity. The Council is comprised of senior leadership and those who drive and review various initiatives and metrics related to inclusion then diversity. In a nutshell, these individuals oversee inclusion and diversity within the organization and have decision-making ability.

In many organizations, I have found that the council is not all that diverse in and of itself. However, I strongly advocate for making your I&D Council as diverse as possible—after all, it's in the name. With that in mind, remember that diversity is more than color or gender. Diversity of thought is a big deal to me, as is diversity of departments. You can't have an I&D Council if it's made up of people from just one department. You need a sprinkling of departments represented, so be sure to include someone from information technology and operations, for example. Every department in your organization must have some say in this.

Here's an example of why your council needs to be diverse. *I was called into a company to help create a sustainable ID&E Council as the one they currently had was failing. This is what it looked like: The executive leadership team was on the council, but of the eight leaders, only one was female and one a person of color. Executive leadership had no buy-in to inclusion and diversity; in fact, for them this was just another thing to do, a box to check with the board of directors. Adding to the problem, there were six mid-level leaders on the council, yet none of them had any decision-making ability. Their Employee Resource Groups (ERGs) were not represented.*

In the end, the lack of diversity and decision-making ability created meetings with no outcomes. There was a gap in information-gathering as well. Unfortunately, this council had been in place for three years before I was brought in—that is a lot of time and energy wasted, not to mention the programs that were ineffective at providing the outcomes and solutions the company was looking for.

I wish I could say this example is just a one-off, but sadly, it is not. I am sure that many of you are thinking, "Hey, that sounds like my council!" The problem is not the intent of what you're trying to create within the company, it's the lackluster information that employees are pulling off the internet that lets them think, "Hey, I can put together a diversity council." But if you read the wrong article, you miss a core component. Remember, inclusion councils are as unique as the organizations they work in.

Let's take a closer look at the structure of the I&D Council and the roles and responsibilities of its members (see Figure 7-4).

Figure 7-4 Structure of the I&D Council

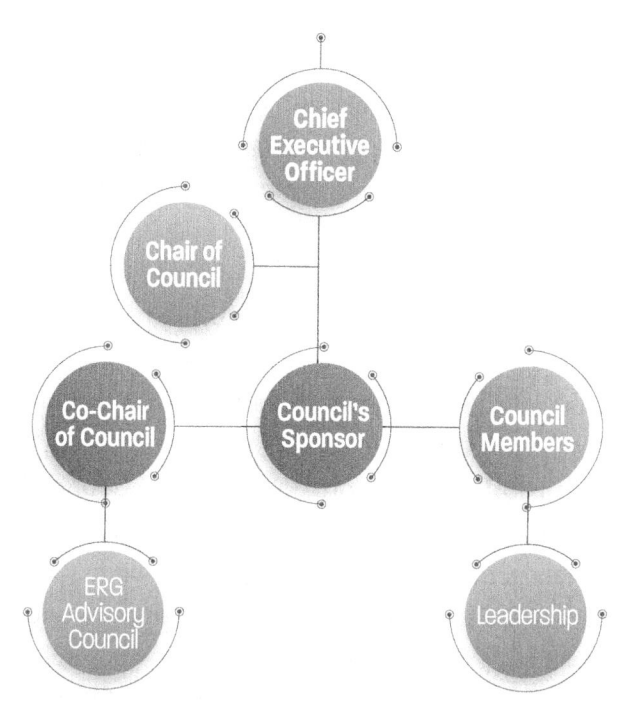

[Diagram showing the structure of the I&D Council with the following connected nodes: Chief Executive Officer at top, connected to Chair of Council, Co-Chair of Council, Council's Sponsor, and Council Members. Co-Chair of Council connects to ERG Advisory Council. Council Members connects to Leadership.]

The I&D Council is the decision and accountability council. The buck stops here. Council members will be made up of the executive leadership team with Senior Vice Presidents and/or Vice Presidents. The council's focus and goal is to create, implement, and make strategic decisions that will drive the inclusion and diversity strategy. In the traditional RACI chart, this council is Responsible and Accountable for all inclusion and diversity decisions and imperatives. It is imperative all members know their role.

Roles and Responsibilities of Council Members:
Chief Executive Officer: Oversees the council.

Chair of Council: Chief Human Resource Officer
- **Direct Responsibilities:** Reports directly to CEO and will provide Inclusion Council updates on what the organization is doing or intends to do to improve the organization's inclusion and diversity strategies, mission and goals.

- **Co-Chair of Council**: Inclusion & Diversity Practitioner (SVP/VP Level), should be the thought leader on inclusion and diversity within the organization.
- **Direct Responsibilities**: Meeting scheduling and preparation, meeting facilitation, follow-up on action items, communication, and messaging, liaising with the executive team and maintaining the organization's inclusion and diversity strategic documents. Report out feedback and insight provided by the ERGs. Creates the year-end I&D Company Report. Co-Chair reports to Council Sponsor.

Council Sponsor: SVP/VP of Human Resources / Organizational Development and Culture
- **Direct Responsibilities**: Supports the Inclusion Council by providing guidance to the co-chairs; serving as the link between the co-chairs and senior management; acting as an arbitrator and making decisions that may be beyond the authority of the co-chairs and Council members; and supporting co-chairs in presentation of recommendations to the executive team. Council Sponsor reports to the Council Chair.

Council Members: Executive Leadership Team / Senior Vice Presidents / Vice Presidents (must have decision-making capability)
- **Direct Responsibilities:** The members' role will be to support current and future inclusion and diversity efforts, embed inclusive best practices, and be accountable in their promotion of inclusion and diversity throughout the organization and their teams. This council is focused on engaging senior leadership, with the goal that they will create and continue to embed inclusion in their areas of responsibility, being active and prominent advocates of inclusive practices and leadership.

Spoke 2 - *The ERG Advisory Council*

The ERG Advisory Council will be made up of the organization's ERG members at the Director level and below. The goal is to update the decision-making council on the ERGs and what they are seeing within the organization, Members are provided with an overview of the I&D Strategy. This council is focused on advising the decision-making council on inclusion and diversity specific to each ERG including barriers, trends, employee engagement, training programs and initiatives within the organization. The advisory council should consist of representatives from different backgrounds within the organization who meet on a regular basis to discuss what is being done on inclusion and diversity, how it's working, and providing advice on what to do next. In the traditional RACI chart, this council's role is to be a **C**onsultant and to **I**nform the I&D Co-Chair of information. It is imperative all members know their role. (See Figure 7-5.)

Co-Chair of Council: This is the same person who is Co-Chair of the I&D Council and is the organization's Inclusion & Diversity Practitioner.
- **Direct Responsibilities:** Responsible for gathering feedback provided by the council members and bringing it to the I&D Council.

Council Members: Individuals who are actively engaged with an ERG. Typically, this council is made up of 15-21 members who are representative of their ERG and job roles/functions. The key, again, is to make this ERG Advisory Council as diverse as possible.
- **Direct Responsibilities**: They are responsible to promote, provide feedback on, facilitate, and support the implementation of the strategic inclusion and diversity initiatives set by the I&D Council. They also provide insight and feedback to both the ERG Sponsors.

Utilize the RACI chart to keep task assignments focused. The mission statement for the ERG Advisory Council is simply to share information and insights on inclusion and diversity programs, initiatives, and feedback gathered through the ERG. Share this with your organization (communication transparency).

Figure 7-5 ERG Advisory Council

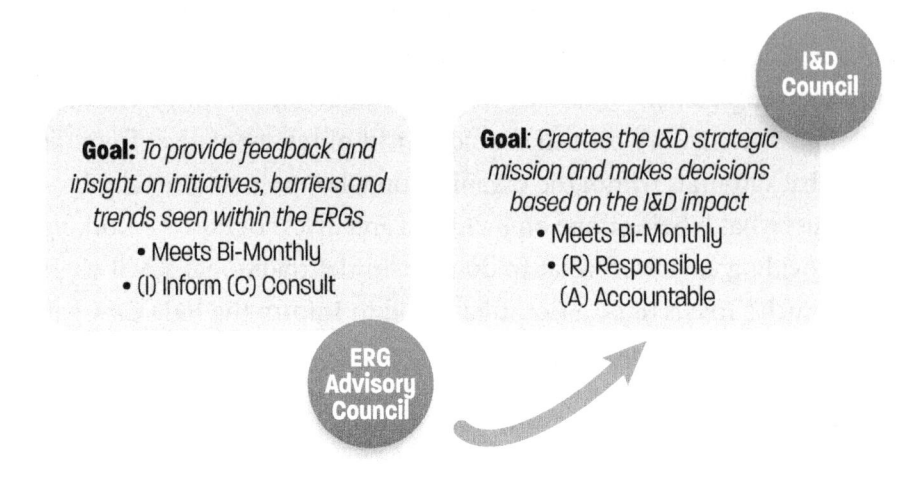

I&D Council
Goal: *Creates the I&D strategic mission and makes decisions based on the I&D impact*
- Meets Bi-Monthly
- (R) Responsible
  (A) Accountable

ERG Advisory Council
Goal: *To provide feedback and insight on initiatives, barriers and trends seen within the ERGs*
- Meets Bi-Monthly
- (I) Inform (C) Consult

Both councils work in tandem with each other, providing a flow of information throughout the organization.

Spoke 3 - *Inclusion & Diversity Statement*

This is the organization's statement on inclusion and diversity (and yes, many include the E as well because it's trendy) and link to the corporate value statement, what the organization business values. Let me ask you, what is your culture brand? If I were to ask several employees at your organization to define your organizational culture, what would they say? What are the themes and is inclusion part of that brand? Moving forward in creating your inclusion and diversity statement, you may find you will need to adapt your current culture brand. This statement must start at the top and align with the organization's values. Take a look at Home Depot's ESG Strategy, which includes a Diversity, Equity & Inclusion Vision Statement.[87] Is there alignment with what you know about the organization? Can you see the alignment on their website? Yes, there is a strong culture brand that includes inclusion and diversity.

As practitioners, we want this statement to be part of the organization's core values. Remembering the RACI approach we discussed previously, here's how it applies to an I&D Statement:

R = Inclusion Team, Executive Leadership
A = Executive Leadership & Leadership
C = Leadership & Management
I = All Employees

Here are several examples of Inclusion & Diversity Value Statements:

Johnson & Johnson

Inclusion at Johnson & Johnson is about creating a deep sense of belonging. It's about a culture where you are valued, your ideas are heard, and you advance this culture for everyone.
Diversity & Inclusion at Johnson & Johnson means - You Belong.

Our Vision
Be yourself, change the world.
Our vision at Johnson & Johnson, is for every person to use their unique experiences and backgrounds, together—to spark solutions that create a better, healthier world.

Our Mission
Make diversity and inclusion how we work every day.
Our mission is to make diversity & inclusion our way of doing business. We will advance our culture of belonging where open hearts and minds combine to unleash the potential of the brilliant mix of people, in every corner of Johnson & Johnson.[88]

Home Depot

Diversity, Equity & Inclusion Vision Statement: *The Home Depot is building a more diverse, equitable and inclusive organization, within our enterprise and the communities we are proud to serve. Grounded in our core values, we have the conviction, capabilities, and tools to make a difference for our associates, community, and suppliers.*

These statements serve as a starting point for your own efforts. You can find other examples of I&D Value Statements on company websites.

Remember that often, such statements are revised over time. Be proud of yours and share it out in the world. Share it with your employees. This statement is your commitment to your employees and your clients around your intent with inclusion and diversity. It is part of your culture brand. This is part of your workplace values AND you must be prepared to be accountable to those values.

This statement also must be part of your talent brand. Potential employees will (I hope) research your organization through its website as well as Glassdoor and other job-hunting sites. Once your statement is created, you are ready to dive into the next phase.

Spoke 4 - *Create Your I&D Strategy*

Figure 7-6 I&D Strategic Pathway

- 01 I&D Organizational Overview
- 02 I&D Strategic Statement
- 03 I&D Strategic Imperative
- 04 I&D Value Proposition
- 05 Organizational I&D Maturity Model
- 06 I&D Strategy Priorities
- 07 I&D Strategic Levers
- 08 I&D Strategy & Stages mapped to the Strategic Levers

The first order of business for the I&D Council is to uncover where the pain points in the organization lie (see the pathway laid out in Figure 7-6). What are the inclusion and diversity issues? Gather the organizational demographic information that will become your human resources/demographic dashboard if one is not already in place. Be sure all information gathered is correct and inclusive of all relevant affinities. Recognize there is intersectionality with all employees (see Chapter 4). What is your organization's inclusion and diversity story? Where is the organization today?

Uncover and create your current I&D Story. As the I&D Council, ask these questions:

- Start with your Inclusion Intent Statement and I&D Statement—now build upon them.
- How does this organization define inclusion and diversity?
- What does the landscape look like within the workplace?
- Can you identify any skill gaps?
- How about intersectionality—what does that look like within the organization and are there gaps?
- What does the workplace look like?
- How would you define the organization's culture?
- What does leadership bench strength mean—and look like—in your organization?

You may be surprised to find that you already have this information at your fingertips. If not, this is a good place to start investing time and energy in gathering that information. This information is your inclusion and diversity starting point. Here's a look at what data matters:

- Look at your organization's demographics; this is the start of creating your human resources/demographic dashboard. Shake out all demographics (gender, age—I do this by generation, ethnicity, veteran status, disabilities, gender, and sexual orientation) at the base level. Then continue to fill in the same demographic information for job function, organizational level (leadership, management, individual contributor).
- Review culture and engagement surveys that have already been done. Note the trends around inclusion and diversity question sets, culture question sets, and engagement question sets. This is a bit more qualitative than quantitative.

- Examine termination reports and look for commonalities based on affinities.
- Examine retention data: who is advancing by affinity, what are the trends?
- Are your inclusion and diversity policies up to date (harassment, discrimination, I&D statement)?
- What about your past diversity goals? Do you have any? If yes, why were they created and what is their story?
- Do your employees have equal access to success and advancement? That's leveling the playing field.
- Do they feel part of the decision-making process?
- Can they talk about barriers?
- Are employees engaged? When there is low engagement, often there's a lack of inclusion.

I tend to be a bit visual, so I like to storyboard an organization's I&D Story. Create a timeline that shows what has been done previously and the results. What levers were pulled? You want to get a sense of the big picture with building blocks for future attention.

Moving forward, now that the I&D Council has gathered all the data, and everyone understands the organizational story of inclusion and diversity, you can now create your strategy. What are the big goals? Keep in mind, this is your strategy, not a list of the initiatives you plan to launch. Create a list of inclusion and diversity priorities for the year, a list of several shifts the I&D Council would like to see happen during the year. You already have your strategic levers and inclusive outcomes (listed above), so now you can begin to formulate priorities around what you can shift within the workplace based on your goals.

Define your inclusion and diversity priorities based on your I&D gaps, issues, and companywide goals. Here are some examples of what this looks like:

- Evolve the I&D Strategy by crystalizing key strategic levers and supporting initiatives that target actions to support a strong culture of inclusion and diversity.

- Define Strategic Levers: Organizational Culture, Leadership Commitment, HRIS, Employee Benefits, Recruitment, Development, Advancement & Retention, Accommodations, Employee Engagement, Supplier Diversity, External Partnership & Outreach.
- Launch the I&D Council to ensure alignment on mission, broaden awareness, and model behaviors to foster an inclusive environment.
- Create and launch Inclusion ERGs for the purpose of creating an opportunity for all employees to feel empowered in bringing inclusion excellence to the organizational culture. Leverage and expand the membership of ERGs, learning programs and external association relationships to increase engagement, reinforce community and networking, and foster brand awareness of your organization as an employer of choice and your approach to employee development.
- Develop and integrate strategies with broader talent strategies that support and target strategies for best-in-class recruiting and retention.
- Implement foundational inclusion and diversity training—level setting, cultural intelligence, implicit bias, and microaggression—with the focus on knowledge gain.
- Improve leadership diversity by creating and launching the high-potential development program with a focus on diversity to improve diversity levels within leadership.

Initiatives are the programs you will create and launch to reach these goals.

Spoke 5 - *Understand Your Strategic Levers*

I often have been asked how inclusion and diversity are impacting the organization, by what means. Being visual, I like to see the organization through levers of impact followed by focused outcomes. These levers will change based on the organization, as will their outcome focus. Below are the basic levers. Examine your organizational strategic levers and what outcomes are important for the lever based on driving inclusion and diversity. When breaking it all down to levers, we also can see the direct leadership role in this change and create teams to manage programs and initiatives. I have to give credit where credit is due, in the past I referred to these as strategic pulls however, strategic levers is a term a good friend of mine uses. Thank you, Janette Suffern.

Table 7-1 Strategic Levers

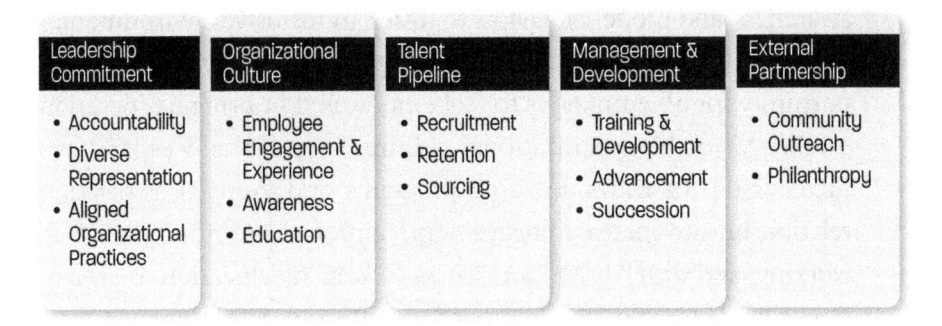

Leadership Commitment	Organizational Culture	Talent Pipeline	Management & Development	External Partmership
• Accountability • Diverse Representation • Aligned Organizational Practices	• Employee Engagement & Experience • Awareness • Education	• Recruitment • Retention • Sourcing	• Training & Development • Advancement • Succession	• Community Outreach • Philanthropy

It is easy to create a strategic company scorecard for inclusion and diversity when we focus on levers. The focus outcomes can be discussed and measured, then further defined based on what the organization needs. In Chapter 9 I demonstrate how to measure the focus outcomes of each lever.

Spoke 6 - *Create the I&D Communication Strategy*
Phew! Now that the I&D Strategy is taking shape, we need to examine how to communicate inclusion and diversity. In Chapter 6 we examined the communication matrix; now we need a communication strategy. Communication is a critical part of any culture change, especially inclusion. There needs to be a process in place for communication to be current and flow from top to bottom and then back up to the top. Transparency is critical.

There are many ways to create this strategy. Personally, I like a cross-function communication team made up of a person from your communication department, your Co-Chair of the Inclusion Council, a member of your senior leadership, mid-level director leadership and two to three managers (from different departments). You could also include your communication leads from your ERGs if you desire. Here is my four-prong approach to communicating inclusion, which I have used several times with great success!

Prong 1: Intranet Page. After creating a solid communication team, think of communication as a window, where the first pane is incorporating an Inclusion & Diversity page on the company intranet. This becomes the go-to for all inclusion and diversity with the theme of inclusion. Include everything inclusion and diversity related so it really is one-stop shopping for knowledge.

On this page/intranet site, place your demographic data and keep it updated. You can also add a calendar of events, podcasts, and resources or a library. Have fun with this. Create a logo. Post your I&D Statement, add the I&D Strategy and the Inclusion Council, and so on. Again, it is important that you have RACI in place, so everyone clearly understands their role and deliverables. Questions should be routed to the Co-Chair's mailbox for answering.

Prong 2: Monthly Newsletter. Someone on the communication team should be responsible for creating and updating a branded Inclusion Newsletter. Remember to keep it simple. Here is where you celebrate your ERGs. You can link to a calendar of events for ERGs and anything you wish to add, such as news. What is new, what new initiative are you focused on? What about your ERGs' activities?

Prong 3: Add a section called Inclusion Corner to the organization's bimonthly or monthly newsletter that is strictly for the Inclusion Council—keep it short.

Prong 4: Organizational Assets. Here's where to keep assets such as email banners and notification tools, internal social media, manager/leadership meetings, etc., that the organization runs for its employees. One company I worked with had an amazing social media platform on their intranet, so we added an Inclusion posting page and encouraged everyone to share information. Another company had banners on the bottom of emails that could be updated (like for snow days) where we put event reminders.

The point of these four prongs is frequency and openness. Did I mention we linked, linked, linked away, to ERG pages, the Inclusion page, policies, etc.? Now comes the hard part: What will you share? What metrics will you share? What is in it for the employees? Why engage? This must be crystal clear.

Over the years, I've learned there are several keys to successful communication on culture shifts, starting with understanding what needs to be communicated and how. Choose the right frequency (trust me, more is better), and know that content needs to be inclusive of everyone and contain the benefits of what the communication is focused on. You must be accountable and listen to feedback and create a sense of openness and safe space for all to share.

Spoke 7 -*Employee Resource Groups*

ERGs have proven to be an essential tool for advancing inclusion and diversity within the workplace. Their impact has been demonstrated in increased retention and employee engagement, the removal of advancement barriers for affinity groups, improved problem-solving, promotion of cultural awareness and improved company innovation. Yet how to establish them is not clearly defined. While I could write an entire book on ERGs, this book focuses on the needle of inclusion. I have seen all different types of ERGs, and some work, some do not. The ERG provides membership to the ERG Advisory Council.

Rather than preach here, I would like to list the top things to keep in mind when creating an ERG:

- Executive sponsorship matters. Each ERG should have an executive sponsor who is engaged with the ERG. The sponsor needs to show up, coach the leadership team, and raise the visibility of this ERG. Hold the executive sponsor accountable (maybe on their leadership scorecard, covered in Chapter 8).

- Clearly define the roles of leadership within the ERG.
- Help create the charter and mission of each ERG—be sure it is clear and concise. Spell out the goals and be transparent.
- Have goals for each ERG (i.e., number of speaker, social, and community outreach events).
- Create a succession plan for the leadership change—please do not leave this to guesswork.
- Please help provide structure. While it is well known that ERGs are employee led, that does not mean leaving the ERG leadership alone. Help them succeed. Remember that the leadership of the ERG is a leadership development role that should include solid coaching
- Help create a communication plan for ERG events.
- Support, support, and then support some more.
- ERGs need funding. Typically, I have seen $125/person allotted to ERGs for programs. This money provides for programs, speakers, and events.
- Link your ERGs to Environmental, Social and Governance (ESG) goals.
- Identify best ways to measure the ERG's impact (programs, attendance, enrollment, ESG, Corporate Social Responsibility).
- Celebrate your ERG!
- When your ERGs are doing community work, whether it's paid or not, giving your people eight hours of pay for community work is a great attraction/retention tool, especially for members of the Millennial generation.

Please feel free to go to the book's website to find an ERG slide deck and more.

Spoke 8 - *Policy Review*
Part of building your inclusion framework is examining your organizational policies to see if they use inclusive language that is also non-gendered. This usually falls under human resources. Be sure these policies are

in a place where employees can find them easily (the employee handbook is a great spot). Here's a list of the types of policies to examine:

- **Generic:** policies that address inclusion and diversity inequalities in the workplace
- **Targeted recruitment:** policies that actively recruit minorities to apply for job openings
- **Voluntary training:** policies that offer voluntary diversity training to employees
- **Mandatory training:** policies that require diversity training for all employees
- **Mentorship:** policies that provide underrepresented workers with mentors who can assist them with job and career changes
- **Formal hiring policies:** policies that rely on formalized/documented criteria for making decisions about hiring and promotion
- **Diversity office:** policies that establish a special office or committee that identifies barriers to diversity and works to remove those barriers
- **Diversity goals**: policies that establish numerical goals for addressing the underrepresentation of certain groups in the workplace
- **Disability and accommodation policy:** there is a complimentary PDF policy on the Federal Communications Commission website (https://www.fcc.gov/sites/default/files/reasonable_accommodation_policy_and_procedures_eeoc_final_2019.pdf)
- Inclusion and diversity language should be added to Anti-Harassment / Anti-Discrimination and Code of Conduct Policy.

Moving Forward

The framework is important as it will help focus your initiative on impact rather than on just "doing." Spend time here to be sure the organization has a solid I&D Value Statement that stands within the company's values. Focus on involving the right people in both the I&D Council and ERG leadership. The I&D Council will be busy during foundation work, as they will need to create the inclusion and diversity strategy that aligns with the Strategic I&D Statement. Keep in mind that you'll need to use the framework of levers to move forward.

The ERGs are now starting to shape up with great leadership and clear role refinement. Once leadership is in place, launch the ERGs and begin to bring in members through the communication strategy. Host an ERG launch party where employees learn about the ERGs and their charter and mission statements.

Outside the I&D Council, level-setting training is needed. Level set the organization on the terms and strategic I&D Statement. Focus on training that provides the tools to your employees around awareness of biases and microaggression. The goal is to have all employees on the same page.

As the organization continues to share with its employees about inclusion and diversity, your employees feel like they're part of something bigger. They believe in the organization's mission and understand the goal. They understand where their impact is. They are part of the decision-making process and feel like they are helping to sail the ship. You know it's an inclusive organization when it trickles out into the community.

You may be asking, are we done with the strategic framework phase? Yes and no, as inclusion and culture are ever changing. It is perfectly fine to go back into this framework to make changes. This process is not rigid; it is more fluid. Be flexible. The more insight, the better the outcomes, as you can craft programs that fit your organization.

Moving forward to the next chapter, we will examine the four pillars of driving inclusion: leadership, human resources, organizational development and learning, and managers. It is important to begin to see this change as holistic and impacting the entire organization, driven by all.

8

Inclusion as the Intersection of Employee Engagement and Culture: The 4 Pillars

Inclusion is NOT a solo task. The four pillars that are essential to making this pivot to inclusion are leaders, human resources, organizational development and learning, and managers. These are the four functional areas that will lead inclusion within the organization through programs and initiatives.

I know I have said this before, but it is so important: all inclusion and diversity work must start at the top and be fully supported by leadership. Without this, everyone will just be spinning their wheels. However, leaders are not alone in the journey of inclusion. The four pillars that are essential to making this pivot to inclusion are leaders, human resources, organizational development and learning, and managers. These are the four functional areas that will lead inclusion within the organization through programs and initiatives. Let us look at each more deeply.

Pillar #1: Leaders

"Diversity is a fact, but inclusion is a choice we make every day. As leaders, we have to put out the message that we embrace and not just tolerate diversity."
—Nellie Borrero, Managing Director, Senior Strategic Advisor
Global Inclusion & Diversity at Accenture

As mentioned earlier, change starts with leadership, and they must understand the why and how as well as lead the shift to inclusion. Who are these leaders, you ask? It starts in the C-suite with executives and includes anyone in the organization who holds a leadership title. Let me be a bit clearer, as the team "leadership" is also a moving target these days as we have managing leaders, leaders, and everyone is a leader in one way. For the sake of this change process, a leader is someone who has decision-making capability, is focused on the larger picture, leads people rather than tasks, innovates and inspires, leads by example, and shapes the organizational culture.

If leadership is not behind the shift to inclusion, then nothing will happen. This is more than just a word shift, from "diversity" to "inclusion." Leadership needs to understand the difference between the two as well as the business case and must be the sponsors of this change. When this is missing, an organization may need to go back to the steps in Chapter 5. Remember, it all starts with leadership.

As a leader, do you:

- seek out different views to gain a better perspective, especially when making a decision?
- share in the decision-making process with diversity of thoughts?
- encourage diverse perspectives and thoughts within your team?
- acknowledge and value people, understanding and appreciating everyone's apparent worth?
- understand the person—who they are, how they think—and are you prepared to communicate and influence with that in mind?
- review advancement with a lens of intersectionality?

If you answered yes to all of the above, you are an inclusive leader. Leadership must be inclusive, meaning inclusive leaders understand their own biases and are constantly working on shifting their perception.

Inclusive Leadership

Inclusive leadership is the ability to lead through understanding all parameters of the problem and considering the needs of **all individuals.** Inclusive leaders openly understand all who report to them beyond their job description and understand how intersectionality plays a role in perspectives and decision-making. They create a safe environment for all to share, understanding and reviewing different points of view to provide better innovation and solutions. They have superior vision to guide change, to inspire and motivate others toward greatness. This leader is trustworthy and ethical, a role model to all, and one who empowers others to take ownership of their work. They are not without fault but are flexible enough to overcome shortcomings and embrace accountability. They are big-picture thinkers and feel there is no box.

With inclusive leadership, there is an elevated level of emotional intelligence and productivity, which results in lower employee turnover, greater job satisfaction, and more effectiveness associated with this leadership style. Business Emotional Intelligence is the adaptive interaction between emotion and cognition that includes the ability to perceive, assimilate, understand, and manage one's own emotions and detect/interpret the emotions of others. Inclusive leaders have this tenfold and are always working to improve their skills and are focused on their team members' skills.

Inclusive leadership raises awareness at the individual level—raising awareness of the importance of the organization's goals; thus, individuals rise above their own needs for the organization's success. They are leaders who are admired, trusted, and respected by the organization's employees. These leaders can connect with their team and can impose the self-concept of organizational visions within the organization, thus lending themselves to strong Emotional Intelligence scores.

Traits of Inclusive Leaders[89]
If you are an inclusive leader, you exhibit the following traits:

- **Authenticity:** Know who you are and where your values lie. Honesty and integrity build trust.
- **Accountability:** Be transparent. Inclusion is part of your own authentic leadership style. Your commitment to diversity and inclusion is

contagious as you share with others. You challenge the status quo or your own perspective on inclusion and diversity. You are accountable and embrace inclusion and diversity as both a company and personal priority.
- **Courage:** Little fear of admitting mistakes and have the ability to speak truth to power (say what needs to be said). You stand up for what is right, placing the employee's rights first.
- **Cognizance:** Elevated level of blind-spot awareness. Ability to see the flaws and gaps within the workflow process. Constantly working on your own self-awareness, and you help others work on it as well. Aware of and adjusting for your own self biases.
- **Curiosity:** Have the wonder of a four-year-old. Able to be open to all and can lock away judgment. Powerful sense of empathy for other people. Curious about and open to difference and perspectives.
- **Cultural Intelligence (CQ):** Aware of and can adapt to culture shifts in the workplace—both business and people. Have the resiliency to be flexible and adaptable in any situation. .
- **Collaboration:** Connecting with others in the workplace through empowerment. You provide psychological safety to your teams, and drive team cohesion through honesty and intent. Well attuned to the layers of inclusion and drivers.

Figure 8-1 Roles of Inclusive Leaders

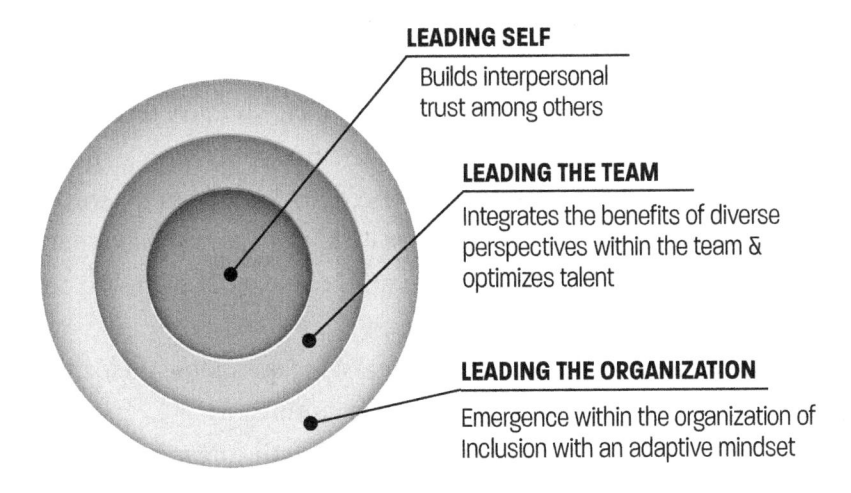

LEADING SELF
Builds interpersonal trust among others

LEADING THE TEAM
Integrates the benefits of diverse perspectives within the team & optimizes talent

LEADING THE ORGANIZATION
Emergence within the organization of Inclusion with an adaptive mindset

Leadership Pillars

Leadership Inclusion Focus: Empowerment, Courage, Accountability, Humility

- Keep the organization focused on inclusion rather than diversity. Be sure the company is focused on more than two affinities (gender and ethnicity).
- Create a pipeline of diverse talent through development and succession planning to improve leadership bench strength.
- Identify and address subtle discrimination such as micro-inequalities or microaggressions.[90]
- Identify and leverage diversity as a platform to increase business performance, aligning behind an unobstructed vision tied to business strategy (Inclusion Intent Statement).
- Utilize ERGs for greater understanding of employees and customers, take an active role in the ERGs.
- Improve performance management by including inclusion metrics based on the following: recruiting, promotion rates, compensation levels, turnover, participation in ERGs, customer gains, and supplier diversity.[91]
- Strategic Corporate Social Responsibility programs (CSR) and Environmental, Social and Governance (ESG) programs leading to community partnerships that ties into your ERGs and Sponsorship.
- Identify (and address barriers to) high-potential employees for advancement.
- Supplier diversification.
- Transparency: Share the organization's inclusion and diversity progress and updates, be sure to separate the two—inclusion goals are different from diversity goals. This all needs to come from the top down. Communicate the business case for inclusion and diversity internally and externally, integrate messages on the impact of inclusion and diversity on the business in meetings.
- Identify the barriers to advancement, asking questions and identifying resistance to the change to an inclusive culture.
- Model the behaviors you want to see within the organization.

- Monitor, reward, and recognize inclusion and diversity efforts among direct reports and other staff.
- Focus on ALL affinities, not just gender and ethnicity, within the workplace.

A note: Leadership scorecards work impressively well when examining the impact of your leadership team on inclusion. Examples of leadership scorecards can be found on the book's website.

Pillar #2: Human Resources

If you work in human resources, you are an organizational hero. Human resources is the heart of the organization and culture is one of its largest focuses (or should be). This department is a cross function of inner departments, all focused on the employees' experience and driving performance. From defining and driving the talent and culture brand of the organization to organizational development and learning, everything that touches the organization's employees has been touched by human resources. No other department within an organization has so many inner departments focused on the same outcomes.

The Many Hats of Human Resources

For those who are reading this book and are not human resource professionals, please let me share the many hats your human resources contact wears (see Figure 8-2).

Figure 8-2 Human Resources Wears Many Hats

	Human Resources	
Talent Management		Business Partners / Strategists
Compensation & Benefits		Workplace Safety
Employee Informatics		Performance Management
Employee Retention		Change Management
Organizational Development		Workflow
Training		Strategy and Processes
Leadership & Management Development		Workplace Negotiation and Conflict Management
Compliance		
Employee Relations		Coaching and Mentoring

And this list just names a few of the roles that human resources professionals take on. My message to all human resources professionals: you are my heroes—I hear and see you.

Human resources professionals can also be caught in a tug-of-war, as they are trying to do the right thing to protect both the organization AND they are there to protect the employee. Sometimes those two missions can conflict. I like to share all this because often human resources people are also seen negatively or viewed as an adversary rather than a friend.[92] This critical role within an organization is constantly changing in tandem with the way we do business. HR professionals are the heart of the organization, and the organization is only as good as its heart.

Today it is not surprising this department now takes on the heavy lifting of inclusion and diversity. From strategy and initiatives to measured outcomes, inclusion and diversity practitioners are found under the human resources umbrella—and all too often this role is not clearly or well defined enough to hire the right person. I went to LinkedIn to uncover what requirements were needed to hire a high-level inclusion and diversity practitioner, such as VP of Culture and Inclusion, SVP of ID&E and People, or Chief DE&I Officer. Here are the most common requirements I discovered:

Requirements
- Bachelor's degree required. Master's degree preferred. (Majoring in whatever.)
- Five to ten years related work experience required in driving diversity and/or organizational development and one to three years supervisory/management experience required.
- Experience leading initiatives promoting inclusion and diversity, and that build organizational culture.
- Demonstrated ability to build partnerships with team members at all levels of an organization.
- Ability to identify organizational development needs and deliver relevant coaching or training as needed.
- Excellent organizational, problem-solving and project management skills.

- Excellent communication skills, both written and spoken, to create a free flow of information at all levels of the organization.

There is not much in the above list regarding expertise in inclusion and diversity. However, the flavor of the next three years for professional development is all about diversity, equity and belonging (must love the trend words). There is a plethora of new programs being offered, yet their focus is on diversity.

What happens when the organization promotes internally—does the company send that person for training? I am not saying we need inclusion and diversity practitioners to all have advanced degrees, as less than 0.7% of all PhDs specialize in or concentrate on inclusion and diversity. And in typical industrial/organizational psychology programs (master's and PhD), the student is lucky to get one class in diversity.

Inclusion and diversity practitioners must constantly be learning within this space. That often means self-directed learning, as online coursework is often focused on selling you the next-level course rather than providing you with tangible information. (I often scratch my own head looking at these courses: if they were getting it right, we would not have the problem we have today with confusion around inclusion and diversity. Heck, many programs are still focused on diversity?) How is the organization supporting this individual? Are we setting up our own inclusion and diversity leaders for failure? Today human resources professionals are leading the business imperative of inclusion and diversity, but they struggle with leadership access, information, seeing the big picture, and more, in large part because the organization and department lack expertise in and understanding of inclusion and diversity.[93]

This is as good a place as any to note this: Successful inclusion and diversity within an organization is colorblind. What I mean is that you do not have to be a person of color to successfully steward inclusion and diversity. Why do I need to say this? Because, recently, I was present to the following rant:

The organization's VP of Culture decided to promote a very talented human resources professional to Manager of Belonging. Kara had worked for this organization for five years as a human resources business partner. Here is her rant:

"Seriously, I want to continue to focus on strategy. Am I being demoted? Now adding belonging in—how much more do you want me to do? You want me to now institute 'belonging'? But belonging goes against half of the rules and policies we have in place, right? Who is going to train me? Is there money to send me back to school?"

And this is where I actually applauded Kara, when she verbally said, "No thank you—this is not in my wheelhouse."

Here's the thing: Nobody wants to say, "I can't do this." If anything, I think that's where the industry has stumbled. That's where the onus is falling on those out there who are doing or trying to do inclusion and diversity, and they're not stepping up and saying, "I can't do this," or "I can't do this alone." Instead, we have created what I call the online learning culture where employees are looking things up online. "Oh, that's how this company did it. How do I set up my diversity council?" I have seen others go online and grab strategy statements without understanding that document is part four of a much larger document—the final stage. You've missed stages one, two and three.

Or they'll get an example from a completely different industry that has totally different workforce issues or that needs to think strategically in a different way, and it doesn't just translate automatically. An initiative that you find on the internet that's less than 750 words is not the solution. But, yes, that's what companies are doing. You may be wondering why they are doing this. Simply put, they have no time or expertise to do fundamental research. And yes, they are gaining "expert knowledge"—however, that knowledge has been pared down to bite-sized media pieces.

Stepping into a technology firm that had four ERGs running—notice I said "running," not "thriving"—I had to ask, *"How did you set these ERGs up?"* The director of diversity simply stated that they found the "instructions" in an article in *Forbes*. That article was less than 750 words on ERG best practices, and they set up four ERGs based on the article. As you know from Chapter 7, there is a lot more to ERGs than can be covered in 750 words. If it were that simple, we'd all have thriving ERGs, and organizations would already be focused on inclusion rather than diversity.

One of the main causes for this gap is how diversity has been spelled out, especially with affirmative action. What did that do to diversity work? It threw it right into human resources' wheelhouse. Human resources staffers are responsible for hiring and employee tracking. Here is my own pushback:

Inclusion is not a human resources function alone. Inclusion and diversity should be the foundation of organizational culture, thus making it a function of every employee within the organization.

Yes, it may fall under the human resources umbrella; however, it is linked to every department within the company, from marketing and operations to information technology and research and design. Inclusion and diversity are driven by culture and mindset.

Human Resources Pillars
Inclusion Focus: Commitment, Policy, Engagement, Safety

- Keep the organization focused on inclusion rather than diversity—be sure the company is focused on more than two affinities while utilizing the lens of intersectionality.
- Create a pipeline of diverse talent through development.
- Create and share a strategic Talent Acquisition Strategy that includes unbiased interviewing (such as Behavioral Interviewing Skills); integrating inclusion and diversity questions and strategies in recruitment and assessment; inclusive job descriptions; inclusive language throughout policy; and reasonable disabilities accommodations.
- Training on how to hire without your biases getting in the way.
- Identify and address subtle discrimination such as micro-inequalities or microaggressions. Have a plan in place to minimize them. Also be well trained in what microaggressions look like.
- Link benefits to attract inclusive employees (i.e., childcare, transgender healthcare, flexible work hours).
- Strengthen anti-discrimination policies by including every affinity

group. Be sure these policies are posted where all can access them easily.
- Uncover hiring demographic trends. Where are the applications coming from (who is applying by affinity)?
- Reinforce the idea that inclusion is about ensuring that everyone's voice is heard, opinions are considered, and value to the team is evident with business leaders.
- Identify underrepresented groups' needs and support them in workforce planning as well as the employee career path. Utilize the lens of intersectionality.
- Provide workers with a safe space to voice their concerns.
- Review exit interviews and passed-over applications and note the trends.

Pillar #3: Organizational Development and Learning

Training builds knowledge ... it does not change attitudes, behaviors, or organizational culture

Organizational development and learning often fall under the human resources umbrella; however, the people responsible for this are highly skilled professionals at training, leadership development, and understanding the employee path throughout the organization. They are content experts and creators, strategic partners and, if I may say, in many organizations, underutilized. Their work directly impacts the culture—as they tend to be the organizational culture driver and touchpoint.

One of the larger focus area this department hosts is training. The role of level setting the organization around terms and effective training is a continuous pain point in the world of inclusion and diversity. Many of the reasons for this have been covered in previous chapters.

Here, I need to address the elephant in the room: Organizations need to understand what diversity training is, how to do it well, and what the outcome is. Why? Because often companies see diversity training as the solution to driving diversity. I cannot tell you how many times I have turned down contracts in the past because all they wanted was inclusion and diversity training. Let me again level set **Training builds knowledge ... it does not change attitudes, behaviors, or organizational culture.** Please feel free to read my dissertation on this!

Solutions: Evidence-Based Diversity Training

Too often, organizations seek to put into place diversity training as the driver for inclusion, yet when training fails, resistance to diversity change is imminent.[94] There is an overwhelming lack of evidence on new diversity initiatives and training trends,[95] yet organizations are quickly adopting these works without evidence that supports or dismisses the training. When training is done incorrectly, with the wrong content, out-of-date data, and/or instructor bias, an organization can see a polarization of attitudes and behaviors that creates the "us-versus-them" workplace environment. And, no surprise, this is *not* how you create a diverse and inclusive organization!

Resistance is the primary negative impact of poorly designed diversity-training programs. When resistance is present, employees rebel and do the opposite of what was expected.[96] Often just the phrase "diversity training" shuts employees down. If you were to offer voluntary diversity training in your organization, how many would attend? It is important to be cautious when instituting diversity training, as it may backfire or have negative results, thus promoting resistance. However, when training is done correctly and for the correct goal, which is knowledge, it can create a win for the organization and employees. Diversity training should level set the workplace's knowledge and expectations while providing an environment of psychological safety in which its employees can learn and grow.

A second impact to be aware of is a negative attitude shift. This negative attitude may be due in part to training resistance or rationale. When the focus of the diversity training is financially based or linked to the organization's bottom line, it may create a backlash of negative attitudes. One client offered gift cards as an incentive to not skip work and attend the diversity training they created. They were surprised by how many employees still did not show up and how those who did attend spent a large amount of time on their phones or computers and stepping out to make "business calls."

Poor goal alignment of why an organization is facilitating the training allows for biases on the rationale for completing the diversity training versus achieving personal growth and understanding.[97] This means we need to be transparent about why we are doing this training and what you expect your employees to gain from attending.

Let me say this again: The goal of diversity training is to improve knowledge, and that knowledge MAY led to a) improving positive intergroup interactions and interpersonal relationships; (b) decreasing discrimination through knowledge; and (c) improving participants' knowledge and motivation to interact with diverse others, dependent upon the focus.[98]

Diversity training is a knowledge tool. There is no data that supports or suggests that diversity training shifts attitudes or behaviors. If you would like more information on this, please feel free to email me and I will send you more data, including my dissertation. I truly would welcome the opportunity to have a conversation with you about this (Lauran@DrLauranStar.com).

Doing Diversity Training Right

So, you may now be wondering whether doing diversity training is worth it. It is, if you do it correctly. *Diversity training done right* includes instructional courses with a focus on (a) improving positive intergroup interactions and interpersonal relationships, (b) decreasing discrimination through knowledge, and (c) improving participants' knowledge and motivation to interact with diverse others. The training program's goals should include positive intergroup interactions and reduced post-training prejudice and discrimination. Diversity training provides participants with knowledge and tools that help diverse individuals understand how to work together effectively, thereby raising personal awareness. Furthermore, diversity training refers to training or solutions designed to increase cultural-diversity awareness, attitude, knowledge, and skills.[99]

Research has determined there are several essential components to consider when creating and implementing diversity training: composition of training and context (approach, setting, duration), design (attendance, focus, type, instruction), group selection (trainee characteristics), and evaluations.[100]

Figure 8-3 A Construct for Effective Diversity Training

Context	Employees are brought into a safe learning environment
	Positive and ethical language, absent blame; moral awareness part of decision-making process, inclusive language
Approach	Integrated approach uses hands-on group activities and retention messages
Setting	Organizational setting with an educational theme of learning, face-to-face as well as online (retention) mix
Duration	2-4 hours face-to-face or virtual in small time increments (no longer than 20 minutes content focuses, break/shift, 20 minutes) for retention, biweekly
Design	Inclusion focus highlights customer needs, conflict management, and problem-solving
Attendance	Voluntary
Focus	Group focus
	Focus will be team-based
Type	Integrated training; metacognitive awareness, attitudinal and behavioral
Instruction	Focus on themes, not people (focus on the outcome theme versus the "ism" or protected groups); consider the instructors (are they biased, knowledgeable, engaging); consider the diversity voice (is the message inclusive and embraced by the organization?); and the strategic integration of majority allies (include their stories and experiences)
Trainee characteristics	Integrated

Organizational Development and Learning Pillars
Inclusion Focus: Encouragement, Enhancement, Commitment, Safety

- Keep the organization focused on inclusion rather than diversity. Be sure the company is focused on more than two affinities (gender and ethnicity).
- Training for knowledge and level setting/inclusion and diversity training increases knowledge and skills. Training topics include level setting inclusion and diversity at _____, cultural intelligence, self-awareness,

affinity training (generation, gender, disabilities, etc.), inclusive leadership, coaching with intersectionality, pronoun usage, and more.
- Create a learning strategy specific to inclusion and diversity and blend into the overall organizational learning strategy.
- Integrate inclusion and diversity into the organization's competencies (i.e., communication), utilizing inclusive language.
- Integrating inclusion and diversity strategies in all training and leadership development is not a check-the-box activity.
- Train managers—on inclusion and as a core competency.
- Inclusive leadership skill-building starts here.
- Create an environment where differences are explored through programming.
- Identify underrepresented groups' needs and support.[101]
- Identify and address barriers to and high-potential employees for advancement through the ERGs.
- External reach into professional associations.
- Ensure the learning strategy includes inclusion and diversity, as well as intersectionality.

Pillar #4: Managers

Managers are the air traffic controllers of the workplace and have direct influence with most individual contributors (the workforce).

Managers are critical to building an inclusive workplace as they are right in the thick of everything. Managers are the air traffic controllers of the workplace and have direct influence with most individual contributors (the workforce). They know the pulse of the organization. Typically, when pulled into a contract, I ask to speak with several managers before I begin any work—they are a large part of the diagnostic phase in understanding the organizational culture. For the most part, they know what will work and what won't, and will also have solutions to change resistance. They are also very trusted by the employees as they are seen as an alignment of themselves.

Keep your managers close—have them engage in the ERGs and the ERG Advisory Council. Ask them for feedback.

Managers' Pillars
Inclusion Focus: Encouragement, Commitment, Enhancement, Safety

- Keep the organization focused on inclusion rather than diversity—be sure the company is focused on more than two affinities (gender and ethnicity).
- People development is critical. Create a pipeline of diverse talent through development and succession planning.
- Identify and address subtle discrimination such as micro-inequalities or microaggressions within your team.
- Integrate diversity and inclusion strategies in performance management.
- Be accountable—show that inclusivity is a core competency.
- Identify underrepresented groups' needs and give them necessary support and resources.
- Provide a safe space for people to voice their concerns.
- Hold "what makes you unique" conversations.
- Identify (and address barriers to) high-potential employees for advancement.

Now that we have uncovered the four essential pillars with action items, I would be remiss if I did not remind you that regardless of which pillar group you work in, one key to inclusion is cross-functional collaboration. Inclusion is a company focus, not a departmental one. Each new initiative should have cross-functional collaboration. Each pillar should work in tandem with the other pillars.

I have made the business case for inclusion as well as defined what it looks like within an organization. Now it comes down to measuring the outcomes. How do we know we have an inclusive culture, did the programs have an impact, and what about our goals—where did we land? For a change within the culture, I prefer to use simple scorecards, be it leadership, ERGs or companywide. Remember, words tell but pictures sell. All outcomes should be shared and transparent. We are asking your employees to adapt to a new culture lens—therefore they should know the results. The harm in not being transparent is resistance.

We are now moving towards the immersion stage of inclusion and diversity, where outcomes are measured, and inclusion and diversity are all becoming part of the cultural fabric. Typically, I will bounce between the four pillars of inclusion and the outcomes covered in Chapter 9. However, just because we are now moving into Chapter 9 does not mean we are done. Think back to the Inclusion Paradigm framework, and now we see the full cycle of engagement.

Figure 8-4 Inclusion Paradigm Framework

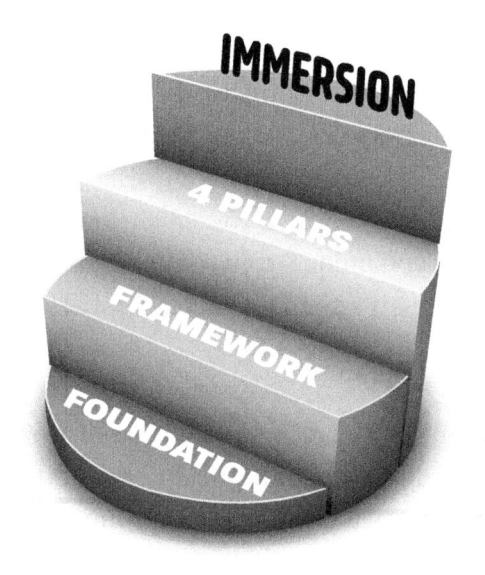

9

Inclusion Immersion—Resulting in Performance Outcome

The immersion stage, when inclusion becomes apparent and fluid within an organization, is a repeatable phase, in that performance and inclusion and diversity outcomes are repeatedly measured.

What does it look like, when all the work done to pivot to an inclusive organizational culture begins to bear fruit? Let's explore the possible outcomes and how you can measure them, so you have evidence to share internally and externally and that will inform your organization's actions as you move through the cycle again as circumstances and conditions change.

Intent Leading to Immersion

The immersion stage—when inclusion becomes apparent and fluid within an organization—is a repeatable phase, in that performance and inclusion and diversity outcomes are repeatedly measured. Once you have made it to outcome measurement, now you can go back to each pillar and tweak what needs adjusting (based on the feedback). If you are reviewing your leadership scorecard, celebrate your successes and strategize about where improvements are needed. The immersion of inclusion and the performance outcomes are all about intent with everyday work.

And we have now come full circle. I started this section of the book focusing on inclusion intent, and we end this section talking once again about intent leading to the emergence of inclusion. "Progress" is a word that encompasses intent; progress happens because we are constantly looking to improve upon where we currently stand. Intent should be present in every phase and aspect of advancing inclusion in your organization.

What is the outcome of this process? That is intent. Intent leads to immersion through intent, flexibility and adaptability. Reviewing the data (outcome intent) allows us to go back to step 1 and make any necessary adjustments. Those adjustments become outcome intent focused. The end goal is to advance inclusion, which has been demonstrated to lead to diversity. This is a process of immersion. Yes, it took me eight chapters to get to the greatest secret of inclusion—it is immersion.

Immersion

Practitioners, professionals, and organizations have been so inundated and focused on diversity, that immersion in inclusion is not possible. One cannot immerse themselves in another's walk or life experience. Yet often the goal in inclusion and diversity is immersion or reaching an organizational state where people are deeply engaged or involved in the inclusion and diversity mission. This is another reason focusing on diversity does not work.

At this point in your inclusion and diversity journey, the organization should be becoming immersed within its inclusive culture. In that immersion of an inclusive culture, the culture will drive your organizational diversity. Organizational immersion of inclusion, sounds like heaven, right? The kicker with inclusion is that what it looks like within an organization is in a state of constant change and flow with how the workplace functions. Why? Well, think about this, for example: what does inclusion look like today versus before COVID-19? It's a bit different today as the workforce is shifting toward a mix of remote, hybrid, and in-office work, dependent upon the company and industry. At inclusion's core, it has a very specific look:

Again, what inclusion looks like:

- There is a level playing field.
- The decision-making process is inclusive not exclusive.

- Employees feel comfortable and safe sharing concerns and issues.
- Employees feel part of the community.
- There is a diverse supply chain and customer base.

Yet, depending on the company, there will be inclusive nuances. These might have to do with remote workers, location, a specialized skill workers need, or consumer base.

At this phase of your journey, you are starting to measure your inclusion and diversity outcomes. When it comes to measuring outcomes, should we be transparent? Yes, so the question is more about the degree of transparency. **The key to gathering and sharing information is knowing what to share throughout the organization and the intent of sharing such information.** I am of the mindset to be as transparent as my audience allows. I also have found the best means to share information is from the top down. All information needs a path to be shared through the C-suite via the I&D Council to senior leadership to leadership, and then from the ERG Advisory Council to managers and employees.

Human Resources Dashboard: Measuring Diversity

Diversity is easy to measure; just run an organizational demographic report or have in place a human resources/demographic dashboard. Be sure to measure all affinities and their progress. As technology advances, you may find your learning management system or talent acquisition platform may already have a dashboard feature. It is also important that the data you are measuring is up to date. Encourage your employees to go in and update their personal information. Believe it or not, often disabilities are not reported. That especially includes learning disabilities like ADHD, ADD, and dyslexia, and mental disorders like depression, bipolar disorder, and anxiety. Be sure your employees feel safe reporting disabilities (as well as sexual identity and gender orientation). Often it is the *"what's in it for me?"* that organizations do not address—why do we want the most up-to-date information? What is the benefit to the employee? The organization?

I like to run an annual "It's All About Me" campaign where I highlight the need to update personal and demographic information through the payroll system. I highlight the fact that the information is confidential, and any output data gathered is based on groupings and no self-identification is provided. In asking for the updates, I share that the benefit for the employee is that the organization can meet employees' needs better if we know who is working for us. For example, if we note an increase in transgender employees, the company can allocate funds to increase the number of gender-neutral bathrooms. Or, if we see an increase in overall disabilities within our employee base, I can create a separate survey looking at new programs to bring into the organization that focus on disabilities, like mental health support.

Human Resources Dashboards are an amazing way to see the organization. Often the organization's payroll and/or hiring platforms come with workforce analytics and are built on key performance indicators (KPIs). When you're creating a dashboard, it's important to understand what you need to measure.

- Common Dashboards
- Human Resource Demographics
- Workplace Inclusion & Diversity Dashboard
- Development Dashboard, from your learning management system (LMS)
- Performance Dashboard
- Executive Dashboard

There are more. As you can see, we can create a dashboard on pretty much anything workplace related.

Your demographic dashboard is important as it gives you a look at the company's affinities as well as important information for succession planning—where is your bench strength and is it diverse? This is an important measurement tool. Yes, affinity data provides us with trends we can often change. Affinity data tells us where gaps are within the organization on diversity of thought. It also tells us how inclusive an organization is—that's right, affinity data is also a measurement tool for inclusion. If your organization has an inclusive culture, word gets out and draws high-level talent with multiple affinities to your workspace.

Figure 9-2 Demographic Dashboard[102]

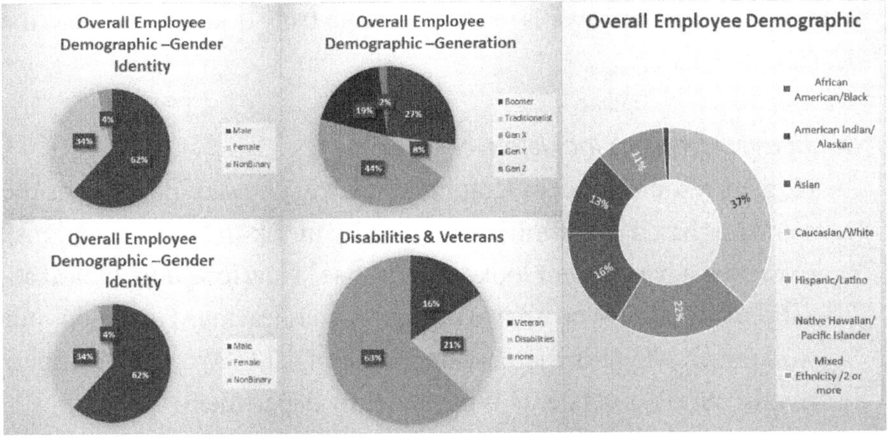

[Source credit for graphic: The Diversity Dashboard, PeopleInsight.com]

In 2011, when I examined the demographic data for a medical device company in Utah, I noticed that the reporting showed a strong trend in talent acquisition that this company's matrix was very diverse. However, the largest affinity this organization had was LGBTQ+. Not only was this number surprisingly high, but the overall demographic data also demonstrated a high level of intersectionality, meaning it was common to have a gay Asian veteran working for this company. Wow! Seriously, at the time of this contract, employers had the state government's backing to terminate LGBTQ+ employees for no cause. The state allowed this until March 2015. Imagine going to work and having your employment terminated because you are gay.

This company's demographic data also showed very high bench strength in leadership, low turnover by any affinity group, and that the average length of a job posting was 7 days. Read that again—the average job posting was 7 days, meaning positions within this organization either had too many resumes to review or were filled in 7 days.

This data was clearly demonstrating the immersion of inclusion. It showed that inclusion was part of everyday life within the organization. It was and still is a core value for the company—not diversity, but inclusion.

Measuring Inclusion

I believe this is where my inner geek comes out to play. I love data. Be it quantitative or qualitative, data rocks! However, not all data is equal and it is imperative that whoever is reading the data truly understands what the data is telling us.

Quantitative Data for Inclusion

- Human resources / demographic: This will show trends within the company based on affinities (provided you ask the right questions). How does advancement look—is it diverse? How long does typical advancement take? Who are we hiring? Who is leaving? How old is our workforce? Where is the next big hole in talent? Are there turnover trends? Who is top talent? What about by department?
- Diversity of leadership board: Examines the overall health of an organization's leadership bench strength and diversity of perspectives.
- Trends in grievances, complaints, and labor relations issues: In an inclusive organization we tend to see these number drop.
- Overall performance: Inclusive organizations are 3.6 times more able to deal with personnel performance problems and 2.9 times more likely to identify and build leaders.[103]
- Innovation, creativity, and agility: Inclusive organizations are 1.8 times more likely to be change ready and 1.7 times more likely to be innovation leaders in their market. This promotes increased productivity leading to increased 2X cash flows for the organization.[104]
- Retention rates, who is staying and more importantly, who is leaving the organization. What is the reason for leaving the organization?
- Program attendance rates: Review ERGs' programs and attendance, as well as new enrollment.

Qualitative Data for Inclusion

- Scorecards: I love scorecards for leadership, management, and company-wide. The scorecard is based on the overall goals of inclusion and diversity for the organization.
- Training survey: I am a fan of surveys being linked in with any train-

ing course, noting the question, what did we miss? Or, what else would you have liked to have learned? Correlate this data quarterly so you can see the impact on knowledge through training as well as the gaps.
- Employee engagement and culture surveys: These can be both quantitative and qualitative. I encourage you to dive in and read comments, look at current trends, and notice what has changed when you examine year-to-year data. If you are using an engagement or survey platform, often it will correlate the data for you. Be sure comments are also correlated within the survey platform.
- Exit interviews: Be sure to ask the right questions and allow for open comments. Why are you leaving? What could the organization improve?
- Retention conversations: Managers should be asking their employees why they stay at the organization and where the employee sees issues that need to be addressed. This information needs to be gathered and reported up.
- Focus groups: Keep this simple with only three questions. Focus on the company's I&D Values Statement and culture.
- Feedback from leadership and management, ERGs, the ERG Advisory Council, and the I&D Council.

In reviewing the data, I always ask, what is the story this is telling? We need both qualitative and quantitative data to compile a true narrative of inclusion and diversity within the organization. Utilize all the data to create a single source of truth for that year, half-year or quarter.[105] The same truth should be heard throughout the organization. That especially includes the brutal truth; please do not paint a rosy picture if it's not warranted, because your employees want what is true. If they don't get that, trust may be lost.

Company Diversity Dashboard

Think back to your levers in Chapter 7. Now combine these with the company- wide scorecard, which is often shared with leadership alone. However, I do recommend sharing a high-level overview of where the company is for inclusion and diversity. A company-wide review should be an overview of all KPIs for I&D, with the Demographic and Advancement Dashboard included. Here's an example in Figure 9-3.

Figure 9-3 Company Diversity Dashboard

Strategic Lever	Focused Outcomes	KPI	Goal	Attainment
Leadership Commitment	Representation	Leadership Diversity	22%	
		Management Diversity	26%	
		Overall Retention	7%	
	Accountability	Metrics from the I&D Strategic Plan	See Plan	
Organizational Culture	Awareness & Education	Engagement Survey	Above 87%	
		Culture Survey	Above 87%	
		Participation of Training Courses	Above 95%	
	ERG's	Employee Enrollment	36%	
		Community Outreach Programs	6	
		Speaker Programs	6	
		Social Program	6	
Talent Pipeline Management & Development	Acquisition	Sourcing Diverse Candidates	34%	
		Hiring Diverse Candidates	41%	
		Retention of Diverse Employees	90%	
	Advancement / Succession	Advancement of Diverse Employees		
Supplier Diversity	Diverse Procurement / Spend	% Supplier Diversity	33%	
		Supplier Diversity Spend	$XXX	

Leadership Scorecard

For inclusion to thrive, there is an accountability piece that is imperative for success. We need to hold leaders accountable for the inclusive culture and workforce diversity. This can be strategically done through a leadership scorecard. Scorecards provide a transparent leader and manager tool that shows a meaningful visualization of data. It also sets leadership and management up for success, as this tool is a living, breathing document that has clearly defined goals.

A leadership scorecard is focused on key performance indicators (KPIs), as shown in Table 9-1. Utilizing the organization's inclusion and diversity levers, KPIs are easy to see. **Remember, we are looking for awareness, application, appreciation, and accountability within the KPIs.**

These scorecards serve a second purpose. They provide transparent expectations and data on organizational trends. When you aggregate the data, look for trends. An organization can utilize this data in forecasting and strategy sessions. What is happening in engagement, retention, talent development, and the market space?

Here are elements and characteristics a scorecard must have:

- Be aligned with strategy with intentional focus on inclusion and diversity outcomes. Looking back at the I&D Strategy, what are the goals and how can leadership bring awareness, application, appreciation, and accountability to those goals?
- Clearly show progress and trends related to those I&D Strategy goals.
- Focus on process not just outcomes; this is critical in understanding how scorecards work. They do more than rate an individual; the process by which goals are being attained is also noted.
- Make sure these scorecards are done on a timely basis and refreshed/reviewed quarterly, Think of the scorecard as a working document. I recommend that my leads examine their scorecards weekly, asking themselves: What needle did I move, even if it was just a little? Where did I struggle?
- Metrics are tied to compensation. This is the most challenging aspect of the scorecard. It comes down to how important inclusion and diversity is to the organization and being reasonable. I have seen success

when the scorecard is linked to an increase in merit by 2% or part of the overall bonus structure. **Caution!** Do not make this a penalty box. As this is a working document, senior leadership should be reviewing this with you biweekly. If you fail, they fail.
- Strategic Levers: Organizational Culture, Leadership Commitment, HRIS, Employee Benefits, Recruitment, Development, Advancement & Retention, Accommodations, Employee Engagement, Supplier Diversity, External Partnership & Outreach, Accountability, Diverse Representation, Aligned Organizational Practices

Table 9-1 Leadership Scorecard

Strategic Lever	Focused Outcomes	KPI	Goal	Attainment
Leadership Commitment	Representation	Increase diversity leadership		
		Increase diversity management		
		Retention of diversity /leadership		
		Representation within the ERGs		
	Accountability	I&D Council		
		Sponsorship of the ERGs*		
		Use of Intersectionality Lens in decision/ process		
		Outreach and support/contributions and engagement with nonprofit organizations focused on people from underrepresented groups.		
		Visibility within ERGs		
		Sharing I&D cross functional		
	Aligned Practices, Policies & Access	Strategic Statement		
		Policy Review		
		HRIS Dashboard Update—to include ALL Affinities		

Inclusion Goals

*Inclusion & diversity had different goals and outcomes—
be sure you know what and why you are measuring.*

I would be remiss if I did not touch briefly upon inclusion goals. As a data junkie myself, I know and appreciate that thriving organizations rely on goals and outcomes to move the needle and see progress. Regardless of what or how you are measuring outcomes, there must be intent. With every goal, be sure to ask these questions:

- Why are we doing this?
- What outcome do we wish to drive?
- What does success look like?
- How will we measure that success?

Now let's remember to examine intent: Do you have inclusion intent outcomes or diversity goals? Yes, they are different. Let me show you.

Goal: Increase the number of veterans in company leadership by 4%. This is a diversity goal. We can simply review the human resources / demographic dashboard to see if there is a shift. Let me ask you ... what is their intent? What does this goal do?

Intent Outcomes: Increase the number of veterans in company leadership by 4%, to understand this community's pain point and gain better strategizing skills. Now we have inclusion intent outcomes. Not only are we looking to increase the number of veterans in leadership positions, but we also understand some of the benefits—so we can measure this (customer survey, team skills assessments and human resources / demographic dashboard).

To have a goal with only an affinity percentage is missing the boat. It further drives the wedge between us and them, and it polarizes your workforce. Please stop doing this. Creating goals that focus on one or two affinities without purpose (intent) is a waste of time and damaging to your organization.

Here's a case in point. MVP Staffing hired employees in part based on affinity/diversity goals. The desire was to hire more Hispanics and Latinos.[106] Unfortunately, this was the outcome: "A class action lawsuit, filed in the United States District Court for the Northern District of Illinois, alleges that the agency, MVP Staffing, used a range of discriminatory practices, including code words for job applicants of different races, to honor the requests of corporate clients who refused to employ African Americans in temporary positions. The company operates about 60 offices in 38 states."

The practice of affinity goals is not good. You are stepping into a puddle that is continuously growing. This practice alienates your employees and can increase unconscious biases and microaggression. If you are focused on diversity, you are wasting your time. Focus on inclusion instead!

Figure 9-4 The Inclusion Paradigm®

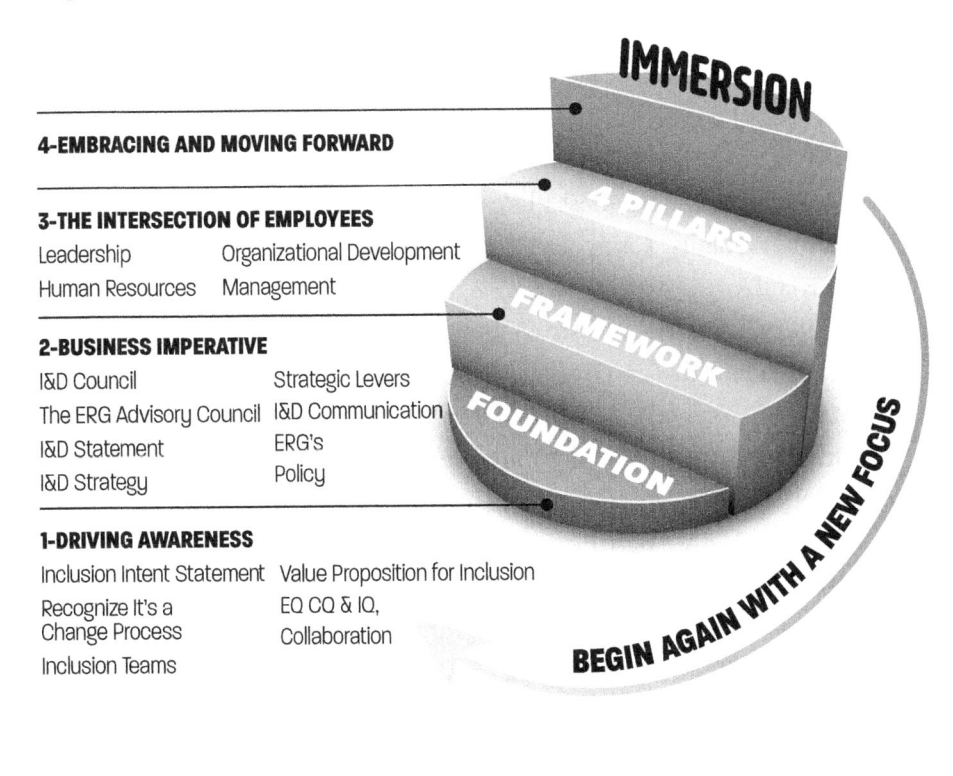

4-EMBRACING AND MOVING FORWARD

3-THE INTERSECTION OF EMPLOYEES
Leadership   Organizational Development
Human Resources   Management

2-BUSINESS IMPERATIVE
I&D Council   Strategic Levers
The ERG Advisory Council I&D Communication
I&D Statement   ERG's
I&D Strategy   Policy

1-DRIVING AWARENESS
Inclusion Intent Statement Value Proposition for Inclusion
Recognize It's a   EQ CQ & IQ,
Change Process   Collaboration
Inclusion Teams

IMMERSION
4 PILLARS
FRAMEWORK
FOUNDATION
BEGIN AGAIN WITH A NEW FOCUS

Wrapping the Inclusion Paradigm with the Return on Investment

We as practitioners have been begging for a workplace inclusion model for diversity when what we should have been asking for is a workplace inclusion model. Ta-da! Now you have a proven workplace inclusion model of how to bring inclusion to your organization—and a process for maintaining it. It has been researched and has strongly demonstrated results. It is evidence based and has successfully been implemented in many organizations that now can reap the benefits of inclusion AND diversity of thought.

You can go to this book's website and download the workplace inclusion model—and yes, go step by step. Keep in mind this is a journey with amazing outcomes. Organizations that embrace inclusion first create a sustainable foundation within their culture that will adapt to the 21st-century employee. Furthermore, by having the inclusion paradigm in your pocket, you will be able to remain on course and not lose sight of the end goal. The following is a list of awards won by companies I have worked with that embraced the Inclusion Paradigm:

- Disability In Index—Best Places to Work with a Disability
- Human Rights Campaign Equality Index—Best Places to Work LGBTQIA+
- Military Friendly Company—Best Places to Work for Veterans
- Modern Health Top Diversity Executives
- Military Times—Best Places to Work for Veterans
- Diversity MBA—Diversity Index Top 50
- Diversity MBA—Inclusive Leadership Index
- Diversity MBA—Best Place to Work for Women
- Diversity Inc—Top 50
- Forbes—Top Places to Work for Women
- Fortune—Best Places to Work for Women
- Fortune—Best Places to Work for Healthcare
- And more

Inclusion Paradigm Are Recognized and See Measurable Improvements

Want more? Here are metrics changes, comparing data from before I started working with them and then two years afterward:

Evidence-Based Improvements after 2 years*

Talent Pool Attraction 49%	Job Satisfaction 39%
Engagement Survey Results 45%	Leadership Diversity 37%
ERG Enrollment & Engagement 39%	Employee Retention 36%

*Aggregate averages

Once you have the know-how, the right focus, leadership support and attainable goals, the Inclusion Paradigm does the rest and yes, this takes work. So you may be thinking, what do I do next? Here are next steps:

- Visit the book's website (https://www.drlauranstar.com/evidencebased-inclusion) and download away. Why should you recreate the wheel when it has been made for you?
- Create your support community both in and out of the workplace. Feel free to put me on speed dial or email me, as I am in your corner. I know you're thinking, "Wait, this is too good to be true—no one just supports other practitioners without asking for something in return." However, that is what I am doing, as we need to shift this focus together rather than solo.
- Keep a copy of your inclusion business case posted somewhere, as there will be times where you may want to take a breather from inclusion and diversity work, or others you are working with may want to take a breather.
- Use the Inclusion Paradigm as a guide,
- Continue to foster your own development in this space. As inclusion and diversity is ever changing, we all need to stay up to date on the evidence of what works and what does not.
- Have fun and celebrate your organizational culture! Enjoy the rewards of your work. Small changes make big impacts!

We are not done yet; heck, I am just starting! :) In the next section we will examine the ever-challenging issue of equity, which, as is only fitting, comes last in the inclusion and diversity journey. However, you may become uncomfortable again (but that's okay). From there, I examine future trends in inclusion and diversity based on the research.

It is time to turn the page!

SECTION 4

Equity and Trends

10

To Be or Not To Be: Equality vs. Equity Is the Question

There is not solid proof that improving diversity will do anything for equity or equality. Furthermore, discussions need to be had around both, and what the organization wants. Personally, I am cheering equality on. But I don't want to get ahead of myself.

I would be remiss if I left the topic of equality and equity out of this book. Equity, much like diversity, is a confusing concept within the workplace. However, it appears the definitions for equality and equity in the workplace have stayed the same. As I have noted, inclusion leads to improved diversity which may lead to workplace equity and/or equality—or will it?

So, what is workplace equity? Is it realistic? How does equality fit in? With equity in the mix, how does equality get measured? The United States has a capitalistic national culture—isn't equity a conflict? Is equity just another tagline? How do we measure equity? How does the legal framework of discrimination fit with equity? Why is traditional DE&I so darn confusing?

To do equality and equity justice, I would have to write a follow-up book to this one (hint). Yet, let me provide some insight and controversy in this one.

The Difference Between Equality and Equity

Let me start by level setting workplace equality, equity, and fairness:

🔄 *Equality seeks to provide all employees with access to the same resources, regardless of the pre-existing barriers they may face. This can refer to an equal distribution of money, resources, or opportunity between workers at a similar level. Equality is in many ways a beneficial concept that can push company culture in the right direction.*[107]

However, the equality lens does not address the problems of underrepresentation or an unfair status quo (a cognitive bias involving leaders, managers and employees preferring things stay as they are or that the current situation remains the same; think of work hours, for example). Moreover, what equality does not address is socioeconomic differences in society and the effect of socioeconomics in the workplace. That begs the question, is equality then only a societal framework, not meant for the workplace? I do not believe that, however, I will dig into that in the next book.

● ***A System of Equity*** *(yes, it is a system) does not provide the same resources and opportunities that equality provides. With equity, an organization will recognize that each employee has varying access to resources and privileges due to socioeconomics. And those with less access may need more support to take fair advantage of opportunities within a given company.*[108]

Let me take this a bit further. The creation of the system of equity is a legal framework within business that allows us to reach a balance in the workplace between fair results for employees and separate circumstances.[109] To that end however, equity can also lead to an us-versus-them workplace as it may drive tokenism, which decreases equality in the workplace. Think of the employee who has not taken advantage of management development provided equally to all employees, but who is now given an opportunity to have special development specific to their needs. What about the 60 employees who completed the management development program? How does the organization explain this? Company X gave employee #173 specialized training, due to gaps from lived experience—and the rest of you are good to go ...

I am often wondering if equity is a scapegoat for not taking accountability to develop oneself. Yes, I just wrote that and I am aware I will get nastygrams—sorry not sorry; feel free to email me your thoughts on all of this, as I welcome the discussion (Lauran@DrLauranStar.com)!

● ***Workplace Fairness*** *is an aspect of organizational justice focused on both process and outcome impartiality. Factors that support fair treatment in-*

clude *mutual respect, strong interpersonal relationships, perceived organization support, and honest communication.* Data also supports that when fairness is found within the workplace, there is an increase in employee commitment and job satisfaction.[110]

Clearly, with these three definitions, you may be scratching your head and may already see an issue. If you have a system of equity in place within an organization, can you have workplace equality or a workplace that is fair? The simple answer is no, because once the system of equity is embraced, equality and fairness leave the building as selected others are receiving special attention. The moment the organization has an exclusive offering to specific affinity groups, equality and fairness are gone.

The more complicated, nuanced answer is maybe, if an organization can frame equity in such a way within its development programs. So, if I may, please let me reframe equity.

The system of equity within an organization recognizes all employees have varying access to resources and privileges, and therefore provides employees with additional support for development. However, the employee is accountable for the ask and the ownership of that development falls to the employee, with the organization being responsible for utilizing the lens of equity in development.

This definition provides more clarity around the scope, leaving ambiguity out. It also provides a bit more accountability around the process. The way equity is currently understood allows for employee to demand the organization take ownership.

Here's an example. I was brought into a large financial organization with the goal of creating an equity framework. The issue that brought me in focused on its lower-level employees without degrees who wanted professional advancement, a common issue. Through the lack of defined roles and accountability, the employees argued that through the system of equity, they deemed the organization should send minority employees to college and pay for it. This begs the question, what is the responsibility of the organization?

From the equality lens, we all have access to education. Some may have to go to community colleges or state colleges while others may go to private schools. Colleges try to neutralize the overall spend based on need and merit. Keeping in mind one reason college has gotten more expensive is the additional supports put in place for equity (reading, writing, math tutoring, first-year experience, additional advisors—heck, my son is an engineering student and has four advisors, and more).[111] One must work hard and apply themselves.

Caution! Please take emotions out of this discussion. This is not an "I suffered; you suffer" argument. My educational background story is built on repeated hard work to get the degree. Coming from a household of five kids with the overall family income in the mid-$60K range, there was no money (back in 1991). I joined the military to help offset the cost of college, worked full time while going to class, attended both community college and a state school, and yes, it took me five-plus years to graduate. Socioeconomically, I had to pay for my own education. I am also the only one of the five who decided to go to college. There is nothing wrong with going to college one class at a time, supplementing courses with community college, taking a credit union loan (federal loans are a whole other topic we won't debate here). My point is that today there are programs and solutions for education regardless of your income level. While it may take a bit of time and energy to find these programs, nothing is free—that is the system of equity working for you. Again, I argue the ownership must fall to the individual.

I am sure we have all seen this well-known graphic from The Equity

Tool website[112] Many trainings use this photo to demonstrate equity versus equality. In the image of equality, we all get invited to the game and are given the same "tool" (a box to stand on). While all three people each have a box to stand on, the spectator in the wheelchair and the shorter spectator still face the obstacle of seeing over the fence.

Here is where confusion sets in. In the image of equity, it's clear that the tools that help each of the spectators see are moved so that the shorter spectator can see; I argue that it is up to the individual to move or ask for help to move those tools over (boxes). Furthermore **the ramp that is utilized is not equity—that is accessibility and MUST be provided per the American Disabilities Act (ADA).**

My point is that both the organization (providing the box or workplace development and the accessibility ramp) and the employee (ask for help or grabbing the box) need to be accountable and take responsibility to drive the organization's system of equity. Better yet, hold a ticket to the game and you will have a seat inside the fence. This goes back to equality, as the individuals are technically watching the game from the outside when they could have just sat inside the fence.

Moreover, equity is not a guarantee in any organization. Yet, I would certainly hope equality is a guarantee within the organization. We all have the right to be treated equally according to the EEOC. Or do we? The Equal Rights Amendment #28, proposed over 50 years ago, has yet to be added to the US Constitution.[113] It was approved by the US House and Senate, but not enough states ratified it by the deadline, so we are still waiting. Oh, by the way, this amendment directly affects women's rights. *According to Congress: The Equal Right Amendment #28—This joint resolution proposes a constitutional amendment declaring that women shall have equal rights in the United States and every place subject to its jurisdiction. The amendment prohibits the United States or any state from denying or abridging equal rights under the law on account of sex.*[114] The amendment has again become a hot topic—stay tuned and get active.

Equity in the Workplace

I think the bigger question within the workplace surrounding equity, just by legal definition, is this: what is the organization's role in providing equity solutions that address those employees who have been marginalized by society? How much cost is acceptable to the organization? How does the system of equity fit with employees who utilized resources that are colored by socioeconomic background or developed skills regardless of their socioeconomic upbringing? Where does privilege fit in the workplace? How do employees stay competitive when workplace equity is a foundation? Where does equity fit from an accountability and ownness point of view? Who defines each employee's system of equity and the organization's system of equity? If equity is not a social norm, then what happens to the employee when they leave work, and what happens to their family?

When I was working with one organization a few years back, they decided they wanted a high-potential program specifically created for their Hispanic/Latino women. Now understand, I am all about employee development; however, the minute you separate out affinities you negate diversity of thought. Developing your employees should be holistic and inclusive, not selective and reductionist, focusing on parts and pieces. Development should be inclusive so the benefit of diversity of thought comes to the table. It also needs to be customizable based on the cohort's skill set. So, for this organization, rather than creating a high-potential program for employees of one particular affinity, we put together a leadership program that was comprehensive and adaptive. It was a program where employees who participated could develop based on their own skill level. It also created employee accountability around skill and career development.

Equity in a job description–YES! This is one of the better ways to reach a diverse employee population in recruitment in the workplace (add inclusive language and bingo!). From an equity lens, when posting a job, ask, is the degree a must-have? If yes, why? What does it demonstrate? What skills does the degree provide? Is the degree a barrier to hiring diverse candidates or is the degree needed for a particular skill (i.e., nursing, practicing medicine, accounting)? If the degree is not for acquiring a skill, then the actual need for a degree may not be there, so then what skills or competencies are a must? This should be the focus of the job posting: the must-haves.

In addition, having blinded resumes when a degree is necessary, redact where the individual attend college. I will share it is difficult to redact names and ethnicities as you will see and hear the candidate during the interview. Also, with artificial intelligence having become more prominent in hiring, allow the criteria you enable to be equitable as well. That criteria should be focused on the must-haves. Additional skills the candidate brings to the table are the basis for negotiation of salary.

And since I am just putting this all out there and exploring the research, let me say this: Base salary is equity—the rest is up for grabs. We already have salary equity the minute we include a salary range in a job posting. If you want more money, it is up to you to negotiate it based on what you, the candidate, bring to the table. In creating an equitable/inclusive job posting, the base salary should meet the demands (must-haves) for the position. If a candidate brings more to the table, they should be paid their worth.

Yes, salary equity is a bone of contention for me, as I am tired of hearing the "women get paid less than men" argument for salary equity. And yes, the data certainly shows women do in fact make less than men, and black women make even less. There is a disproportion here and the only way that goes away is if women recognize their own worth and demand it.

In my mid-twenties, while in the Army Reserves, I took my first professional position in pharmaceutical sales. I have an extensive medical background thanks to my military experience and yes, I am a trainer and educator at heart. Upon going to training, I learned my male counterpart was making $10K more than me. I was at $38K, and he was at $48K. He did not have any experience in healthcare or sales. Moreover, he was really struggling with the medical understanding of the organization's products and potentially would fail out of training. However, he was smart, business-wise, as this was his third professional position, and his first in sales; before that he worked in strategy management.

While we were sharing a beer, I came right out and asked how the hell did he get $10K more than me? His response changed my money mindset around self-worth. He asked me if I negotiated my salary. Remember, I had just finished several tours of duty with the US Army, and I had never negotiated my salary before (the military pays on level/grade of job; they nailed salary equity). Yes, my response was, "What, you mean you can ask for more money?" We made a pact: I would get him through the medical aspect of training, and he would teach me how to negotiate my salary. It was a skill set I had to learn, and boy, did I. From that day forward I can say I have been paid my worth.

Don't feel bad. Even Sheryl Sandberg had to learn the lesson of negotiation when she took on the role of Chief Operating Officer at Facebook. She noted when the offer came in she just wanted to take it, out of excitement and not knowing her own worth. It was her husband at the time who stepped up and negotiated the contract with her.[115] Her background prior to Facebook included going to Harvard University, working as a management consultant for McKinsey & Company, working for Lawrence Summers (then the United States Secretary of the Treasury under President Bill Clinton), and joining Google in 2001. One would think she would have known her worth by 2007 as well as how to negotiate salary, but that was not the case. Negotiation is a skill we all should develop if we wish to get paid our worth. Salary equity is not enough (it's the base of a salary, not the range).

This skills training should be available to all employees. Now, who gets to attend specific skills training? Through the equity lens, I have to ask whether we are targeting affinities or employee readiness, and this is where equity falls apart. When we focus on affinities first, we lose equality and talent. Quota attainment is certainly a factor that drives tokenism.[116]

Risks of Workplace Equity

Equity definitely poses a risk in the workplace. What is interesting in assessing the organizational risks of workplace equity is that they are the same risks for diversity discussed back in Chapter 1. Equity has an inherent risk of equity fatigue, alienation and exclusion, lost trust, and sustainability. The risks do not stop there, as research has demonstrated a focus on equity can trigger a decrease in employee motivation, promoting affinities over skill, and inequality in hiring, salary, and promotion, leaving the organization open to legal action.

Decrease in Employee Motivation

When equity comes into play, the organization may face a decrease in motivation from employees as they all perform the same function, lacking variation and authority level. "We all get paid the same to do the same job, regardless of skill level."[117] Prospective employees may ask themselves, why bother to apply as the opportunities are going to a select few? I often see this when leadership places a goal around promotions and affinities, like 25% women on boards by 2025. Hey, I am all over more women on boards, but that must be the woman's choice–not a quota. The quota demand sets all up for failure, because the goal is to meet quota rather than hiring the best person for the position.

This can also ding your talent brand, which is not surprising as there are organizations out there that specifically target affinity hires and may pass over talented employees who may not be X (female, veterans, person of color, white, male, etc.). In one conversation with a CEO of a midsize financial company, they told me they had a VP role open for two years because they wished to hire a woman of color for the position. The recruiter screened over 200 resumes, yet the hiring process did not move forward because they did not have a woman of color in the mix. Think of the business implication there, including the time and money lost.

Promoting for Affinity, Not Skill

Tokenism comes into play when we promote based on affinity rather than skill. When skill gaps become apparent, the promoted affinity loses credibility, resulting all too in often being placed in the token box by others. It is hard to come out of that box and regain credibility and trust. The organization may also lose its top talent as employees are smarter than we often give them credit for.

Measuring Equity

There is a definite need for more research around how to measure workplace equity and fairness, as often the questions in surveys posed to measure outcomes have no validation. The typical equity questions fall to how you are treated (fairly with respect?) and whether your compensation is fair. Therefore, if you are paying your employees fairly and treating them well, then ta-da, you have workplace equity—or not.

The evidence on equity in the workplace has yet to be determined beneficial, in large part due to research design. Often a study will note inclusion criteria such as inclusive organizational culture, equality in salary and skills development all the same, but then look at advancement numbers. Does this study show equity impact? No. Going back to the definition, what was provided to level the playing field? What are equity initiatives that have been studied? Is there a clear pathway to provide organizational equality and the system of equity? How does society balance equity? Can we have workplace equity and social equality? At the risk of repeating myself, the United States is a capitalist country.

Hofstede's evaluation of the US national culture (see Figure 10-1) finds we are highly individualistic (one of the highest scores for ALL countries) and score high in masculinity (focus on competitiveness and success).[118] So based on our national culture how does equity fit in socially?

Figure 10-1 Hofstede on US National Culture

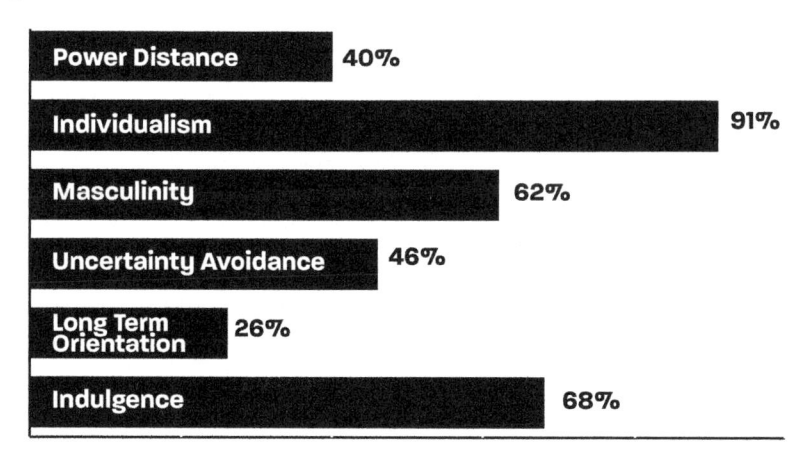

Power Distance	40%
Individualism	91%
Masculinity	62%
Uncertainty Avoidance	46%
Long Term Orientation	26%
Indulgence	68%

Taking emotions out of the equality versus equity versus workplace fairness equation, equity has nothing to do with empathy; all three should not have emotional strings. Yet, due to the polarization of the American political system, ID&E are becoming an emotional nightmare. So many more questions need to be asked and answered. More thought leadership is needed, and it needs to be evidence based. Let's not waste another 60 years figuring out this aspect of ID&E! I would love to hear or read your thoughts and questions on this section. Please feel free to shoot me an email at Lauran@DrLauranStar.com and let's engage.

11

Future Trends in ID&E

Those who focus on the past learn and understand where we have been. Those focused on today know where we currently are. However, those who embrace the past and present and look to the future with evidence will create a business future that is sustainable AND beneficial for all.

We know that inclusion, diversity, and equity are moving targets. However, by level setting and focusing on inclusion, you have a clear strategic path to building ID&E within your organization. In this chapter, to wrap up the book, I'm providing evidence-based initiatives that have proven return on investment and future trends for ID&E.

Evidence-Based Initiatives

Masterminds

As an inclusion and diversity practitioner, who do you turn to when you have a question or concern around ID&E? Bringing ID&E into an organization is a journey, and no one has all the answers. As I mentioned in Chapter 6, I strongly suggest that you create a mastermind group of inclusion and diversity practitioners you have met in the field or at a conference. Remember that creating a mastermind takes intent and the results will only be as good as your group focus.

I created a mastermind through my LinkedIn contacts—all are inclusion and diversity practitioners working in that role, have at least a master's degree in industrial/organizational psychology, and have the stamp of thought leadership, meaning there is research, authorship, and stewardship on the topic of inclusion and diversity. We all have different affinities and perspectives on ID&E. We meet monthly via Zoom, with a formal agenda and a beverage of choice (each taking a turn running the meeting). I love this group—we discuss everything, both with and without political correctness. It is a safe space to challenge each other as well as share concerns and yes, insecurities. Here we can be vulnerable with each other.

Benefits of a Mastermind
- Safe space to challenge perspectives and research
- Support each other and act as a sounding board for new ideas and thoughts
- Ongoing learning in the ID&E space
- Stay current on trends such as the law of ID&E, due to members having specialization in different areas
- Accountable
- Research updates
- And more

Employee Resource Groups
While I did touch on this earlier in Chapter 7, here are specific actions ERGs can take to drive inclusion. Although ERGs are an amazing tool for ID&E, most organizations do not use them effectively. Beyond them being part of the Inclusion Advisory Team, they are the eyes and ears of ID&E.

- Training: Utilize your ERG for new training rollout. Have them peer review training slide decks to ensure organizational alignment. I find all my trainers in the ERG for any and all ID&E company-wide training initiatives.
- Professional Associations: Link professional associations to your ERG. Assign one or two to each group and see who wants to join. Create a partnership with that association for both learning and recruiting.

- Link your ERGs to your CSR / ESG, which will allow better measurement of impact that all will be able to see.
- Launch a podcast through your ERG.
- Have the ERG create inclusion and diversity videos, representing their own affinity group.
- Educate and promote awareness through the different holidays and awareness months. This is one of the easiest ways to drive inclusion, celebrating our differences, but it is often left to the side. Institute ID&E awareness every chance you get. This is where social media is our friend. When your ERG celebrates, post it! Give recognition to the ERGs.
- Allow your ERG to grow and adapt to the changing business times. Employees are remote, hybrid and/or in person, so the ERG must adapt.

ID&E Learning Strategy

When creating learning activities, be sure they align with the inclusion learning strategy. It is important when learning that there is a consistent message, regardless of training topic. If one slide deck calls it ID&E, all decks should refer to ID&E. Limit the confusion. Training elements should build upon each other rather than a single out, check-the-box training. An example of this is sexual harassment training; it's a check-the-box training because all it focuses on is sexual harassment—not inclusion. Is it customized to your organization? Does it discuss different affinities and social norms that can lead to sexual harassment? Is there a prevention business case? What about the organization's process for handling sexual harassment? Is the training transparent to the organization, sharing information such as how many harassment cases have been brought forth?

Infuse inclusion and diversity into leadership, management training, sales, new employee onboarding, and competency trainings. This will create better buy-in from all. It also advances inclusion company-wide. I encourage you to partner with your learning and development team to review ALL training and apply both intersectionality and inclusion lenses to find gaps and/or add inclusion and diversity content with intent.

This means you should add content when it is needed and it improves the training, rather than just adding content for the sake of doing so.

Interviewing without Biases

Infuse interviewing without biases into your organization's talent acquisition strategy. Below are the cornerstones:

- **Recognize your biases before the interview:** We typically find 8 different types of biases in the workplace. Create a file or training around these biases. Ask managers and leaders what biases they have used before when interviewing. Did they move a candidate forward because they went to the same college or belong to the same fraternity, sorority or civic group?
- **Inclusive Process Mapping:** Map out your current recruiting workflow and seek opportunities to be more inclusive at each step of the hiring process. Understand the members' demographics to better provide a diverse hiring pool of candidates. Anonymize a step in your process or resume review (i.e., remove college name and gender, assign a candidate a number and remove the name). Review your candidate rejection reasons to look for patterns that indicate bias. Review your offer negotiation policy to see if you're making biased compensation decisions.
- **Inclusive Job Descriptions:** Review job descriptions to see gaps in attraction, list only must-haves, ensure the language is gender neutral.
- **Structured Hiring—Competency—Behavioral Style Interviewing Method:** Adding structure to the hiring process will help reduce bias in decision-making. Implementing structured hiring means creating a deliberate process where you consistently assess candidates on a set of attributes necessary for success in the role. This inherently shifts the focus from bias-driven decisions to data-driven decisions. Train all managers and above on Behavioral Style Interviewing. Create goals for accountability scorecards as part of the Behavioral Style Interview.
- **Diverse Interview Panel:** Ensure there is a diverse representation of thought, departments, ethnicity, and gender identities on all interview

panels. This will reduce bias in your final decisions and show candidates from underrepresented groups that they are represented at your company.

Even if we are working to create a fair and equitable hiring process, undetected biases can have a negative impact on your screening and selection decisions.

Performance Mentorship & Coaching

Create a mentorship and coaching program with a focused-on minority affinity. This will help create visibility for those who are underrepresented. Start with your ERGs and branch out. Keep in mind, however, from an inclusion lens, all are welcome.

Be sure you know the difference between coaching and mentoring. They are not the same. Both are performance improvement tools; however, coaching asks more questions and is focused on skill development, where mentoring is more about sharing ideas and career advancement. Coaching is a learnable skill and requires development/ training on the coach's part. In launching a coach training program, be sure it is inclusive. Mentoring, on the other hand, tends to be less formal and there is no set training needed. The mentor must, however, have a passion for advancing others.

The Centers for Talent Innovation demonstrated that 81% of minorities who were mentored reported positive job satisfaction. There is plenty of data supporting and demonstrating the benefits of coaching. Several studies are posted on this book's website.

Inclusive Language

Pronouns are important. They are part of our identity, so let's be sure to use them correctly. Utilizing inclusive language, I tend to use "them" or "they" instead of "him" or "her." Wait, did you just do an eye roll? I get it—pronouns are a new focal language. Think of it this way: If you have children, when they were infants, were they ever misidentified? Did you quickly correct the person who misidentified your child? Remind your employees to be patient, as pronoun utilization is built on awareness and the ability to make corrections.

Diversity Statement

Improve your diversity statement, accommodation procedure and all harassment policies. Remove reporting barriers, make them easy to find. Did you know, according to *Human Resources Director*, 65% of all harassment cases stem from ID&E?[119]

Build up your organization's Employee Assistance Program (EAP) to include mental health, childcare, disability support, and so forth. Ask: what do my employees need to thrive in this position from a support lens? I have seen several organizations put in childcare to attract employees with children.

Impact of Inclusion on the Community

Once you build the inclusive foundation, and continue to follow that, then your diversity of thought candidates will find you. When an organization is strong on inclusion, it trickles out into the community with social responsibility benefits. Word spreads that a company's affinity groups are doing community service because they WANT to, not because it's expected, and that has benefits.

You do not have to look far to see how inclusion trickles into the community. Look at Dow. The work they are doing within the organization around inclusion moved beyond the company and is having a global impact. Below are a few impactful outreach programs being done through their ERGs:[120]

> **Recycling shoes while helping students learn new skills**
> *The Singapore Permanent Shoes Waste Recycling Ecosystem project collects school and athletic shoes to be recycled and made into sports infrastructure such as jogging tracks and playgrounds. Leveraging this project, DEN recently raised S$34,200 ($25,000 USD) for the* **Autism Association Singapore** *to partner with a local school serving autistic students and a tailor-instructor, who teaches graduates how to sew the casings for pads and mats that are made from the recycled shoes. These pads and mats are then used to enhance safety at the school. This partnership helps the students learn a new skillset and prepare for future job opportunities.*

Team Rubicon serves communities by mobilizing military veterans to continue their service, leveraging their skills and experiences to help people prepare, respond and recover from disasters and humanitarian crises.

Eight Dow employees *from* **Team Rubicon** *were deployed in 2021, with participants coming from Texas, Michigan and Louisiana in the United States, and from Alberta, Canada. Team members helped* <u>Little Warriors</u>, *a nonprofit camp near Fort Saskatchewan, supporting children who were victims of sexual assault. They also supported the Louisiana communities of Hammond, Houma and La Place following Hurricane Ida. Team Dow contributed more than 400 volunteer hours to Team Rubicon's efforts in 2021.*

VetNet welcomed Dow Canada to Team Rubicon for the first time. Twelve Dow Canada employees were trained and are now ready to deploy and volunteer.

ID&E Trends

Hiring Diversity Professionals to Prepare for Systematic Change[121]

Consultants are fading in this space, in large part due to organizations recognizing ID&E are separate and should drive different outcomes the organization needs to thrive. Many of us saw this change coming and, like me, are joining the workplace again full time. Inclusion and diversity practitioners need to be change agents. They need to understand how to launch company-wide change initiatives that go beyond training. They must be stewards and influencers in the ID&E space. There is a full range of skills needed to be effective.

As a practitioner, the challenge is finding organizations that are truly looking for change. Every company is yelling "DE&I" but few are actually committed; most are going through the motions.[122] SHRM reported that roughly 80% of companies are just going through the motions and not holding themselves accountable, according to the report, *Elevating Equity: The Real Story of Diversity and Inclusion*.[123] Additionally, according to SHRM, the study concluded:

- 76% of companies have no diversity or inclusion goals;.
- 75% of companies do not have DE&I included in the company's leadership development or overall learning and development curricula;
- 40% of companies view diversity work to mitigate legal, compliance or reputational risks, with HR in an enforcer role; and
- 32% of companies require some form of DE&I training for employees; 34% offer training to managers.

Clearly there is a need for more work. Where does your company fall? How are you gaining impact?

It is important to note another factor in seeking inclusion and diversity practitioners is the trends in human resources. According to Workvivo survey of 520 HR professionals, looking at workplace trends and behaviors, over 98% of HR professionals were feeling burnt out, with 94% stating they felt overwhelmed.[124] Further, 90% reported emotional fatigue and dreading coming to work. More importantly, 73% felt they did not have the proper tools to impact the workplace from the ID&E lens.

Evidence-Based Metric Decisions

ID&E can be costly, and companies are now asking for the return on investment. How and what are you measuring? Why? How are you gathering data and what is the initiative supposed to solve? Organizations want more from their inclusion and diversity practitioner. As practitioners, we must be business-savvy and financially savvy as well as up on the latest research. In the future, do not be surprised to hear company executives say, "Show me the data."

Remote and Hybrid Work Impacts ID&E

A new lens of work has come into play as COVID-19 has driven employees home and opened the door to remote and hybrid work. According to Global Workforce Analytics, over 56% of the US workforce can work—and already is working—from home and the current trends demonstrate over 30% will continue working from home through 2023.[125] This is not surprising, as there are cost savings from having your workforce remaining out of the office (we also see productivity increases). This shift in the workforce may create openings for those with disabilities to remain at home.

The overall workforce and its culture has to shift to accommodate the changes of a remote/hybrid workplace. The process of engagement will need to be examined as everyone will need to adapt. This is another great place where ERGs can help facilitate inclusion and engagement through outreach.

Gender Identity

According to Purdue, gender identity and expression of identity is heightened.[126] Awareness is a critical component for the LGBRQIA+ community. The understanding and utilization of pronouns, gender-neutral language, and partner benefits and health benefits for transitioning individuals are hot buttons, as the political atmosphere is heating up. New laws are being put in place, some pro and some con.

Multigenerational Workplace

While I explored this in detail in Chapter 2, the rationale for doing so was based on the trend of four to five generations sharing today's workplace. There needs to be intent to understand and relate to the different perspectives each generation has. Moreover, we need to embrace rather than label the differences and begin to process the differences, especially when it comes to workflow and problem-solving.

Deeper Focus on Biases and Microaggressions

"We already run training on these two topics, so why more now?" I receive this comment quite a bit, and here's why. If you look at the history of diversity initiatives, organizations try to focus on the quick fixes and yes, unconscious bias training falls into this category. After videos of racist behavior, such as two black men getting arrested in a Starbucks store, went viral in 2018,[127] Starbucks brought in a consulting firm to launch an unconscious bias program. They closed 8,000 shops for a full day of bias training. Unfortunately, the question has been raised and answered: Did this training work? The simple answer is no. The *Harvard Business Review* examined bias training through the last 30 years at over 800 US firms and concluded that bias training alone does not shift biases or perspectives.[128] Furthermore, this type of training may in fact have the reverse effect in that it may activate unconscious biases.[129] What is heartbreaking is that the evidence against a one-day training was already out there, but Starbucks and the contracting consulting firm did not look for it.

One day of training is not enough to shift biases and attitudes and to process knowledge. Great intentions with no return on investment, as this type of training was already shown not to work. We need to stop looking at quick fixes.

I am not saying training is not needed; we know it is needed and again only provides knowledge when done correctly. I tend to argue that before you implement training, ask what the overarching goal is and how to best support the training program. Training should be stackable, meaning one unit leads into the next to build knowledge. There is a reason that just leading a horse to water is not enough to get it to drink.

Ethnicity and Practitioners

Gone are the days where you had to be a person of color to work in the field of ID&E. In the workplace and education, we are starting to see people of color stepping back from ID&E and focusing on their passion. The reverse can also be said; I am a white woman who does ID&E and being so no longer dings my credibility. We are seeing partnerships among all ethnic, gender, veteran, disabilities and sexual/gender identification affinities, when a diversity of different perspectives is needed.

The belief that only a person of color can successfully do ID&E is very outdated, and let me just say it, we still work in a very white business world (due to population and socioeconomics). The role of the inclusion and diversity practitioner is not about ethnicity or gender; it is about ensuring whoever holds this position has the knowledge and influence to deliver the right results. We need to stop putting employees in career boxes based on their affinities.

Equity

The research certainly is showing equity is an area if interest. As to where we go with equity, the jury is still out, regardless of the DE&I rhetoric on equity. I am excited to see where we go with equity versus equality.

These are all trends. However, as we know, trends can be derailed quickly, thus there is a need to remain focused on the end goal. Yes, the goal is to build an inclusive organizational culture and diversity will follow. More to come.

Your ID&E Journey

Believe it or not, we have come to the end of the book. You now have more foundational knowledge and some advanced knowledge around inclusion and diversity. If you began reading this book a bit confused or unfocused, I hope this work has helped you find some clarity. You also have the Inclusion Paradigm in your back pocket, a *researched and application-proven workplace inclusion model that provides a clear pathway for creating an inclusive organizational culture. It's an innovative scaffolding of steps that have been strategically layered, resulting in sustainable success. This model also recommends inclusion initiatives that have proven to have the desired impact of driving inclusion within the organization. This paradigm is based on research (on workplace culture, diversity, and inclusion) followed by real-world application with proven, measured results.*

However, it really is just the start or perhaps the midsection of your own ID&E journey. There is still so much to learn when it comes to the workplace (outside of a lab or academia) and we are now digging below the surface. We need to keep focused and have intent in the work we do, as ID&E impacts more than the organization's culture; it impacts all employees within said culture.

The best part of ID&E is that we do not have to do it alone. In fact, quite the opposite. Learn how to influence and engage others. Create teams to tackle issues. Utilize your ERGs for insights. Look for evidence, or proof that a program will work.

ID&E are business imperatives. It is also a business framework. We as practitioners need to change the focus from diversity to inclusion and allow inclusion to work for us, rather than diversity working against us.

Finally, know when to get out. This is hard, intense, and sometimes downright emotional work. Take care of yourself. Take some "me time" for yourself. If ID&E are not your passions, you will most definitely feel the ID&E fatigue. Know when to tap others to pick up passion and focus. It is okay to step back and recognize ID&E may not be your passion area. You deserve to be happy and engaged professionally.

ID&E is a team sports, and we all need to share our successes and best practices. That is the goal of the *Evidence-Based Inclusion* website, where I will share and ask you to share as well, what has worked, what has not, and the evidence for both. I believe doing so will help us all, in the work of creating and fostering ID&E success.

Appendix A: Dissertation Abstract

"The Effect of Gender-Diversity Training on
Perceived Organizational Justice"
by Lauran Star Raduazo
Doctoral Dissertation for Walden University (2021)
https://scholarworks.waldenu.edu/dissertations/10535/

The purpose of this quantitative study was to examine gender-diversity training content and design and their effect on employees perceived organizational justice. A total of 205 employees specializing in science, technology, engineering, mathematics, and finance (STEM&F) participated in this study. A quantitative quasi-experimental study design occurred with a baseline, posttraining, and 2-month final follow-up. A mixed ANOVA was run to test for mean differences for Colquitt's Organizational Justice Scale (COJS) overall and subscale scores. Baseline, posttraining, and final scores were compared by intervention and control group. There was a statistically significant interaction within intervention between time and groups ($F(2,406) = 12.247$, $p < .01$, partial $\eta2 = .057$), as well as overall COJS score ($F(2,406) = 7.57$, $p < .01$, partial $\eta2 = .036$). Interpersonal justice results demonstrated there was not a statistically significant interaction within intervention between time and groups; however, there was a statistically significant interaction between the intervention and time on interpersonal score. Informational justice results demonstrated a statistically significant interaction within intervention between time and groups; however, there was no statistically significant interaction between the intervention and time on informational justice score. More research is needed to determine if the results are applicable for other protected classes, STEM&F, and/or other industries. The results can help promote positive social change through diversity training in local governments and businesses. It may also provide new pathways to encourage women in the STEM&F system by decreasing gender stereotypes.

Appendix B: Training Framework

Context	Employees are brought into a safe learning environment
	Language—Positive and ethical language, absent blame; moral awareness part of decision-making process
	Gender inclusion training
Approach	Integrated approach uses hands-on group activities and retention messages
Setting	Organizational setting with an educational theme of learning, face-to-face as well as online (retention) mix
Duration	2-4 hours face-to-face; retention biweekly
Design	Inclusion focus highlights customer needs, conflict management and problem-solving
Attendance	Voluntary
Focus	Group focus—gender and ethnicity
	Focus will be team-based
Type	Integrated training; metacognitive awareness, attitudinal and behavioral
Instruction	Focus on: themes, not people (focus on the outcome theme versus the "ism" or protected groups); consider the instructors (are they biased, knowledgeable, engaging); consider the diversity voice (is the message inclusive and embraced by the organization?); and the strategic integration of majority allies (include their stories and experiences)
Trainee characteristics	Integrated
Measuring effectiveness of diversity training	Perceived organizational justice scale

Appendix C: Inclusion Paradigm Human Resources / Demographic Dashboard

ALL employee demographics breakdown:

Label	# Employees
Females	
Males	
LGBT/Transgender	
Black Male (BM)	
White Male (WM)	
Hispanic Male (HM)	
Black Female (BF)	
White Female (WF)	
Hispanic Female (HF)	
Black	
White	
Hispanic/Latino	
Asian	
1 or more ethnicities	
Other	
Veteran	
Disability	
Baby Boomer (1946-64) Ages: 55 & up	
Generation X (1965-80) Ages: 39-54	
Millennials (1981-96) Ages: 23-38	
Generation Z (1997-2012) Ages: 22 or below	

Leadership only demographics breakdown:

Label	# Employees
Females	
Males	
LGBT/Transgender	
Black Male (BM)	
White Male (WM)	
Hispanic Male (HM)	
Black Female (BF)	
White Female (WF)	
Hispanic Female (HF)	
Black	
White	
Hispanic/Latino	
Asian	
1 or more ethnicities	
Other	
Veteran	
Disability	
Baby Boomer (1946-64) Ages: 55 & up	
Generation X (1965-80) Ages: 39-54	
Millennials (1981-96) Ages: 23-38	
Generation Z (1997-2012) Ages: 22 or below	

What is the 1-year retention rate / by level – and the demographic breakdown
Company-wide Retention Rate for (yr.): _____

Gender and Ethnicity Aspect:

FIRST LEVEL EMPLOYEES: Male

First Level Employee Label	Retention Rate	Total First Level	Promoting	Hiring
Black Male				
White Male				
Hispanic Male				
LGBTQ				

FIRST LEVEL EMPLOYEES: Female

First Level Employee Label	Retention Rate	Total First Level	Promoting	Hiring
Black Female				
White Female				
Hispanic Female				
LGBTQ				

MANAGERS: Male

Manager Employee Label	Retention Rate	Total First Level	Promoting	Hiring
Black Male				
White Male				
Hispanic Male				
LGBTQ				

MANAGERS: Female

Manager Employee Label	Retention Rate	Total First Level	Promoting	Hiring
Black Female				
White Female				
Hispanic Female				
LGBTQ				

Gender and Ethnicity Aspect: *(continued)*

LEADERS: Male

Leader Employee Label	Retention Rate	Total First Level	Promoting	Hiring
Black Male				
White Male				
Hispanic Male				
LGBTQ				

LEADERS: Female

Leader Employee Label	Retention Rate	Total First Level	Promoting	Hiring
Black Female				
White Female				
Hispanic Female				
LGBTQ				

LEADERS DEMOGRAPHICS

Generational Aspects:

Employment Level	Retention Rate	Baby Boomers	Gen X	Gen Y– Millennials	Gen Z
First Level Employees					
Manager					
Leaders					

Results of last employee engagement survey

What benefits do you offer—the benefit package?

Define the organization's inclusion goals (HR lens)?

Is your workplace/ safe space certified? _____ Yes _____ No

Anything else we should know?

How should the company measure success in inclusion (HR lens)?

What are the reasons for those measurements?

How are leaders currently being held accountable for inclusion (Performance Management)?

Copy of Performance Management System

Training and Development

The person in charge:

What diversity and inclusion training has the company offered?

What was the employee feedback?

What were the outcomes?

Appendix D: Glossary

Affinities: Characteristics that make a person unique.

Attitude shifts: A change in behavior or feelings toward an issue or diverse group of individuals.

Colquitt Organizational Justice Scale (COJS): The measurement tool for perceived organizational justice. COJS has already demonstrated validity as a measurement tool in perceived organizational justice and is customizable toward the type of training participants receive (Enoksen, 2015).

Distributive justice (DJ): Employees' perceptions of fairness associated with decision outcomes and distribution of organizational resources such as salary, praise, and promotions (Enoksen, 2015).

Diversity training: Instructional courses with focus on (a) improving positive intergroup interactions and interpersonal relationships, (b) decreasing discrimination, and (c) improving participants' knowledge and motivation to interact with diverse others. Goals should include positive intergroup interactions and reduced post-training judice and discrimination. Diversity training provides participants with tools that help diverse individuals understand how to work together effectively, thereby raising personal awareness. Furthermore, diversity training refers to training or solutions designed to increase cultural diversity awareness, attitude, knowledge, and skills.

Emersion: the process of emerging from or being out of water after being submerged, or in this case, emerging from the confusion around DE&I.

Ethnicity: Cultural characteristics that define a person as being a member of a specific group.

Heterogeneity: Dimensions of diversity (including gender, age, sexual orientation, and ethnicity) within organizational employees.

Informational justice (IFJ): Employees' perceptions of how information is shared in organizations as timely, truthful, and specific (Enoksen, 2015).

Interpersonal justice (IPJ): Employees' perceptions of respect and how they are treated in the organization (Enoksen, 2015).

Nationality: The legal sense of belonging to a specific political nation state.

Neurodivergent (sometimes abbreviated as ND): Having a brain that functions in ways that diverge significantly from the dominant societal standards of "normal."

Neurodiversity: The diversity of human minds, the infinite variation in neurocognitive functioning within our species.

Neurominority: Any group, such as people with autism, which differs from the majority of a population in terms of behavioral traits and brain function.

Neurotypical (often abbreviated as NT): Having a style of neurocognitive functioning that falls within the dominant societal standards of "normal."

Organizational diversity: Differences in employees in an organization that may include gender, religion, ethnicity, and culture.

Perceived organizational justice: Any employee's perception of fairness or equality in an organization (Enoksen, 2015).

Race: A social construct. We are all part of the human race.

Workplace diversity: Refers to the individual affinity's employees have that make them unique. These characteristics can include gender, race, ethnicity, religion, age, sexual orientation, sexual identification, veteran status, disabilities, physical abilities, and ideologies.

Workplace inclusion: refers to creating a work environment where all people are truly welcomed, valued, and respected, for all of who they are, regardless of differences. The feeling of accepted, understanding, and being valued in a group or team of individuals in the workplace; being of value based on other factors than diversity.

Workplace intersectionality: Employees have more than one affinity and those affinities combine shape that employee's perspective.

Workplace meritocracy: an organizational performance management system built into the organizational culture, in which employees advance into positions of success, power, and influence based on their demonstrated abilities and merit.

Appendix E:
Intersectionality Exercise

Team Activity—Intersectionality

This is an open-source activity created by the Canada Life Assurance Company and it is my favorite exercise.[130] Intersectionality focuses on the overlap of the various social identities one person may hold. This activity can help reveal areas where we may hold an unconscious bias towards particular groups.

Time required: 20 minutes.

Preparation

In advance of the meeting, send each participant the Intersectionality worksheet PDF for a virtual meeting or print one for each participant for an in-person meeting. (Download a copy from the book's website.)

Suggested wording:

Intersectionality focuses on the overlap of the various social identities one person would hold. This can include skin color, ethnicity, gender, sexuality, and class. Different combinations may increase or decrease the likelihood that you will experience systemic oppression and discrimination. For example, you may consider a white male to be in the majority in your workplace, but if a white male is also gay, the intersection of his sexual orientation may increase the likelihood that he will face discrimination.

In your handout is a list of social identities.

Focusing only on the first column, I'd like you to name your intersection in each group. For example, under gender, state the gender which you identify with. In skin color, put down how you would describe yourself. You will not be asked to share any of this, it's simply to help you identify your own intersections.

[You can ask participants to let you know when they're finished. If you're doing the activity face-to-face, you can ask the participants to put down their pens. If you're facilitating this virtually, you can ask participants to raise their hands or use whatever signaling method is available through your virtual meeting platform.]

In the next column in your handout, identify which of your social identities are part of the majority at work. Consider those you interact with on a regular basis and count if the number of people who have the same intersection as you add up to more or less than 50 percent. If the majority share that particular intersection, check the box in that row.
You have one minute.

Whenever an intersection is shared by the majority, it's easier for implicit bias against those not in this group to go unnoticed.

(In one workshop, a participant said they would not know if anyone at work is gay because they would never ask. Since there were approximately 1,000 employees in the workplace, statistically speaking there would have been around 100 people who were gay. The participant was asked if people at work ever talked about heterosexual experiences related to husbands, wives, wedding anniversaries or pregnancies. Of course, the answer was yes.

In this workplace, it's likely that those who are gay just remained silent and excluded from these conversations. By thinking more inclusively, we can expand our conversations to validate and acknowledge other social identities. In this example, simply talking about a same-sex wedding that you attended or a same-sex couple with children can make the conversation more inclusive. It doesn't mean that everyone within that social identity will speak out, but it does mean that they are more likely to feel included in the conversation.)

By now I hope you have some idea of what implicit bias and microaggressions are.
In the next column of the handout, I want you to think about

potential acts of implicit bias towards the social identities in your workplace that are not part of the majority. This requires you to first identify the minority social identities in each category and then to list a few potential microaggressions or acts of implicit bias.

You do not have to have witnessed this, just imagine what they might experience. While there may be several other social identities in each category, you are thinking generally about those at work who are in the minority. Let me give you a few examples:

An Asian person who was third-generation Canadian had people move away from them during the COVID-19 pandemic because they were assumed to be more likely to have the virus and be contagious than others. The implicit bias was being shunned or excluded and presumed to be a foreigner.

A Canadian of East Indian descent was detained at the airport 9 times out of 10, while the average is less than 3 times out of 10 for random selection. The implicit bias resulted in a person having to always spend more time at the airport because someone thought they looked like a person who might be engaged in criminal activity.

A highly qualified person who is nonbinary and dresses differently than the majority is told they are "not management material" because they won't command respect. The implicit bias is being judged by their appearance rather than their capabilities.

You now have 3 minutes to complete this column.

Hopefully this exercise has helped you to think through some of the experiences of those in the workplace who are in the minority. If you have a relationship with anyone in these groups, ask them what their experience has been with implicit bias or microaggressions. You may be surprised.

Now I want you to think about the people you hang out with when you are not working. For each of the categories, record the various social identities that are not part of your social circle.

To be included in your social circle means you interact with them at least 6 times a year outside of work. Also ask yourself why nobody from these particular identities is included in your social circle. As with the rest of the questions, you won't be asked to share your answers. **You have 3 minutes.**

Hopefully by now you will have more awareness of the unconscious bias that is unique to you.

Appendix F: Culture / Engagement Survey

Based on a scale of 1- 5 where
(1) Strongly Disagree, (2) Somewhat Disagree, (3) Neutral,
(4) Somewhat Agree, (5) Strongly Agree

Culture

Questions	Theme	Suggested Action
If I raised a concern about discrimination to my manager, I am confident my company would do what is right.	Policy	Update employee handbook on policies Share policies
There is a level and transparent playing field within the organization for salary, bonus, and promotion	Inclusion	Transparent communication on salary reporting processes, where the company ranks on salary compared to others within the marketspace. Review how and who is advancing within the organization
This company respects individuals and values their differences	Covering Inclusion	TNG on Covering TNG Communication TNG Unified Language—Inclusion TNG DiSC Personality TNG EI—Self Awareness Strategic I&D transparency
The decision-making process at _____ is inclusive; meaning the process include all employees in decisions that affect my work.	Inclusion Transparency	Review how decisions are made and who is in the room- where are the gaps? TNG on Collaboration and Decision-Making Level set training on the why for I&D

Overall, employees, including myself, feel part of the organizational community.	Inclusion Culture	Transparent communication on the why for I&D Employee Resource Groups
Employees of diverse backgrounds are encouraged and interact well in this company.	Culture EQ	TNG Culture Intelligence CQ® TNG on Inclusion Coaching Coaching to MGT to crease a safe space Sharing at town forums—discussing no silos—assigned seating Leverage Inclusion Council
This company provides an environment for the free and open expression of ideas, opinions, and beliefs.	Communication *Why"	TNG Coaching for Mgt and LDR TNG Inclusive Leadership ERG's Inclusion Council
Please list the strengths of the _____ culture—OPEN Ended—fill-in	Open	Brainstorm and find the gaps

Management / Leadership

Question	Theme	Suggested Action
Leadership is prepared to effectively manage a culturally diverse workforce	Leadership	Leadership Coaching TNG Inclusive Leadership Create and share the strategic plan Unified Language in Inclusion
My immediate manager encourages people with different ideas and opinions to speak up	Power to Speak Truth	TNG EI—Communication Skillset Coaching Communication Example Mgt/ LDR video
People at _____ are managed as if they can always improve their talents and abilities	Development	Utilize the Intersectional lens Collaboration

Overall, employees, including myself, feel comfortable and safe to share concerns/ issues with management, leadership, and human resources	Inclusion Communication	Transparent communication plan TNG DiSC on Communication and Teambuilding
On my team, we can have discussions on difficult/uncomfortable topics	Culture	TNG DiSC on Communication and Teambuilding TNG CQ TNG Difficult Conversations and Conflict Management (TKI-Thomas Kilmann Inventory)
The leadership at this company encourages inclusion	Leadership	Leadership coaching Strategic plan Unified language in inclusion Quarterly townhalls
Management shows that diversity is important through its action	Transparency Communication	Transparency for the Strategic message Coaching Leadership Example videos series of quarterly video
What is one priority the leadership should consider to continuously improve _____ organization culture, focusing on inclusion?— Open ended—fill in	Open	Brainstorm

Career Development

Employees of diverse backgrounds are encouraged to apply for higher positions	Career Pathways	Cross Function TNG Career / MGT pathways LDR awareness of pipeline MGT/LDR Coaching
List some of the way _____ leadership can help employees grow in your position and career.—OPEN SCALE	Open	Brainstorm

Survey Complete

Voluntary Information
- What is your gender?
- What is your ethnicity?
- Are you a veteran?
- Do you have or have you had a disability?

Which of the following best describes your role in the organization?
- First-level supervisor
- Manager/supervisor higher than first level (including senior management positions)
- Not a manager or supervisor

Appendix G:
Listing of Tools on Book Website

- White paper on generations in the workplace (Chapter 2)
- Disability Policy
- Editable Reasonable Accommodation Policy
- Culture/Engagement Survey (Ch 3 and here in Appendix)
- PowerPoint on business case for inclusion
- Psychological Safety in the Workplace
- Templates and Examples listed at end of Chapter 6
- ERG slide deck (Chapter 7)
- Leadership Scorecards
- Workplace Inclusion Model (Chapter 9)
- Studies on Coaching (Chapter 11)
- Blank RACI Template
- Human Resource Dashboards
- Diversity- History Demographic
- Affinity Iceberg
- Racial/ Ethnicity Diversity Index by State 2020
- Intersectionality Worksheet
- Shore Model of Inclusion
- LGBTQ+ Youth Population by State 2020
- I&D Strategy
- Up-To-Date Research Articles
- Links to Best Practices

Endnotes

1. Joanne Lipman. (2018, January 25). "How Diversity Training Infuriates Men and Fails Women." *Time, 191*(4), 17–19. http://time.com/5118035/diversity-training-infuriates-men-fails-women/ (Excerpted from *THAT'S WHAT SHE SAID: What Men Need to Know (and Women Need to Tell Them) About Working Together* by Joanne Lipman. HarperCollins Publishers, 2018).

2. Lauran Star Raduazo, "The Effect of Gender-Diversity Training on Perceived Organizational Justice" (2021). *Walden Dissertations and Doctoral Studies*. 10535. https://scholarworks.waldenu.edu/dissertations/10535/

3. Aduk Rasool, Ghani Khatir, and Nadir Shah Nadir (2018). "Diversity and Its Impact on Employee Satisfaction and Performance." *International Journal of Research in Commerce & Management, 9*(7), 12–15. https://ijrcm.org

4. Rohini Anand and Mary-Frances Winters (2008). "A Retrospective View of Corporate Diversity Training from 1964 to the Present," *Academy of Management Learning & Education, 7*, 356–372. https://doi.org/10.5465/AMLE.2008.34251673

5. Anand and Winters, 2008.

6. Rebecca Blumenstein and Jessica Bennett (2018, October 1). "For Women, the Climb to the Top Has Sputtered," *The New York Times*, p. F1.

7. Frank J. Cavico and Bahaudin Mujtaba (2017). "Diversity, Disparate Impact, and Discrimination Pursuant to Title VII of US Civil Rights Laws: A Primer for Management," *Equality, Diversity, and Inclusion: An International Journal, 36*, 670–691. https://doi.org/10.1108/EDI-04-2017-0091; see also Rasool et al., 2018.

8. A quick history can be found here: https://www.vsource.io/blog/evolution-of-diversity-in-the-workplace

9. Mike Schneider, "Census Data: US Is Diversifying, White Population Shrinking," Associated Press, August 13, 2021, https://apnews.com/article/race-and-ethnicity-census-2020-7264a653037e38df7ba67d3a324fc90d

10. Bailey Reiners, "57 Diversity in the Workplace Statistics You Should Know," BuiltIn.com, October 20, 2021, updated March 4, 2022, https://builtin.com/diversity-inclusion/diversity-in-the-workplace-statistics

11. D'Vera Cohn, "Future Immigration Will Change the Face of America by 2065," Pew Research Center, October 5, 2015, https://www.pewresearch.org/fact-tank/2015/10/05/future-immigration-will-change-the-face-of-america-by-2065/

12. Patricia Buckley and Daniel Bachman, "Meet the US Workforce of the Future: Older, More Diverse, and More Educated," *Deloitte Review*, Issue 21, July 31, 2017, https://www2.deloitte.com/us/en/insights/deloitte-review/issue-21/meet-the-us-workforce-of-the-future.html

13 Emma Hinchliffe, "The Female CEOs on This Year's Fortune 500 Just Broke Three All-time Records," *Fortune*, June 2, 2021, https://fortune.com/2021/06/02/female-ceos-fortune-500-2021-women-ceo-list-roz-brewer-walgreens-karen-lynch-cvs-thasunda-brown-duckett-tiaa/

14 *Women in the Workplace 2021*, McKinsey & Company, https://womenintheworkplace.com/

15 John Csiszar, "There Are Only 4 Black Fortune 500 CEOs," February 21, 2021, https://www.yahoo.com/now/only-4-black-fortune-500-200024302.html

16 Glassdoor's Diversity and Inclusion Workplace Survey, Last Updated September 29, 2020, https://www.glassdoor.com/blog/glassdoors-diversity-and-inclusion-workplace-survey/

17 Joanne Lipman (2018, January 25). "How Diversity Training Infuriates Men and Fails Women," *Time, 191*(4), 17–19. http://time.com/5118035/diversity-training-infuriates-men-fails-women/

18 https://www.dol.gov/general/topic/hiring/affirmativeact
https://definitions.uslegal.com/a/affirmative-action/https://en.wikipedia.org/wiki/Affirmative_action#Origins

19 Fidan Ana Kurtulus, (2012), "Affirmative Action and the Occupational Advancement of Minorities and Women During 1973–2003," *Industrial Relations: A Journal of Economy and Society 51*(2):213–246.

20 Kurtulus (2012), "Affirmative Action"

21 EEO-1 Data Collection, US Equal Employment Opportunity Commission, https://www.eeoc.gov/employers/eeo-1-data-collection

22 "Discussing Human Capital: A Survey of the S&P 500's Compliance with the New SEC Disclosure Requirement One Year After Adoption," Gibson Dunn, November 10, 2021, https://www.gibsondunn.com/discussing-human-capital-survey-of-sp-500-compliance-with-new-sec-disclosure-requirement-one-year-after-adoption/

23 Alhejji et al. (2016), "Diversity Training Programmed Outcomes: A Systematic Review," *Human Resource Development Quarterly, 27*, 95–149. https://doi.org/10.1002/hrdq.21221; Bezrukova et al. (2016), "A Meta-analytical Integration of Over 40 Years of Research on Diversity Training Evaluation," *Psychological Bulletin, 142*, 1227–1274. https://doi.org/10.1037/bul0000067; Buengeler et al. (2018), "How Leaders Shape the Impact of HR's Diversity Practices on Employee Inclusion," *Human Resource Management Review, 28*, 289–303. https://doi.org/10.1016/j.hrmr.2018.02.005; Gundemir et al. (2017), "Multicultural Meritocracy: The Synergistic Benefits of Valuing Diversity and Merit," *Journal of Experimental Social Psychology, 73*, 34–41. https://doi.org/10.1016/j.jesp.2017.06.002; Mariam B. Lam (2018), "Diversity Fatigue is Real: And It Afflicts the Very People Who Are Most Committed to Diversity Work," *Chronicle of Higher Education, 64*(5), 28. https://www.chronicle.com/article/diversity-fatigue-is-real/; Lipman, 2018; Moss-Racusin et al. (2018), "Gender Bias Produces Gender Gaps in STEM Engagement," *Sex Roles, 79*(11/12), 651. https://search-ebscohost-com.ezp.waldenulibrary.org/login.aspx?direct=true&db=edb&AN=132945897&site=eds-live&scope=site

24 Lipman, 2018; Moss-Racusin et al., 2018.

25   Lam, 2018.

26   Mariah Bohanon (2018), "Diversity Fatigue: How Ineffective Training Hurts Workplace Inclusiveness," *Insight into Diversity*, 90(8), 20–21. https://www.insightintodiversity.com/diversity-fatigue-how-ineffective-training-hurts-workplace-inclusiveness/

27   "The Myth of Race, Debunked in 3 Minutes," Vox, January 13, 2015. https://www.youtube.com/watch?v=VnfKgffCZ7U

28   Megan Gannon, "Race Is a Social Construct, Scientists Argue," *Live Science*, Scientific American, February 5, 2016, https://www.scientificamerican.com/article/race-is-a-social-construct-scientists-argue/

29   "New AMA Policies Recognize Race as a Social, Not Biological, Construct," American Medical Association, November 16, 2020, https://www.ama-assn.org/press-center/press-releases/new-ama-policies-recognize-race-social-not-biological-construct

30   Background Readings: Interview with Alan Goodman, *Race: The Power of an Illusion*, California Newsreel, on PBS, 2003, https://www.pbs.org/race/000_About/002_04-background-01-07.htm

31   Race, United States Census Bureau, https://www.census.gov/quickfacts/fact/note/US/RHI625221

32   Eric Jensen et al., "Measuring Racial and Ethnic Diversity for the 2020 Census," United States Census Bureau, August 4, 2021, https://www.census.gov/newsroom/blogs/random-samplings/2021/08/measuring-racial-ethnic-diversity-2020-census.html

33   Jennifer J. Deal et al. (2013). "Motivation At Work: Which Matters More, Generation Or Managerial Level?." *Consulting Psychology Journal: Practice & Research* 65(1): 1-16.

34   Jacob Martin and William A. Gentry (2011). "Derailment Signs Across Generations: More in Common Than Expected." *Psychologist-Manager Journal* 14(3): 177-195.

35   Brenda J. Kowske, Rena Rasch, and Jack Wiley (2010). "Millennials' (Lack of) Attitude Problem: An Empirical Examination of Generational Effects on Work Attitudes," *Journal of Business and Psychology* 25(2): 265-79.

36   Jennifer J. Deal et al. (2013). "Motivation At Work: Which Matters More, Generation Or Managerial Level?." *Consulting Psychology Journal: Practice & Research* 65(1): 1-16.

37   https://listingcenter.nasdaq.com/assets/RuleBook/Nasdaq/filings/SR-NASDAQ-2020-081.pdf

38   Sharon Perley Masling, "Focusing on Reporting the 'S' in Environment, Social & Governance," Bloomberg Law, July 22, 2022, https://news.bloomberglaw.com/securities-law/focusing-on-reporting-the-s-in-environment-social-governance.

39   Attracting Veterans to Your Workplace, Society for Human Resource Management, https://webcache.googleusercontent.com/search?q=cache:WBjXlKXlYKEJ:https://www.shrm.org/resourcesandtools/tools-and-samples/hr-forms/pages/attracting_veterans.aspx+&cd=1&hl=en&ct=clnk&gl=us

40   Understanding Military Skill Sets and How They Apply to Business, Recruit Military, https://recruitmilitary.com/employers/resource/172-understanding-military-skill-sets-and-how-they-apply-to-business

41 Nash Riggins, "15 Benefits of Hiring Military Veterans," Small Business Trends, November 2, 2017, https://smallbiztrends.com/2017/03/benefits-of-hiring-veterans.html

42 Employer Financial Incentives, Employer Assistance and Resource Network on Disability Inclusion, https://askearn.org/page/employer-financial-incentives

43 Top Companies for People with Disabilities, DiversityInc, https://www.diversityinc.com/2021-top-50-specialty-lists/people-with-disabilities/

44 Robert D. Austin and Gary P. Pisano, "Neurodiversity as a Competitive Advantage," *Harvard Business Review*, May-June 2017, https://hbr.org/2017/05/neurodiversity-as-a-competitive-advantage#_blank

45 Celia Daniels, "Benefits of Neurodiversity in the Workplace," Daivergent, November 20, 2019, https://daivergent.com/blog/neurodiversity-in-the-workplace#_blank

46 Carol A. Adams, "Neurodiversity at Work Benefits Everyone—Why Companies Are Hiring Autistic People," The Conversation, September 24, 2020, https://theconversation.com/neurodiversity-at-work-benefits-everyone-why-companies-are-hiring-autistic-people-146788#_blank

47 "Fostering Neurodiversity in Teams," Nesta, https://www.nesta.org.uk/feature/innovation-squared/fostering-neurodiversity-teams/#_blank

48 Louise Meehan, "How Neurodiversity in the Workplace Can Benefit Business," CPL, May 2020, https://www.cpl.com/blog/2020/05/what-is-neurodiversity-and-how-does-it-benefit-business#_blank

49 Austin and Pisano, 2017.

50 Ted Smith, "Why Hiring Upside Down Thinkers is a Competitive Advantage," ADDitude, March 30, 2022, https://www.additudemag.com/workplace-neurodiversity-benefits-adhd-talent/#_blank

51 David Altman and Joanne Dias, "Psychological Safety: An Overlooked Secret to Organizational Performance," Talent Management, December 1, 2020, https://www.talentmgt.com/articles/2020/12/01/psychological-safety-an-overlooked-secret-to-organizational-performance/#_blank

52 Jennifer Liu, "Companies Are Speaking Out Against Racism, But Here's What It Really Looks Like to Lead an Anti-racist Organization," CNBC, June 15, 2020, https://www.cnbc.com/2020/06/15/what-it-means-to-be-an-anti-racist-company.html.

53 Laura Morgan Roberts, "Race and Leadership: The Black Experience in the Workplace," December 17, 2019, Darden School of Business, University of Virginia, https://ideas.darden.virginia.edu/race-and-leadership

54 "Values Matters: New Study Finds Company Stances on Social-Political Issues Can Only Hurt Employee Work Performance," July 21, 2020, Columbia Business School, https://www8.gsb.columbia.edu/newsroom/newsn/9407/values-matters-new-study-finds-company-stances-on-social-political-issues-can-only-hurt-employee-work-performance

55 "Exxon Mobil Will Ban 'External Position Flags' Like the LGBTQ Rainbow Pride Flag from Being Flown Outside Its Offices," Business Insider, April 24, 2022, https://www.businessinsider.com/exxon-mobil-ban-lgbtq-pride-flag-flown-outside-offices-2022-4

56 "Great Expectations: Americans Want More From Companies," MetLife, November 27, 2018, https://www.metlife.com/about-us/newsroom/2018/november/great-expectations-americans-want-more-from-companies/

57 Katarzyna Szczepańska and Dariusz Kosiorek. (2017). "Factors Influencing Organizational Culture." Scientific Papers of Silesian University of Technology. Organization and Management Series. 2017. 457-468. 10.29119/1641-3466.2017.100.34, p. 459.

58 Edward Segal, "Why Employees Don't Trust HR Staff—And What Can Be Done About It," Forbes, November 28, 2021, https://www.forbes.com/sites/edwardsegal/2021/11/28/why-employees-dont-trust-hr-staff-and-what-can-be-done-about-it/?sh=76a4ac33179f

59 "75+ Eye-Opening Company Culture Statistics For 2022, GreenThumbs (HR blog), January 9, 2022, https://blog.greenthumbs.in/company-culture-stats.php

60 Emilio J. Castilla, "Achieving Meritocracy in the Workplace," *MIT Sloan Management Review*, June 13, 2016, https://sloanreview.mit.edu/article/achieving-meritocracy-in-the-workplace/

61 "Meritocracy: Unraveling the Paradox," Deloitte, November 28, 2016, https://www2.deloitte.com/au/en/blog/diversity-inclusion-blog/2019/meritocracy-unraveling-paradox.html

62 Chris Drew, 15 Meritocracy Examples, Helpful Professor, September 6, 2022 https://helpfulprofessor.com/meritocracy-examples/

63 Dr. Doyin Atewologun, Dr. Fatima Tresh, and Dr. Manjari Prashar, "Diversity Versus Meritocracy: An Unhelpful (Harmful?) Narrative," Delta Alpha Psi Services Ltd., https://deltaalphapsi.com/our-insights/diversity-versus-meritocracy-an-unhelpful-harmful-narrative/

64 David Barol, "Feeling Part of the Team: The Importance of Building an Inclusive Culture in the Workplace," PeopleScout, https://www.peoplescout.com/insights/inclusive-culture-in-the-workplace/

65 "Stop Saying Diverse When You Mean Something Else," Rakshitha Arni Ravishankar, *Harvard Business Review*, June 21, 2021, https://hbr.org/2021/06/stop-saying-diverse-when-you-mean-something-else

66 "The Deloitte Global 2022 Gen Z and Millennial Survey," Deloitte, https://www2.deloitte.com/global/en/pages/about-deloitte/articles/genzmillennialsurvey.html?icid=wn_

67 *Diversity Wins; How Inclusion Matters*, McKinsey & Company, May 2020, https://www.mckinsey.com/~/media/mckinsey/featured%20insights/diversity%20and%20inclusion/diversity%20wins%20how%20inclusion%20matters/diversity-wins-how-inclusion-matters-vf.pdf

68   Devyn Hinchee, "Which Comes First, Diversity or Inclusion?" Hiring Solved, May 18, 2021, https://hiringsolved.com/blog/which-comes-first-diversity-or-inclusion/

69   Valerie Bolden-Barrett, "Companies Are Investing in Diversity but Many Workers Don't Reap the Benefit," HR Dive, January 23, 2019, https://www.hrdive.com/news/companies-are-investing-in-diversity-but-many-workers-dont-reap-the-benef/546376/

70   Turnover Cost Calculation Spreadsheet, Society for Human Resource Management, https://www.shrm.org/resourcesandtools/tools-and-samples/hr-forms/pages/turnover-cost-calculation-spreadsheet.aspx. See also "The Cost of Replacing an Employee and the Role of Financial Wellness," Enrich, https://www.enrich.org/blog/The-true-cost-of-employee-turnover-financial-wellness-enrich

71   "Affirmative Action Policies Throughout History," American Association for Access Equity & Diversity, https://www.aaaed.org/aaaed/History_of_Affirmative_Action.asp

72   "Affirmative Action," Legal Information Institute, Cornell Law School, https://www.law.cornell.edu/wex/affirmative_action

73   Cindy-Ann Thomas and Brandon R. Mita, "$10 Million 'Reverse' Race & Gender Discrimination Verdict Gives DE&I Programs a Halloween Fright," Littler News & Analysis, October 29, 2021, https://www.littler.com/publication-press/publication/10-million-reverse-race-gender-discrimination-verdict-gives-dei

74   Lindsey M. Lavaysse, Tahira M. Probst, and David F. Arena Jr. 2018. "Is More Always Merrier? Intersectionality as an Antecedent of Job Insecurity," *International Journal of Environmental Research and Public Health* 15(11): 2559. https://doi.org/10.3390/ijerph15112559

75   "Kimberlé Crenshaw on Intersectionality, More Than Two Decades Later," Columbia Law School, June 8, 2017, https://www.law.columbia.edu/news/archive/kimberle-crenshaw-intersectionality-more-two-decades-later#:~:text=Crenshaw%3A%20Intersectionality%20is%20a%20lens,class%20or%20LBGTQ%20problem%20there

76   Quote from Reddit user Amarkov, in "Intersectionality at Work: Why Focusing on Women Isn't Enough," Culture Amp, https://www.cultureamp.com/blog/intersectionality-at-work

77   Adwoa Bagalini, "5 Ways Intersectionality Affects Diversity and Inclusion at Work," World Economic Forum, July 22, 2020, https://www.weforum.org/agenda/2020/07/diversity-inclusion-equality-intersectionality/

78   "What Does Inclusion Really Mean for Your Business?" Justworks, December 18, 2020, https://justworks.com/blog/what-does-inclusion-really-mean-for-your-business

79   Vijay Eswaran "The Business Case for Diversity in the Workplace Is Now Overwhelming," World Economic Forum, April 29, 2019, https://www.weforum.org/agenda/2019/04/business-case-for-diversity-in-the-workplace/

80   "How to Measure Inclusion in the Workplace," Lauren Romansky, Mia Garrod, Katie Brown, and Kartik Deo, *Harvard Business Review*, May 27, 2021, https://hbr.org/2021/05/how-to-measure-inclusion-in-the-workplace

81   "Culture vs. Engagement: Avoiding the Runaway Strategy Bus (or Getting It Under Control Before It Crashes)," Deloitte, 2016, https://www.google.com/

url?sa=t&rct=j&q=&esrc=s&source=web&cd=&ved=2ahUKEwju7pyfjNP3AhXfkokEHUYSBtgQFnoECAwQAw&url=https%3A%2F%2Fwww2.deloitte.com%2Fcontent%2Fdam%2FDeloitte%2Fus%2FDocuments%2Fhuman-capital%2Fus-cons-culture-vs-engagement.pdf&usg=AOvVaw2fzGd_y1-xX9pvVLEMyf37

82 Kumar Parakala, "How to Overcome Barriers to Inclusion and Diversity," *Forbes*, June 17, 2021, https://www.forbes.com/sites/forbestechcouncil/2021/06/17/how-to-overcome-barriers-to-inclusion-and-diversity/?sh=29c53f476075

83 Kathy Gurchiek (March 19, 2018). "6 Steps for Building an Inclusive Workplace," Society for Human Resource Management, https://webcache.googleusercontent.com/search?q=cache:adyH3N2LZJgJ:https://www.shrm.org/hr-today/news/hr-magazine/0418/pages/6-steps-for-building-an-inclusive-workplace.aspx+&cd=1&hl=en&ct=clnk&gl=us

84 Sundiatu Dixon-Fyle, Kevin Dolan, Vivian Hunt, & Sara Prince (2020). *Diversity Wins: How Inclusion Matters.* McKinsey Report, 2020. Retrieved from https://www.mckinsey.com/featured-insights/diversity-and-inclusion/diversity-wins-how-inclusion-matters#. See also Vijay Eswarah (2019). "The Business Case for Diversity in the Workplace Is Now Overwhelming," WeForum, 29 Apr 2019. Retrieved from https://www.weforum.org/agenda/2019/04/business-case-for-diversity-in-the-workplace/.

85 Cultural Intelligence Center, https://culturalq.com/about-cultural-intelligence/

86 Lynn M. Shore, Jeanette N. Cleveland, and Diana Sanchez, "Inclusive Workplaces: A Review and Model," *Human Resource Management Review*, Vol. 28, Issue 2, 2018, Pages 176-189,. https://www.sciencedirect.com/science/article/abs/pii/S1053482217300529

87 Home Depot, ESG Statement, https://corporate.homedepot.com/responsibility

88 "Diversity, Equity & Inclusion," Johnson & Johnson, https://www.jnj.com/about-jnj/diversity

89 Juliet Bourke, "The Six Signature Traits of Inclusive Leadership: Thriving in a Diverse New World," Deloitte Insights, April 14, 2016, https://www2.deloitte.com/us/en/insights/topics/talent/six-signature-traits-of-inclusive-leadership.html. See also: Develop Inclusive Leaders at Scale, Korn Ferry, March 9, 2022, https://www.kornferry.com/insights/featured-topics/diversity-equity-inclusion/develop-inclusive-leaders-at-scale?utm_source=linkedin&utm_medium=paidsoc&utm_term=link&utm_content=dei-remarketing-website-conversions-develop-inclusive-leaders-at-scale-1&utm_campaign=22-04-dei&li_fat_id=3868f746-130c-49f9-9621-1cd4d48d4aff

90 Kathy Gurchiek (March 19, 2018). "6 Steps for Building an Inclusive Workplace," Society for Human Resource Management, https://webcache.googleusercontent.com/search?q=cache:adyH3N2LZJgJ:https://www.shrm.org/hr-today/news/hr-magazine/0418/pages/6-steps-for-building-an-inclusive-workplace.aspx+&cd=1&hl=en&ct=clnk&gl=us

91 Gurchiek (2018), "6 Steps for Building an Inclusive Workplace."

92 Bridget Miller, "Why Is HR Often Viewed Negatively by Employees?" HR Daily Advisor, February 18, 2020, https://hrdailyadvisor.blr.com/2020/02/18/why-is-hr-often-viewed-negatively-by-employees/

93 The Future of Diversity, Equity, & Inclusion 2022, Circa, https://circaworks.com/resources-diversity-future-of-dei-2022-research-whitepaper/?creative=572667386865&keyword=diversity%20and%20inclusion&matchtype=p&network=g&device=c&gclid=Cj0KCQjwspKUBhCvARIsAB2IYut7tN-rKQCaeGaD7nDVU_QaIHsTvvtcTuoxJSeVhQ1yWWb_CbOWWSYaAgJ0EALw_wcB

94 Frank Dobbin and Alexandra Kalev, "Why Diversity Programs Fail—And What Works Better," *Harvard Business Review*, 94(7–8):52–60, July-August 2016. www.hbr.org

95 Mike Noon, "Pointless Diversity Training: Unconscious Bias, New Racism, and Agency," *Work, Employment and Society*, 32(1):198–209, 2018. https://doi.org/10.1177/0950017017719841.

96 Mariah Bohanon, "Diversity Fatigue: How Ineffective Training Hurts Workplace Inclusiveness," *Insight into Diversity*, 90(8):20-21, April 17, 2018. https://www.insightintodiversity.com/diversity-fatigue-how-ineffective-training-hurts-workplace-inclusiveness/.

97 Kristen P. Jones, Eden B. King, Jonathan Nelson, David S. Geller, and Lynn Bowes-Sperry (2013). "Beyond the Business Case: An Ethical Perspective of Diversity Training," *Human Resource Management*, 52, 55–74. https://doi.org/10.1002/hrm.21517.

98 Hussain Alhejji,, Thomas Garavan, Ronan Carbery, Fergal O'Brien, and David McGuire (2016). "Diversity Training Programme Outcomes: A Systematic Review," *Human Resource Development Quarterly*, 27, 95–149. https://doi.org/10.1002/hrdq.21221

99 Alhejji et al., 2016. See also Pradeepa Dahanayake, Diana Rajendran, Christopher Selvarajah, and Glenda Ballantyne (2018). "Justice and Fairness in the Workplace: A Trajectory for Managing Diversity," *Equality, Diversity, and Inclusion: An International Journal*, 37, 470–490. https://doi.org/10.1108/EDI-11-2016-0105; and Alex Lindsey, Eden King, Michelle Hebl, and Noah Levine (2015). "The Impact of Method, Motivation, and Empathy on Diversity Training Effectiveness," *Journal of Business and Psychology*, 30, 605–617. https://doi.org/10.1007/s10869-014-9384-3.

100 Bezrukova, K., Spell, C. S., Perry, J. L., & Jehn, K. A. (2016). "A Meta-Analytical Integration of Over 40 Years of Research on Diversity Training Evaluation," *Psychological Bulletin*, 142, 1227–1274. https://doi.org/10.1037/bul0000067. See also Yuka Fujimoto and Charmine E. J. Härtel (2017). "Organizational Diversity Learning Framework: Going Beyond Diversity Training Programs," *Personnel Review*, 46, 1120–1141. https://doi.org/10.1108/PR-09-2015-0254

101 Gurchiek, K., (2018)

102 The Diversity Dashboard, PeopleInsight, https://www.peopleinsight.com/blog/diversity-peopleinsight-top-hr-dashboards

103 *Diversity and Inclusion: The Reality Gap –2017 Global Human Capital Trends*, Deloitte Insights, https://www2.deloitte.com/us/en/insights/focus/human-capital-trends/2017/diversity-and-inclusion-at-the-workplace.html

104 *Inclusive HR Toolkit, Part 6: Measuring Success*, Work in Culture, https://www.workinculture.ca/Resources/Inclusion-in-the-Creative-Workplace/Inclusive-HR-Toolkit/Part-6-Measuring-Success/Tools

105 Cindi Howson, "To Make Real Progress on D&I, Move Past Vanity Metrics," *Harvard Business Review*, May 21, 2021, https://hbr.org/2021/05/to-make-real-progress-on-di-move-past-vanity-metrics

106 "Black Workers' Suit Accuses Job Agency of Favoring Hispanic Applicants," *The New York Times*, December 6, 2016, https://www.nytimes.com/2016/12/06/us/lawsuit-alleges-discrimination-against-blacks-at-national-job-agency.html

107 Understanding Workplace Equity vs Equality, Diversio, https://sloanreview.mit.edu/article/how-workplace-fairness-affects-employee-commitment/

108 Understanding Workplace Equity vs Equality, Diversio, https://sloanreview.mit.edu/article/how-workplace-fairness-affects-employee-commitment/

109 Equity, Cornell Law School, https://www.law.cornell.edu/wex/equity

110 Matthias Seifert, Joel Brockner, Emily C. Bianchi, and Henry Moon (Winter 2016). "How Workplace Fairness Affects Employee Commitment," *MIT Sloan Management Review*, https://sloanreview.mit.edu/article/how-workplace-fairness-affects-employee-commitment/

111 Hannah Bareham, "Why Is College So Expensive?" Bankrate, March 25, 2022, https://www.bankrate.com/loans/student-loans/why-is-college-expensive/

112 Equity and Wealth, The Equity Tool, https://www.equitytool.org/equity/

113 Elizabeth Blair, "50 Years Ago, Sex Equality Seemed Destined for the Constitution. What Happened?" *All Things Considered*, National Public Radio, March 22, 2022, https://www.npr.org/2022/03/22/1086978928/50-years-ago-sex-equality-seemed-destined-for-the-constitution-what-happened

114 H.J.Res.28 - Proposing an amendment to the Constitution of the United States relative to equal rights for men and women.117th Congress (2021-2022), https://www.congress.gov/bill/117th-congress/house-joint-resolution/28

115 Aimee Groth, "Facebook Feminist Sheryl Sandberg Candidly Responds To All Of The Haters," March 11, 2013, Business Insider, https://www.businessinsider.com/sheryl-sandberg-60-minutes-interview-2013-3

116 Equity and Wealth, The Equity Tool, https://www.equitytool.org/equity/

117 Ruth Mayhew, "The Disadvantages of Equity in the Workplace," Chron, https://smallbusiness.chron.com/disadvantages-equity-workplace-11499.html

118 United States National Culture, Hofstede Insights, https://www.hofstede-insights.com/country/the-usa/

119 "7 Diversity and Inclusion Initiatives Your Company Can Action Right Now," *Human Resources Director*, June 11,2021, https://www.hcamag.com/us/specialization/diversity-inclusion/7-diversity-and-inclusion-initiatives-your-company-can-action-right-now/257728

120 Advancing with an Intentional Focus on ID&E, Dow, https://corporate.dow.com/en-us/esg/report/inclusion-and-diversity.html

121 "6 Top Trends in DEI for 2022," Purdue University Global, February 2, 2022, https://www.purdueglobal.edu/blog/business/diversity-equity-inclusion-trends/

122 Kathy Gurchiek, "Report: Most Companies Are 'Going Through the Motions' of DE&I, Society for Human Resource Management, February 23, 2021, https://www.shrm.org/resourcesandtools/hr-topics/behavioral-competencies/global-and-cultural-effectiveness/pages/report-most-companies-are-going-through-the-motions-of-dei.aspx

123 Josh Bersin, *Elevating Equity: The Real Story of Diversity and Inclusion*, 2021, https://ss-usa.s3.amazonaws.com/c/308463326/media/27436024f0b84dfd274918375735238/202102%20-%20DEI%20Report.pdf

124 "They're the Unsung Heroes of the Great Resignation, But Who's Looking after HR?" Workvivo, https://www.workvivo.com/hr-breakdown/

125 "Work-at-Home After Covid-19—Our Forecast," Global Workforce Analytics, https://globalworkplaceanalytics.com/work-at-home-after-covid-19-our-forecast

126 "6 Top Trends in DEI for 2022," Purdue University Global, February 2, 2022, https://www.purdueglobal.edu/blog/business/diversity-equity-inclusion-trends/

127 https://www.youtube.com/watch?v=gegA9GsJ26A

128 Frank Dobbin and Alexandra Kalev, "Why Diversity Programs Fail: And what works better" (July–August 2016), *Harvard Business Review*, https://hbr.org/2016/07/why-diversity-programs-fail

129 Patrick S. Forscher, Calvin K. Lai, Jordan R. Axt, Charles R. Ebersole, Michelle Herman, Patricia G. Devine, and Brian A. Nosek (2019). "A Meta-analysis of Procedures to Change Implicit Measures," *Journal of Personality and Social Psychology*, 117(3), 522–559. https://doi.org/10.1037/pspa0000160https://psyarxiv.com/dv8tu/

130 "Team Activity: Intersectionality," Workplace Strategies for Mental Health, Canada Life Assurance Company, https://www.workplacestrategiesformentalhealth.com/resources/team-activity-intersectionality

About the Author

Inclusion & Diversity Strategist, Psychologist & Author

Dr. Lauran Star is known for transforming leadership and organizational culture by pushing the edge of status quo to achieve greater employee engagement, culture, inclusion, and diversity.

As a senior HR leader with 20+ years of success driving high-performing organizational cultures and employees, Dr. Star is raising the ID&E bar while driving measurable change within organizations through data-driven strategies. Known for uncovering blind spots to achieve optimal performance and enhanced retention, she dives in where others tread lightly, yet is insightful, warm, and approachable.

Her own affinities go beyond being a woman, as she is veteran of the United States Armed Forces who served in Operation Desert Storm, has a learning disability, and was raised in a multicultural family. Prior to her corporate life, she performed on and off Broadway.

Dr. Star holds a PhD in Industrial Organizational Psychology specializing in Inclusion, Diversity and Equity. A bestselling author and well-known media expert, her thought leadership touches many. She is a distinguished researcher and practitioner in the field of inclusion, diversity and equality.

During her off time, you can find her enjoying life with her family.

Dr. Lauran Star
INCLUSION • DIVERSITY • EQUITY

www.drlauranstar.com
www.linkedin.com/in/lauranstar
Lauran@DrLauranStar.com

Made in the USA
Middletown, DE
02 April 2023